Architects of Change

Jeremy Ghez

Architects of Change

Designing Strategies for a Turbulent Business Environment

Jeremy Ghez
HEC Paris
Jouy-en-Josas, France

ISBN 978-3-030-20686-4 ISBN 978-3-030-20684-0 (eBook)
https://doi.org/10.1007/978-3-030-20684-0

This Palgrave Macmillan imprint is published by the registered company Springer Nature Switzerland AG.
The registered company address is: Gewerbestrasse 11, 6330 Cham, Switzerland

To A., who helps me try to build a better world, every single day.
To D., E., and B., who remind me why, every single day.

Preface

I wrote this book during the first term of Donald Trump's presidency, as Brexit negotiations were still underway three years after the referendum and as a wave of populist movements shook an already weakened European Union. I found the degree of discontent in countries that significantly benefited from the democratic and free-market system in the past to be a powerful disruptive moment we cannot ignore. In fact, this anger should serve as a powerful reminder of where we've failed collectively. We must remember that demagoguery may soothe short-term pains. But reaching our broader, long-term, collective goals will require a degree of reinvention and transformation of the business environment whose scope we may not have fully grasped yet.

Yet, at the same time, I am also struck by the number of people who want to make a difference, but who believe they cannot do so because of the pressure coming from employers, clients, shareholders and other stakeholders whose metrics of success focus more on short-term profitability than on long-term impact. This book is not only designed to draw attention to the significance of the change that is needed to tackle major threats, most notably weakening social contracts between people and their governments and global warming; it is also meant to provide a toolbox for those individuals wanting to have an impact and who could help transform that anger into a true force of change. It is meant for decision makers in the private sector and the public sector who are looking to transform the way we do business and the way we approach key global challenges we will need to tackle in coming years. And even as those challenges evolve, I hope that this book continues to provide some food for thought, as well as tools and strategies that will help people in continuing to transforming their business environment in a meaningful way.

Every generation seems to believe it is living in an exceptional period, and this generation is no exception. There is nothing illegitimate about that sentiment. But it comes with a responsibility: remembering that, even as individuals, we are empowered to make a difference. I hope this book can be part of the conversation on how we do that, today on the critical questions of weakening social pacts and global warming, and tomorrow, on those issues that will shape the business environment of the next generation.

May 2019 Jeremy Ghez
Jouy-en-Josas, France

Acknowledgments

Writing a book is no easy task—far harder in fact than what I imagined, considering this is a topic I've been teaching for such a long time. In fact, I've come to realize that when you are finally putting on paper what enthralls you, you challenge every word you write, you wonder about the accuracy of every single statement you make, and you question every argument you formulate. Reaching the end of the process is all the more intellectually exhilarating. So you cannot possibly forget who made this possible along the way.

There was, of course, the team at Palgrave Macmillan to whom I am immensely grateful for giving me this opportunity. Liz Barlow initially made this happen and I thank her for her very thoughtful comments at the beginning of the process. Lucy Kidwell provided extremely useful guidance throughout the process and I'm very thankful for that.

There were, as well, the conversations with HEC Paris and RAND colleagues throughout the years. I'd like to thank in particular Matt Bassford, who has always been a reliable friend and who provided extremely helpful comments on the book proposal, as well as Kai Ruggeri, with whom I have taught many classes in managerial economics and business environment over the years. Kai has proven to be not only a great colleague but also an invaluable intellectual partner in this process. I am also thankful for my endless conversations with quite a few colleagues on key topics ranging from global politics and strategy to sustainability and social innovation. Pascal Chaigneau has not only been a wonderful colleague and a great friend but also an invaluable mentor. I was also fortunate to talk about the many issues that this book discusses with many talented people, including Eloic Peyrache, Andrea Masini, Florian Hoos, Nathalie Lugagne, Alejandra Cervio, Olga Hein, Christelle Bitouzet, Alexandre Cadain, Nicolas Lemoine, Jean-Philippe

Couturier, Matthis Schulte, Ai-ting Goh, Eric Mengus, Corey Phelps, Rodolphe Durand, Bénédicte Faivre-Tavignot, Ludovic Subran, and Bernard Garrette. These conversations provided me with more insights than what I could possibly describe here. I am also grateful to Mary-Joyce Ahsue who has been giving me administrative support for the past ten years at HEC, and that is, by no means an easy task. Last, but not least, I'd like to thank Phillipe Oster and his team, including Sophie Garnichat, Julie Dobiecki, Maud Clerc, Aniza Pourtauborde (without forgetting Leyla Douci). They have all done so much in helping me hone my message over time. I am, without a doubt, forgetting to name many other colleagues I have interacted with and do hope they will forgive me.

I would also like to give a special recognition to my colleagues Lise Penillard, Déborah Keraghel, and Sophie Mebo (and all of her crew!) who have become part of my closest professional family in this exploration of sustainability and the global business environment. These words do not do merit to what the three of them represent for me—but somehow, I know that they know what I mean. I'm also grateful to all of the students and participants whom I have interacted with and who shaped the content of this book—far more, in fact, than they will ever know.

There are great interviews in this book as well. I met Jim Thomson, who sat on my dissertation committee, and Greg Treverton, who is the person who taught me almost everything I know about strategic analysis, a very long time ago. It would be hard to overstate what Jim and Greg have represented for me: both have been tremendous mentors over the years, providing me with their continuous and unwavering support. I am also grateful for the time they gave me on this project—and even more so for always answering my emails with such enthusiasm. There is also Alastair Newton; I once reached out to him with a simple email and was surprised to see how someone who was a total stranger to me then could be so generous with his time and his insights. That generosity never ceased. I am thankful to him too, not only for his time on the project, but also for helping me think about these complex issues over time. I have a similar story with Pascal Picq, whom I once met at a conference, thinking I had in front of me someone who was way out of my league. Yet, he never let me think that for a second more and I am grateful to him too for his time and his intellectual generosity in this process and throughout the years. I would also like to thank Joël Barbier who is the most informed observer of the Silicon Valley I have ever met. Joël has not only provided me with invaluable insights about a world that often stumps me; he has also been a thought partner about this changing and, at times, scary world. There is also Justin Vaïsse—yet again another extremely generous person when it comes to intellectual curiosity (in spite of an extremely busy schedule), and to whom I am so grateful for his time and his insights. Finally, there's Jean-Noël Kapferer, a real living legend when it comes to luxury and brands. Those are topics I always thought were very far away from my areas of interest. I just needed to sit through one of Jean-Noël's sessions, watch him bring these topics to life, and be very quickly convinced of the contrary. He, too, will never really know how thankful I am for his time.

There are also the colleagues who gave their time to reviewing drafts of this book. I met Gerard de Maupeou a while back, at a time (and I am not lying) when I was very close to quitting academia. Gerard is one of the people with some of those untold magical powers that transform a very dim reality into a glass half-full. I highly appreciated his comments on this book. Roger Hallowell also provided precious comments on a past draft that helped me bring this book to the next level and I am so grateful for his time. Finally, Randy White provided more help than I could ever hope for. Randy was not only generous with his time and his insights but also extremely supportive in this grueling process during which it feels as if we met a second time.

Any remaining mistakes are mine, and mine alone.

Last but not least, there are those, backstage, who, day by day, do not only provide you with the environment you need to thrive professionally, but who make life just worth living. My parents, obviously, who are here every step of the way. There are also big brothers in the story, as well as in-laws (all kinds of them, in fact, ranging from mother and father, to brothers and sisters), nephews and nieces who may not necessarily see their imprint on this work at a first glance—but they should. And then, there are, of course, the three most wonderful creatures I know: my three children who will always be the achievements I am most proud of and who are the reason why I want to bring change to this world.

And there is, obviously, their mom, my wife and my partner in more ways than she thinks. I could always thank her and say I love her. But those words (or any other words for that matter) would not do any justice to how grateful I am to her and what she does, day in and day out. After all, this book isn't mine; it's ours. And this is just a start. So let's see where life takes us next, shall we?

Contents

1 A Tale of Two Professions 1

2 Case Study: When James Bond Met Q 15

3 The World We Live In 23

4 Case Study: The Change-Maker Game 61

5 The Road to Reinvention 67

6 Case Study: Founding a Popular Pizza Place in Paris 89

7 The Power of Analysis 95

8 Case Study: Strategizing at Amazon When Globalization Comes Under Pressure 111

9 The Significance of Anticipation 127

10 Case Study: Getting Ready for the World in Five Years 151

11 The Purpose of Imagination 159

12 Case Study: Conducting a Pre-Mortem 175

13 The Meaning of Creativity 189

14 Case Study: Looking for Talent in a Chaotic World 201

15 A Tribute to My Kids (the Ultimate Architects of Change) 217

Index 225

List of Figures

Fig. 1.1	Central government debt: total (% of GDP). Source: World Bank	4
Fig. 1.2	World GDP (constant, in billions of 2010 US$)	6
Fig. 1.3	HDI by country group	6
Fig. 3.1	Defense spending compared across the globe. Source: SIPRI Military Expenditure Database (https://www.sipri.org/databases/milex)	26
Fig. 3.2	Two coalitions face-to-face. Source: Adapted from Bruce Bueno de Mesquita, Principles of International Politics, 2007	30
Fig. 3.3	Two (ideological) coalitions face-to-face. Source: Adapted from Bruce Bueno de Mesquita, Principles of International Politics, 2007	31
Fig. 3.4	Europe's contribution to regional and global cooperation. Source: European Commission, 2017. http://europa.eu/rapid/press-release_IP-17-385_en.htm	35
Fig. 3.5	Number of regional trade agreements in force. Source: WTO, Regional Trade Agreements Information System (RTA-IS)	36
Fig. 5.1	Labor productivity in the United States since 1948. Source: Division of Major Sector Productivity, Bureau of Labor Statistics. Data reflects press release of March 7, 2019. Full report: www.bls.gov/news.release/prod2.nr0.htm	71
Fig. 6.1	Popular pizza's market	90
Fig. 8.1	The evolution of trade (as a percentage of GDP) since 1960. Source: World Development Indicators, 2019	113
Fig. 8.2	The effects of WWI on the West. (**a**) Population, mid-year (thousands). (**b**) Real GDP per capita in 2011 US$	115
Fig. 8.3	The volatility of markets since 1990. Source: Yahoo Finance	119
Fig. 9.1	Interest rates on long-term European government bonds (denominated in national currencies): 1992–2018. Source: Eurostat	134
Fig. 9.2	Four scenarios for the future of the European Union	142

List of Tables

Table 1.1	Real GDP growth rate by decade (in %)	4
Table 3.1	2018 global economic powers measured by GDP	27
Table 3.2	Changes in defense spending, 2008–2017	28
Table 5.1	The prisoners' dilemma	80
Table 11.1	Fifteen digital business models create three forms of value	170
Table 12.1	List of Fortune 500 companies	181

1
A Tale of Two Professions

Regardless of where you are from, the industry you work in (or) industry your work is in or your personal political beliefs, chances are that there are plenty of angry people around you. If you think this anger is justified but not unavoidable, if you believe this anger calls for deep transformations in the way we live and do business, and if you are looking for new and meaningful opportunities for change in this easily disrupted business environment, then this book is intended for you.

Reasons to Be Angry

This anger is fueled by legitimate anxieties about a changing world of people who feel they have lost their bearings. In this world, past political systems, that were once beacons of stability and peace, are not providing these people with the comfort about their status and guaranteeing their economic and social prospects anymore. Constant disruptions and challenges to what seemed yesterday's natural order are leading to the advent of a scary, unknown and tempestuous world in which what you deem improbable is likely to happen and in which you thought was likely may actually never happen. The political processes and business models that we often took for granted in the past now appear dysfunctional at best, and obsolete at worse.

The sense that those in power, in business or in government, or those who *influence* those in power, are completely disconnected from the reality of the most vulnerable—or the ones who *feel* the most vulnerable—only compounds this anger. This disconnect often seems to be at the heart of demographic,

J. Ghez, *Architects of Change*, https://doi.org/10.1007/978-3-030-20684-0_1

racial, and generational divides that we observe across the globe. For instance, in the United States as well as in Europe, the opposition between a rural and conservative electorate and a more urban and progressive one may not be new but certainly everlasting and highly relevant when it comes to understanding recent electoral surprises and social tensions. Similarly, we can observe tensions across racial groups that result from differences in narratives about integration and meritocracy: disagreements about how well a society or a political system is working today for all of its citizens stem from opposing (and yet very authentic) views about a society's reality. Last but not least, the generational divide between a relatively older age group that often feels more legitimate because of its experience and a relatively younger age group that feels victimized by the mistakes (and, at times, the recklessness) of its elders is no less significant in explaining this disconnect that can make power transitions between generations all the more complex to manage.

Ultimately, the combination of these anxieties and this disconnect leads public opinions across the globe to feel as if they are losing control of their fate, and perhaps more disturbingly, of that of their children. Anger is not only a natural response; it is, perhaps, the only response possible for those who feel powerless. In turn, in response to this anger, there are two types of influential actors: those looking to surf on that anger and that disconnect in order to obtain some personal gains and consolidate their influence in a broken system and those hoping to transform that anger into meaningful action and transformation, in particular by bridging the disconnects.

This book unapologetically ignores the first category of demagogues and looks to decisively empower the second, the architects of change, looking to bring meaningful and durable change to a business environment that so desperately needs it. Here is why.

The Paradox of Change

There is no dearth of reasons to feel powerless in this business environment.

The Crises of a System

Defining the key characteristics of the business environment we live in is no easy task. Some would use the free-market liberal democracy model that international organizations have promoted since the end of World War II. Yet, that definition excludes a significant part of the world population, not least of which are two major powers, namely China and Russia—the case of India being debatable.

Others would rely on the term "globalization" which describes the gradual process of integration of national and regional economies that accelerated in the nineteenth century before taking a full stop in 1914, before starting again, gradually in 1945 and accelerating once again in the aftermath of the Cold War. This process of integration has significantly increased the degree of *interdependence* between different players. It has lifted huge chunks of the global population out of poverty and has become part of a global reality that no real serious influencer, including a non-western one, can ignore.

Yesterday, globalization was about the promise of a wealthier, a more efficient, and a more transparent world. Today, it faces the risk of losing its momentum, on at least three levels.

First, some of the major actors of globalization, namely the states, may be far more constrained in their ability to act than they ever were. In fact, in the wake of the 2008 Recession, western governments in particular carried out substantial efforts to preserve the global economy. This effort resulted in high levels of public debt, meaning that states do not have the same firepower to influence the global business environment as in the past, at a time at which challenges are no less significant—quite to the contrary. Technological disruptions like automation and artificial intelligence are putting a wide array of workers at risk of losing their jobs if they do not upgrade their skills. Perhaps even more fundamentally, the lack of productivity gains and our inability to retrain those displaced by automation, may have well undermined our ability to bounce back durably in a landscape that is not getting any easier to navigate in—with the growing cost associated to climate change-related crises in particular. The constraints on these governments' ability to act may limit their efforts in tackling these challenges.

The model is undergoing a financial crisis as a result (Fig. 1.1).

Second, low levels of economic growth and increasing political polarization across the globe suggest that the model is not as efficient as it used to be in generating wealth and stability. This is fueling fears about the long-term prospects of economic growth which some economists are describing as a parenthesis of human history. Low or no growth would be the new normal in a system that desperately needs to adapt to the changing political, social, technological and environmental landscape—especially in the new age of social discontent and climate change. This would undermine the system's ability to continue to integrate all populations, in particular the most modest and least skilled ones. It would also undermine humanity's ability as a whole to survive in a world characterized by deep climate instability.

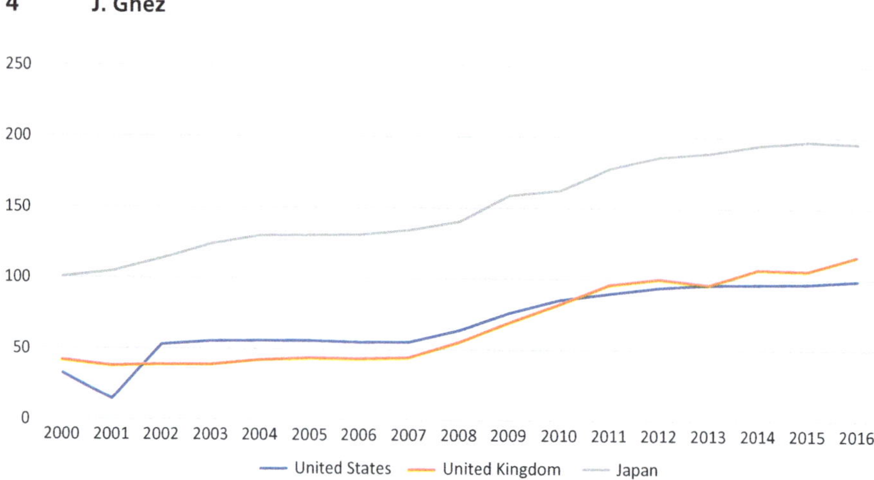

Fig. 1.1 Central government debt: total (% of GDP). Source: World Bank

Table 1.1 Real GDP growth rate by decade (in %)

	1960s	1970s	1980s	1990s	2000s	2010–2017
United States	50	37	36	35	15	16
Japan	144	51	49	11	2	8
European Union	56	35	24	20	13	10
Brazil	67	106	22	24	33	3
China	22	69	134	149	146	67
India	41	26	63	66	87	59

Growth rates have slowed down in OECD (Organisation for Economic Cooperation and Development) economies since the 1960s in a substantial and undeniable way. Recent data suggests emerging economies may be experiencing the same trend, but it is far more recent and on the question of whether it will last, the jury is still out.

The model is undergoing a crisis of efficiency as a result (Table 1.1).

Last, in yesterday's world, wealthier countries could act as if they were models of transparency, political stability, and economic dynamism that other countries could emulate in an increasingly interdependent world. The world has not become any less interdependent—but the model to emulate seems to be increasingly less attractive. In fact, high levels of discontent across western countries are putting into question the traditional mandate of the state. An increasing chunk of public opinions appear disenchanted with the democratic system which is not necessarily the political aspiration it was in the aftermath of the Cold War, a quarter of a century ago. The prospect of durably low growth is also fueling fears of social demotion in populations that once believed in the promise that the prospects of their descendants would always be better than theirs. If that promise in broken, it may be hard for them to consent to the efforts their elders made when in terms of taxes and respect for generally accepted societal norms. As one study has shown, "the proportion of younger citizens who believe it is essential to live in a democracy" is now falling in the minority in countries like the United States, Great Britain, the Netherlands, Sweden, Australia, and New Zealand. The authors add:

> this disaffection with the democratic form of government is accompanied by a wider skepticism toward liberal institutions. Citizens are growing more disaffected with established political parties, representative institutions, and minority rights. Tellingly, they are also increasingly open to authoritarian interpretations of democracy.

The study concludes that public attitudes towards democracy are not the only ones affected; political behavior, too, is changing: "In recent years, parties and candidates that blame an allegedly corrupt political establishment for most problems, seek to concentrate power in the executive, and challenge key norms of democratic politics have achieved unprecedented successes in a large number of liberal democracies across the globe."[1]

The model that once championed transparency and political stability is now undergoing a crisis of legitimacy as a result.

The Other Part of the Glass

These crises are all too real. Yet, here is a paradox: those crises notwithstanding, humanity has never been wealthier, healthier, and more educated, and more empowered than it is currently.

The fact that humanity has never been this wealthy is a very long-term trend that British historian and economist Angus Maddison has illustrated in his well-known dataset (Fig. 1.2).[2] Between 1700 and 2016, the GDP (gross domestic product) per capita measured in 2011 US dollars was multiplied by 21.2 in France, by nearly 16 in the United Kingdom, and by 23.6 in Germany. In the case of the United States, the earliest data dates back to 1720 and GDP per capita was multiplied by 39 between 1720 and 2016. Data is more limited for poorer economies; yet, the trend, over a shorter period of time, is no less significant. The GDP per capita of one of the poorest economies of the African continent, Malawi, was multiplied by 2.35 between 1950 and 2016. Similarly, it was multiplied by 3.22 in Bangladesh and by 2 in Bolivia.

Admittedly, increasing wealth alone is not sufficient to make the argument that humanity is better off. Yet, measures of health and education point to the very same story. In particular, the Human Development Index (HDI) has

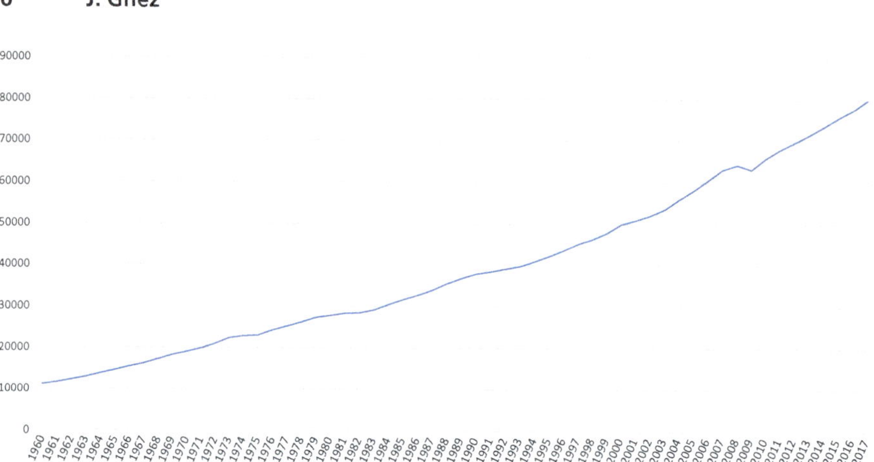

Fig. 1.2 World GDP (constant, in billions of 2010 US$)
The growth of world GDP has been almost continuous since the 1960s. This substantial growth has transformed societies all across the world and has lifted millions out of poverty.

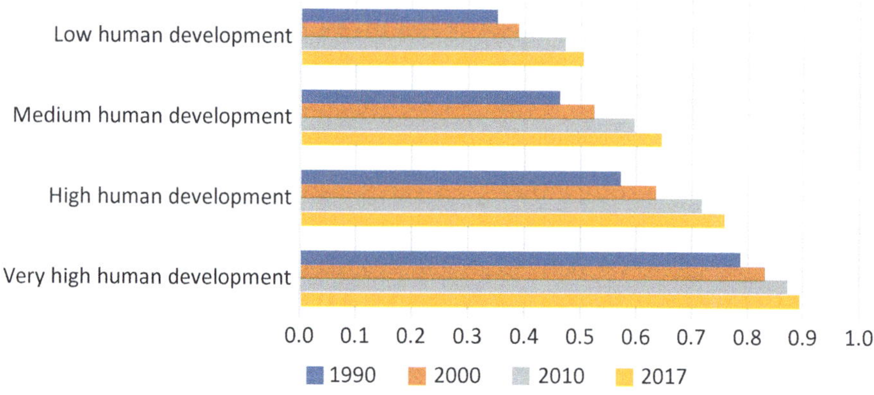

Fig. 1.3 HDI by country group
The progress of HDI indices across the globe between 1900 and 2017 is unquestionable according to UNDP (United Nations Development Programme) data. The lower the level of human development, the bigger the progress made. The gap between the most developed region of the world and the least developed is also closing.

continuously increased worldwide since 1990—at a yearly growth rate of 0.73%. That growth is more modest in OECD economies (0.49%), where there is less room to improve, and yet is still a resilient trend. It was, as expected, far more spectacular in Sub-Saharan Africa (1.12%) and even more so in South Asia (1.39%). These trends point to a healthier and more educated workforce, worldwide (Fig. 1.3).[3]

These trends of increasing wealth and improving health and access to education are significant even over the timespan of a decade. According to World Bank data, global life expectancy went from 69.5 to just over 72 between 2006 and 2016. The global share of the population living with $1.90 per day or less dropped from 20.7% in 2005 to just below 10% in 2015. According to UNICEF (United Nations International Children's Emergency Fund) data, neonatal mortality rate dropped from 24.3 for a thousand in 2007 to 18 for a thousand in 2017. These are not just long-term trends but also changing realities happening under the very eyes of this generation.

Empowerment is certainly harder to measure quantitatively. Yet, there is plenty of evidence suggesting the trend is pointing to the same story: whether it is a more informed population in a Northern African country able to hold truth to a long-lasting dictatorship or the increased ability of a group of citizens in a Western country to organize itself and undermine the traditional influence of political parties and labor unions, the notion that the ever-more connected and knowledgeable citizen is becoming increasingly influential seems widely shared.

The Perspective of History

Ultimately, this business environment was able to improve the fate of an incredibly significant number of people—and the outcome is indisputable here. But it seems ill-prepared to face the new set of challenges that the twenty-first century is bringing to the table and requires significant reinvention. In fact, these three trends on wealth, health, and empowerment cannot erase by themselves the three crises of the system. But they are powerful illustrations of the assets that are at the disposal of those actors seeking to drive change in an environment ripe for disruption.

In fact, as we look to put these challenges in perspective, we must not forget that history can be a useful guide, in particular because we, as humanity, have been at this critical point once before, just prior to the period that historians now refer to the Renaissance. And as two authors Ian Goldin and Chris Kutarna have argued elsewhere, "The forces that converged in Europe 500 years ago to spark genius and upend social order are present again in our lifetime. Only now they are stronger, and global."

The anxieties and the identity crisis that we are going through should not be surprising as a result: populations who thought of themselves as "middle classes" and as pillars of modern societies, driving incremental changes to improve the overall resilience of societies, feel particularly uneasy, dispossessed, and disenfranchised in these uncharted waters. They believed that the system would guarantee the continuous progress of the prospects of those who worked hard and who played by the rules. They may feel they have taken that progress for granted, given fears about unemployment and social demotion, about economic slowdown and rising protectionist and populist sentiments, and about our sense of physical security in the wake of pandemics and acts of violence. So instead of looking to tame these forces upending social orders and upsetting our economies, we are scared stiff by uncertainty.

As Goldin and Kutarna observe:

> The last Renaissance was a time of tremendous upheaval that strained society to, and often past, the breaking point. Now, we risk fumbling badly again, as individuals, as society and as a species—and we've had some big stumbles already. It's made many of us cynical and fearful for the future. If we want to attain the greatness for which humanity is once again eligible, we must keep faith in its possibility. We must do all we can to realize it. We must broaden and share more widely the benefits of progress. And we must help one another to cope with the shocks that none of us will see coming.

This business environment, in other words, is custom-made for architects of change.

Time to Act—But How?

We understand why amid fears about durably low economic growth and about increasing global political, social, societal, technological, and environmental tensions worldwide, it has become fashionable for senior executives to worry and complain about how unstable and turbulent the world has become. How does one thrive in such an unamicable environment?

These fears are legitimate—and documented. But they may drive our focus to the wrong set of priorities: instead of arousing our curiosity, encouraging us to be imaginative and inviting us to be bold in looking for fixes to the most mind-boggling and pressing issues of tomorrow, these fears are forcing us to put the emphasis on the issue of the day, that is, on what is part of our comfort zone. Changing mindsets is essential.

The Story of the (Un)needed Hero

In turbulent times, it is rather natural to look for heroic role models. The fireman easily fits the job: when the house is burning (as executives often argue in times of crisis), who better to fight the flames of the day and to put out the most pressing fires threatening the life of a company, or a country? The figure of the fireman is also impactful because it allows leaders to mobilize and direct resources toward a common, tangible goal and thereby show off their leadership skills. After all, no one ever blames a leader for putting a fire out. That yields immediate results—unlike the much-despised talking heads, who are not especially known to act.

This is why fears about durable economic stagnation and political instability feed the "fireman" mentality: a wide range of actors, who are very happy to fight the flames of the present, often overlook the possibility that the house may have already burnt down. And a fireman rarely has the luxury to maintain the curiosity and the imagination that is required today to act on and fix the most mind-boggling and pressing issues of tomorrow. That is the role of architects, willing to bring about change to the edifice so as to make it more robust and sustainable.

And yet, dysfunctional systems and obsolete models do not necessarily require that fires be put out. Instead, they demand to be redesigned and rebuilt, or even completely reinvented. In fact, firemen, as arduous as they may be in fighting the flames of the day, may not always see that the house has already burned down and may be ill-suited to rebuild it. This is why this world is probably not a fireman's playground but that of an architect's. In practice, it requires far more courage to start thinking and acting like an architect of change.

To be sure, the architect figure may look far less impressive because it may seem far less heroic. Yet, in this turbulent business environment, it may be time to repair this injustice, in particular because we should be especially wary of decision-makers who constantly look for fires to put out, instead of looking for opportunities to repair and to rebuild. Being an architect may be less appealing on paper, given the technical skills, the precision, the attention to detail and the patience it requires. But it is decidedly the figure that deserves more attention in a business environment that we openly describe as ripe for disruption.

Meet the Architects of Change

Meet Daniel, a young banker filled with ambition—and not only financial ones. Daniel understands the conversation about the world entering uncharted waters all too well: traditional measures of risk are not shedding enough light on the phenomena and the transformations he is seeing worldwide. The real challenge to him lies not only in understanding these changes but also in bringing a whole industry to embrace them and to modify its analytical grid accordingly—because the ramifications of the industry failing to do so will be as wide as they are significant.

Meet Emilie, a bright, determined, and newly promoted executive in the procurements department of a big company that is looking to adapt to the new business environment. Everyone inside the company may be, in theory, ready to embrace change, in favor of more sustainable and inclusive practices in particular. Yet, in practice, Emilie still needs to fight against the temptation to revert to yesterday's dogma of short-term benefits and measures of returns. The real challenge for Emilie lies in mobilizing forces of change and describing a sufficiently realistic and yet appealing vision of the future so as to get the company to transform not only its practices but its whole cultural mindset as well.

Meet Anita, a seasoned entrepreneur, with a simple and yet powerful idea in mind: too many old clothes are left unused because they are worn out, or worse, thrown out, when they could actually have a second life. Anita is in a unique position to understand what clients want because she meets with them and works on an existing product that already has a history. The ultimate result is handmade and tailor-made—unlike the many other substitutes for those old clothes. Her challenge is not only about recycling; it is also about giving a second life to a defining object for a person looking forward.

Meet Bella, a young and already successful consultant, helping a wide range of for-profit and non-profit actors worldwide. These actors share a common characteristic: they all hear and understand the injunction to be "innovative"; but they also have the same dirty little secret—they are not even sure anymore what that actually means. As a result, for those for-profit and non-profit actors, business as usual seems like the safest way to operate. Bella knows that not taking any risks is a risk itself. Her challenge lies in going beyond the world is ripe for disruption, and exploring with her clients the unexplored, the unimagined models of tomorrow.

Daniel, Emilie, Anita, and Bella are all architects of change in the making. They are anti-fatalist and anti-conformist by design. This means refusing what destiny has in store for you and constantly seeking to challenge the status quo. They are also agitators, looking to break the consensus of the day by broadening society's horizons and identifying new opportunities to create value. As architects of change, they are not content with just making a short-term profit, in particular because they are not in the business of passively accepting their business environment as it is. Instead, they are trying to actively analyze it in order to bend it. They all have a shared interest in identifying a broken system that they believe they can fix, thereby creating new sources of value and new opportunities, for themselves and for society as a whole. This is not a task they can undertake without considering their surroundings. It is not a task they can tackle without accepting that they will need to explore the unknown.

This Book Is a Tool

In fact, no matter where you stand professionally, if you are convinced that this business environment is an invitation for change rather than an encouragement to protect the status quo, these questions are likely to matter to you.

Being an Architect of Change in This Business Environment

If you are an entrepreneur, developing your ability to be an architect of change can help you identify opportunities in areas that are ripe for disruption. You may in particular be able to create new business opportunities by fixing broken systems that have become unsustainable for a wide range of political, social, and environmental reasons.

If you are working in a big company, being an architect of change can help you transform the way the business and the industry operate so as to create more value not only for shareholders and consumers but for society as a whole as well. Focusing more on shared value as a game-change will not mean forgoing profit but fundamentally changing the equation you rely on to maximize profits.

If you are a banker, thinking like an architect of change can help you identify the relevant trends shaping the most meaningful risks and opportunities in tomorrow's markets. As a game-changer in the banking industry, relying on a non-conformist view of a sector, you may be able to better uncover opportunities that more conventional and traditional approaches may overlook.

If you are a consultant, approaching a business problem like an architect of change can help you determine what is likely to make some business models more successful than others, and what approaches are likely to be disrupted in this business environment. This approach may be better suited for a consultant advising industries that are ripe for change because the traditional way they function may not be sustainable anymore.

What to Expect in This Book

No matter where you find yourself professionally in a disruptive landscape, your ability to think and act like an architect of change is therefore likely to be a key driver of success. This is why this book is designed to help potential business creators, senior executives and, more generally, leading decision-makers and analysts in business and beyond, identify future opportunities to innovate and bring about meaningful and constructive change to obsolete systems and models—in an increasingly complex business environment.

Ultimately, this book looks to empower you, the reader, as an architect of change. It aims at providing you with the roadmap you need to become a driver of change and to transform dysfunctional processes and obsolete models in a wide range of fields into viable and sustainable paradigms in this intimidating, erratic, and turbulent business environment. It is designed for those individuals that are deeply dissatisfied with the status quo and profoundly frustrated with this broken system that is not holding its promise of a better tomorrow—and yet, who still believe in that promise, if anything because of the fact that there can be no other alternative in their mind. This book's objective is to provide architects of change in the making with the toolbox they need to better understand their business environment and thus design meaningful strategies not only to survive but also to strive.

You will find in the following chapters a mix of tools and case studies. The presentation of tools often rely on frameworks and business practices that often already exist, but that have never really been placed side by side. Doing so will help you put together your own roadmap for transformation. The case studies not only apply these tools but also broaden horizons as well as consider alternatives to the status quo and to the existing consensus about the state of the business environment and the opportunities to seize. They often place you in the shoes of an actor facing a significant challenge and provide food for thought on how architects of change can not only transform that challenge into value for themselves but also fix a larger problem in the long run. As you read and ponder the issues raised by these case studies, it is important to remember that, more often than not, it is better to *ask* yourself and others some questions, rather than to pretend to *know* all of the answers.

In particular, in Chaps. 2 and 3, you will learn how to tame the current business landscape. Chapter 2 provides a thought experiment that relies on two very well-known and strikingly different figures of fiction, James Bond and Q, that architects of change will ultimately need to reconcile in order to be successful in this business environment. Chapter 3 will give you an overview of the global business landscape that is designed to help you determine the reality of the business environment you live in order to be in a better position to identify the problems and the most meaningful impact you can have.

In Chap. 4, you will start to imagine, in a game that throws you 20 years ahead, the type of architect of change you really are, given your understanding of global dynamics and the problems you are seeking to solve. Chapter 5 will give you the critical tools you need to find that road to reinvention that you will most probably have already started to look for, unconsciously at the very least. This chapter is designed to help you capture the major microeconomic dynamics shaping your immediate business environment. It will help you identify opportunities to better leverage these dynamics and to act on them, in particular by transforming your activity that is better suited for future challenges. Chapter 6, a case study on a fancy pizza place, will help you put into practice those principles of reinvention in a very practical way.

Chapters 7 through 12 will help you identify and develop the major qualities you need in order to become an architect of change. In particular, an architect of change must be analytical, as opposed to dogmatic, as Chap. 7 illustrates. Chapter 8 provides a case study on a retail giant looking to identify threats and opportunities, beyond the doom and gloom of the most pessimistic voices—but also beyond the blind idealism of the most optimistic. Architects of change must also nurture a strong ability to anticipate, as Chap. 9 shows by introducing you to scenario-planning. Chapter 10, which describes the dilemma of a key actor looking to better anticipate future trends beyond the noise and the scary headlines, will help you put the principles of anticipation into practice. Last but not least, architects of change will need to understand the purpose of imagination, which lies ultimately in strengthening one's resilience. Chapter 11 presents an exercise, the pre-mortem, which will help you not lack imagination in a world in which you will desperately need some.

Chapters 13 through 15, the final chapters of this book, concentrate on the creativity, the ultimate quality of architects of change that results from their ability to remain analytical, to anticipate, and to imagine in this turbulent business environment. Chapter 13 discusses the meaning of creativity and the implications this has for the knowledge economy—a key feature of this business environment. Chapter 14 presents one final case of a Human Resource expert, looking to put together the ultimate team to help a tech giant survive and make a difference in this highly political landscape. Finally, Chap. 15 ends on a more personal note, by describing the lessons this author draws from interacting with children—in particular his own.

It thereby ends on a positive note: children have plenty of energy to bring the change they want to see and plenty of curiosity to imagine alternatives.

They know how to make a difference because they still know how to dream, experiencing no real difficulty in overlooking what adults see as "reality." That behavior may be one of the most empowering and powerful ones to bring change.

In other words, we once knew how to be architects of change. But we forgot along the way. We need to undertake this journey in order to find our own, personal way of being architects of change, once again?

Notes

1. Roberto Stefan Foa and Yasha Mounk, "The Signs of Deconsolidation," *Journal of Democracy* 28, no. 1 (January 2017): 5–16.
2. Maddison Project Database, version 2018. Bolt, Jutta, Robert Inklaar, Herman de Jong and Jan Luiten van Zanden (2018), "Rebasing 'Maddison': new income comparisons and the shape of long-run economic development," Maddison Project Working paper 10.
3. "Human Development Reports—Trends," United Nations Development Programme, September 2018, http://hdr.undp.org/en/composite/trends.

2

Case Study: When James Bond Met Q

Fiction can, at times, be a source of inspiration for architects of change looking for new avenues of reinvention. The stories of the famous British spy, James Bond, are no exception.

It is hard to find two figures of fiction that are more antinomic than James Bond and Q. One is a spy that fulfills his missions on the field, while the other is a researcher who spends his professional life in the lab. Yet, though they may look nothing alike, they need each other to succeed. In fact, when he meets Q, the head of research and development of his intelligence service, MI6, James Bond often seems uninterested in what his colleague has to say: the spy never asks for fancy gadgets; yet, Q always has fancy gadgets to offer. And in the stories, James Bond rarely uses those gadgets for their intended purposes; but he somehow always ends up fulfilling his mission and neutralizing the enemy—thanks to the fancy gadgets.[1]

The Decision-Maker's Struggle

The James Bond analogy with today's business world is striking. Executives are often confident—and legitimately so—about their understanding of the business environment and how they fit in the global picture. But that confidence can also dampen their curiosity and discourage them from broadening their horizons. In fact, too often, executives and decision-makers are tempted to believe they know the right answer, failing to recognize that they are approaching the problem with the baggage of dogma and overlooking what the less sensationalist, yet no less insightful, pieces of analysis are saying.

J. Ghez, *Architects of Change*, https://doi.org/10.1007/978-3-030-20684-0_2

Reconciling Two Contradictory Figures

Acting is what is most exhilarating to them as they ignore, as a result, pieces of evidence that could have suggested viable alternatives. The instant gratification of having an immediate impact by solving the most pressing issue of the day should by no means inspire guilt. Who, after all, never dreamed of being a James Bond-like figure in this business environment? But it should not lead us to copiously ignore Q, as what he has to say can often be game changing. In fact, leaders who do not take courageous decisions like James Bond are unlikely to succeed in being transformative. But, at the same time, leaders who fail to constantly rethink, reimagine, and redesign their toolbox and their approaches, and perhaps more fundamentally, their purpose, may not have a significant long-term impact in this business environment.

The art of being an architect of change lies in reconciling James Bond and Q.

The James Bond Story Versus the Q Story

The James Bond story of a business or organization is fairly straightforward: it is the one that the headlines and the concerns of the day generate. It usually concentrates on issues related to short-term profitability, to the ability of the organization to manage internal crises so as to better function and to meet the challenges set by the competitive landscape. The James Bond story puts the emphasis on the flames of the day the business or the organization must face.

The Q story focuses on the idea of the business or the organization that goes beyond its current activities, that allows it to adapt to the changing business environment and that can make it successful over an extended period of time. It is a story that is interested in broader horizons—both in terms of time and in terms of topics—than the James Bond one, as the key concern is not only the business's or the organization's ability to fulfill the mission of the day, but also its ability to fulfill its long-term purpose.

The challenge architects of change face does not lie in deciding who to listen to. Rather, it lies in striking the right balance between the inspiration we draw from both James Bond and Q, the right balance between the two narratives in order to design transformative strategies that will help a business or an organization out of a stalemate.

Saving Companies from Irrelevance and Stalemates

Thinking about the James Bond and the Q stories of a company can help its leadership understand how, as would-be architects of change, it can put together a meaningful roadmap to increase its impact. The reasoning is applicable to virtually any company or organization looking to durably shape the business environment.

What IBM's Centennial Says About the Company

The instance of IBM is illustrative. Depending on when you are considering this example, the James Bond story you may come up with may vary and depend on possible profit surge or warning, on a change in leadership or on a new market or competitor IBM is entering or facing.

The Q story, on the contrary, is likely to be more complex.

Celebrating IBM's centennial, the British weekly *The Economist* argued that the company's

> secret is that it is built around an idea that transcends any particular product or technology. Its strategy is to package technology for use by businesses. At first this meant making punch-card tabulators, but IBM moved on to magnetic-tape systems, mainframes, PCs, and most recently services and consulting. Building a company around an idea, rather than a specific technology, makes it easier to adapt when industry 'platform shifts' occur.[2]

A company like IBM has and is likely to hit some bumps along the way that shareholders and other stakeholders expect the company's leadership to manage as quickly and as efficiently as possible.

But the company's long-term viability will depend on the leadership's ability to remember its secret, that is, that very "idea that transcends any particular product or technology," namely, the "strategy is to package technology for use by businesses" (see note 2). This is likely to be the only guarantee for success in the wake of a deep, structural crisis driven by the changing business environment. And identifying that idea is what will help the company's leadership be true architects of change.

Uber's Central Idea

The transportation network company Uber has experienced several internal crises related to the fitness of its leaders, to its management of diversity inside the company, to how it has addressed sexual harassment claims and to how it has treated its drivers. Questions related to the company's overall profitability, its impressive ability to raise capital, and its ability to find compromises with city regulators on its operations are also often part of the headlines. It is inconceivable that the company's management could ever ignore those concerns.

But as it seeks to fight the flames of the day and to adapt the company accordingly, it must also keep an eye on the very idea that could make it durably successful, namely *mobility*. This is the very idea that could help the company rethink its purpose in the changing and turbulent business environment, in particular by helping it understand in what way the advent of driverless cars and smart cities for instance should shape its approach in the near future and in the longer run. The example of smart cities is particularly striking: given the significant efforts the company has put in elaborating high-performance algorithms to efficiently allocate drivers and organize resources, Uber could arguably be a key actor of smart cities and work in close collaboration with city regulators—the very people the company is having difficulties finding a compromise with. Putting greater emphasis on the Q story and identifying the broader idea that transcends any particular headline often helps a company move out of the stalemate.

An Exercise for Transformation

The successful architect of change is the individual able to consider any embattled company and find the idea that could transcend any particular product, service or technology that organization is known for. Reconciling James Bond and Q does not mean ignoring one or the other but rather addressing the challenges raised by the former relying on what the latter is seeing.

You may have doubts about the ability of a Chinese tech and retail company like Alibaba to make headway in a Western market, unless you consider what the company can do to build up the "made in China" brand and to create new free-trade areas: the company designed an electronic world trade platform to facilitate the expansion of ecommerce in Asia and to make it easier for small- and medium-sized businesses to trade across borders. These efforts suggest that the concerns of the company's leadership have gone beyond those of traditional ecommerce and tech experts.

You may legitimately wonder about the future of newspapers, and more broadly about news organizations who have experienced substantial financial difficulties in recent times. As the founder of two news organizations Jim

Vandehei once argued, digital media companies find themselves caught in a "crap trap":[3] Instead of producing quality but costly content, they looked to rely on attractive headlines to increase traffic and to contain costs. And yet, observes Vandehei, "revenue never followed because everyone else was doing the same tricks and getting the same spikes—and the simple law of supply and demand drove down the value of their inventory."[4] The James Bond story of the industry, focused on the ability of these organizations to increase traffic and generate ad revenues for instance, was therefore misleading, in particular for those actors looking for transformative impact. Jim Vandehei's Q story about the industry is less about scale than it is about the ability of its actors to create "content of consequence and value."[5] This ability will mean a shift away from paper and to mobile and social networks, a greater focus on informing rather than trying to influence the reader, an effort to make it easy for the reader to grasp complex information efficiently and quickly and a focus on content that is worthy of people's time. This information revolution is one that responds to a large extent to the changing environment of the media industry in the age of rumor, dogma, and speculation.

Lessons for Architects of Change

Ultimately, you may question the viability of a company. Becoming an architect of change requires trying to identify alternative narratives of the business environment that incorporate those doubts about viability, but that also help you bring about meaningful change where others identified stagnation and turmoil. It means, in sum, to be able to constantly reconcile James Bond and Q—and make them work together.

In fact, this discussion provides three key insights for leaders seeking to become architects of change.

First, the James Bond and Q dialog is an invitation to go beyond the linear thinking our human brains may be well-wired to deal with but that is in no way the reality of this business environment. As this author argued elsewhere,

> the conventional, linear minds of traditional leaders are used to extrapolating and predicting. Yet, it is hard to imagine how they can thrive without greater awareness of exponential phenomena. This approach may only induce limited and imperceptible changes initially, but these modifications can be transformative and disruptive once they gather steam. Without curiosity and imagination, many of these leaders are likely to lose their edge and see their activity disrupted.[6]

This is why the Q narrative of a business or an organization is so critical: it drives decision-makers to broaden their horizons and explore alternatives to linear interpretations of their environment, thereby transforming them into architects of change. This form of mental gymnastics is indispensable to architects of change as a result. In this business environment, those delivering the analysis need to push it because it will rarely be pulled—or demanded—by those making the decisions.

Second, the contrast between the James Bond and Q stories sheds light on the significance of analysis and the importance of approaching problems with as few preconceived notions of reality as possible. When we are held hostage by the headlines and the flames of the day, we may very well be suited to fulfill today's mission. But because we pay so little attention to Q's story, to the ideas that are likely to persist regardless of changes of the business environment, we are in no position to bring about transformative change. Architects of change, on the contrary, are able to do so, in spite of the complex business environment and its evolution, because they pay attention to the deeper, structural, and fundamental dynamics of the landscape and its organizations. Their ability to remain analytical in an ideological world puts them in a position to bring about transformative change.

Last, and not unrelated to the previous point, is the fact that we should look to nurture our curiosity and our imagination so as to understand our business environment. In doing so, architects of change are able to better understand—and therefore tame?—their business environment and populate their radar screen with topics that are worthy of attention. This effort is not as straightforward as one might believe: it is often tempting for would-be architects of change to focus on colonizing Mars or putting an end to all wars. But ambition is not only about moonshot projects. More often than not, the impact of architects of change can first be very local before influencing the wider environment. This is why we should not discount incremental change that can actually be transformative ultimately.

Subsequent chapters explore these insights in detail.

But it is first important to note that architects of change can never achieve this, can never accurately state the problem they are trying to solve without a clear understanding of their business environment and all its dimensions that both James Bond and Q would have raised. This is the topic of the next chapter.

Notes

1. This comparison was first discussed in a workshop whose content was described in Gregory F. Treverton and Jeremy J. Ghez, *Making Strategic Analysis Matter*, RAND Corporation Conference Proceedings Series CF287-NIC (Santa Monica, CA: RAND, 2012).
2. "The Test of Time—IBM's Centenary," *The Economist*, June 9, 2011, https://www.economist.com/leaders/2011/06/09/the-test-of-time.
3. Jim VandeHei, "Escaping the Digital Media 'Crap Trap,'" *The Information*, April 19, 2016, https://www.theinformation.com/escaping-the-digital-media-crap-trap.
4. VandeHei.
5. VandeHei.
6. Jeremy J. Ghez, "Training Future Leaders to Be More Like Q, Less Like James Bond," *BizEd Magazine*, August 23, 2018, https://bized.aacsb.edu/articles/2018/08/training-future-leaders-to-be-more-like-q-less-like-james-bond.

3

The World We Live In

No one ever takes a decision in a vacuum. A wide range of forces that shape our business environment can be the reason of early success or failure of any actor, big or small. Unless we understand those forces and the world we live in, we are likely to flounder around in the global landscape, misstating the issue we are seeking to tackle and the objectives we are trying to reach. It is hard to define the problem we want to solve, as architects of change, without understanding first the world we live in.

But analyzing the world we live in, global megatrends and deep underlying forces may feel like an overwhelming, at times herculean task: decision-makers with very worldly preoccupations, facing the urgent demands of consumers, shareholders, and/or other stakeholders, often feel the urgency of the moment lies in fighting the flames of the day, not understanding the broader architecture of the business environment. This is especially true when we feel that our personal weight and specific aims are modest compared to how brutal and impressive the broader business environment seems. This analytical effort could represent at times in a luxury we feel we cannot afford: any piece of analysis is likely to be contingent on current trends and affairs that may seem highly relevant today but that could fast become obsolete. Updating such analysis therefore requires a constant, costly effort.

Yet, this effort is by no means a futile one. Research has shown that companies that adopt a longer-term horizon outperform their peers substantially in terms of revenue and in terms of financial performance, while investing more, including in research and development, and creating more jobs.[1] Excessive focus on short-term dynamics and the current noise comes at a cost, too. When architects of change build the capacity to shed light, get a good grasp

J. Ghez, *Architects of Change*, https://doi.org/10.1007/978-3-030-20684-0_3

of, monitor and perhaps leverage the mega-forces shaping their business environment, they are able to get ahead of their peer competitors as a result.

This chapter explores six of these mega-forces that have the potential to profoundly shape the business environment: geopolitical rivalries, global cooperation, identity politics, inequalities, global warming, and technology.[2] This list may feel incomplete and we may interpret (and even label differently) each of these forces differently depending on the time, the industry or activity, and the region we are located. But it is important to remember that the point of this exploration is not to choose which one of these forces is definitively shaping the business environment contrary to the five others but to develop an ability to capture, at any point in time in the life of a decision-maker, which *combination* is likely to matter most when it comes to your ability to drive change in this business environment.

Conducting such an analytical effort can help you structure the way you think about the world we live in and the forces shaping it. As a result, understanding first the business environment better so as to define the problem you want to solve and to identify the obstacles and the forces you could leverage as an architect of change in the making becomes all the less so costly and laborious.

The objective of this chapter is to help you achieve this effort. The chapter discusses each of the forces and explores its implications for decision-makers looking to drive change.

A World of Geopolitical Rivalries

A conversation about the forces shaping the business environment usually starts with a statement about the power struggles between great global powers seeking to protect, or even consolidate, their positions at the detriment of others. This conversation often focuses on power distribution as a result: whoever has "power" can coerce others to do what it wants them to do, impose its will and its rules to the rest of the world and can even shape norms and standards at the global level. This view argues that, because global powers rarely have overlapping interests, one's win is another one's loss. In this zero-sum game, great power rivalries will shape global outcomes. Whoever wins the struggle gets to set the rules.

Determining who has "power" can therefore be of critical importance to the architect of change looking to understand who will set tomorrow's rules and regulations, and who is likely to be in a position to attract resources tomorrow. But as they do look to determine that, architects of change should be wary of the limits of the definition and the argument about power, as well as the ability to coerce.

First, power is rarely uniform: it can be exercised in expected and straightforward ways, as well as in more surprising and unanticipated ways—including beyond coercion. In addition, the notion that states are the only actors who have the ability to influence outcomes is likely to have its limits in a business environment in which they have fewer financial means and less legitimacy to act. The array of actors we consider is therefore a significant question. The very definition of power matters as a result: it is critical to understand which country *or non-state actor* has leverage to influence outcomes, rather than just focus on which country can actually coerce others.

Second, power analysis usually provides a snapshot of power distribution at a given moment in time, without consideration of changing trends. Another challenge lies in understanding disruptive moments that lead to key changes in the world's power structure—and potentially, as a result, to a new set of norms and standards, set by the new dominant power which successfully challenged the former dominant power.

The complex definition of power suggests that we should handle this argument about how the business environment functions with care.

Defining Power

The most straightforward forms of coercive power are economic and military in nature, in particular because both provide actors with the ability to coerce weaker players into behaving the way they want them to behave.

When a Hegemon Is Able to Coerce

On the military side, the size of the military, measured by defense spending, is the metric that we commonly refer to. On the economic side, the size of the economy, measured by gross domestic product (GDP), provides a picture of leading global powers (Fig. 3.1).

Historically, the existence of a hegemon, that is, a single power dominating the world both in terms of economic and military strengths, has not been uncommon. It has the ability to impose its standards to the rest of the world—even if the legitimacy of the hegemon is not necessarily widely accepted. It presents the advantage of providing clarity about the rules and norms that shape the global landscape. It can therefore be a source of stability for the business environment. For instance, in the aftermath of the fall of the Berlin

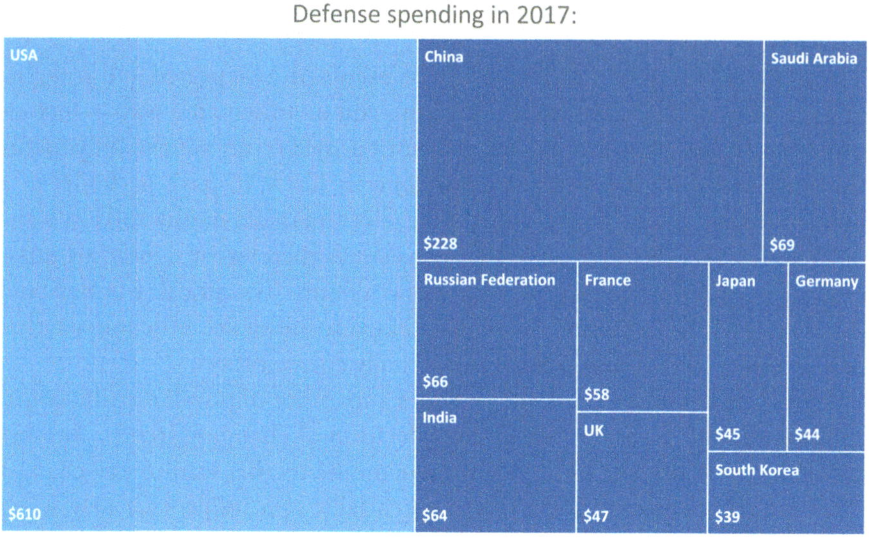

Fig. 3.1 Defense spending compared across the globe. Source: SIPRI Military Expenditure Database (https://www.sipri.org/databases/milex)
When it comes to defense spending, the United States unequivocally outranks all other nations, spending more than the other top seven countries *combined*.

Wall and the subsequent dislocation of the Soviet Union, the United States stood out as the only dominant power capable of shaping the global landscape with a political agenda focused on free markets and democratic standards (Table 3.1).

The Dynamics of Power Are Also Critical

Nevertheless, this dominance has never been eternal. The interests of countries rarely overlap, raising questions about the viability of any status quo. The rise to power of challengers seeking to overturn the current international architecture can undermine the ability of the hegemon to influence outcomes over time as well as its legitimacy to do so in time. Ultimately, when the challenger seeks to overturn the status quo, it is likely that whatever one power is able to win, another will lose in this zero-sum game. Great power rivalries are therefore unavoidable in this logic. They fuel the tensions and the rivalries that historians and geopolitical experts have always been mindful of because their potential to trigger deep, structural changes in how the business environment works is significant. Consider the 2008 financial crisis, which arguably

Table 3.1 2018 global economic powers measured by GDP

Top 10 economic powers in the world in 2018							
Rank	Country	GDP (nominal)	Share of global GDP	Rank	Country	GDP (PPP)	Share of global GDP
1	United States	20,412.87	23.3	1	China	25,238.56	18.7
2	China	14,092.51	16.1	2	United States	20,412.87	15.1
3	Japan	5167.05	5.90	3	India	10,385.43	7.69
4	Germany	4211.64	4.81	4	Japan	5619.49	4.16
5	United Kingdom	2936.29	3.36	5	Germany	4373.95	3.24
6	France	2925.10	3.34	6	Russia	4168.88	3.09
7	India	2848.23	3.25	7	Indonesia	3492.21	2.59
8	Italy	2181.97	2.49	8	Brazil	3388.96	2.51
9	Brazil	2138.92	2.44	9	United Kingdom	3028.57	2.24
10	Canada	1798.51	2.06	10	France	2960.25	2.19

Source: International Monetary Fund World Economic Outlook (April 2018)

The distribution of power measured in economic terms by GDP is more ambiguous. While GDP rankings in nominal value suggest the United States is still by far the most significant economy in the world, GDP rankings relying on PPP, or purchasing power parity, which accounts for differences in living standards, suggest that China has actually overtaken the United States. In both cases, the top economies represent more than two-thirds and more than 60% of the global GDP measured nominally and with PPP respectively. Neither indicator is a perfect measure of economic power in a standalone way as they reflect different realities about the state of respective economies. The fact that China became the leading power in the PPP ranking by 2014 means that the purchasing power inside the country, given the overall level of prices, is more significant there than in the United States. It is an illustration of how big a market the country has become. And yet, it is not in local currencies that we measure international trade and financial flows; it is in dollars. The nominal ranking suggests that in this realm of global finance and trade, the United States remains by far the leading power. Finally, it is also noteworthy that neither indicator captures notions like welfare or happiness that make Scandinavian countries so appealing and attractive. The list of economic indicators is therefore far broader than GDP.

undermined the US ability to durably uphold the standards it held dear, because the crisis put into question the very foundations of those very standards. Combined with the rise of China, often described a revisionist power seeking to challenge the current status quo and potentially overturn it, the financial crisis raised many questions about the viability of a global system dominated by the United States.

Because the dominance of a hegemon has never been eternal, there is a risk in only considering any snapshot of a given power distribution at a specific moment in time: a challenger's successful bid to overturn the status quo and the resulting abrupt changes in norms and standards can blindside any player that is not attentive enough. It is therefore critical to consider trends and momentum as well as less straightforward ways in which some players can exert their influence so as to fully grasp how norms and standards may evolve over time (Table 3.2).

In fact, in addition to absolute forms of power, it is also important to consider the momentum of power distribution. Those powers that have, in recent

Table 3.2 Changes in defense spending, 2008–2017

	2008	2017	% change
China	108,457.126	228,172.636	110
India	41,113.3829	59,757.1062	45
Russia	40,285.9723	55,327.2217	37
Saudi Arabia	51,781.0329	69,521.4499	34
Germany	39,546.0141	43,022.9795	9
France	53,569.1578	56,287.3987	5
Japan	44,600.8091	46,555.9842	4
USA	692,402.045	597,177.905	−14
UK	57,203.4247	48,383.3663	−15
Italy	34,187.5724	28,416.6048	−17

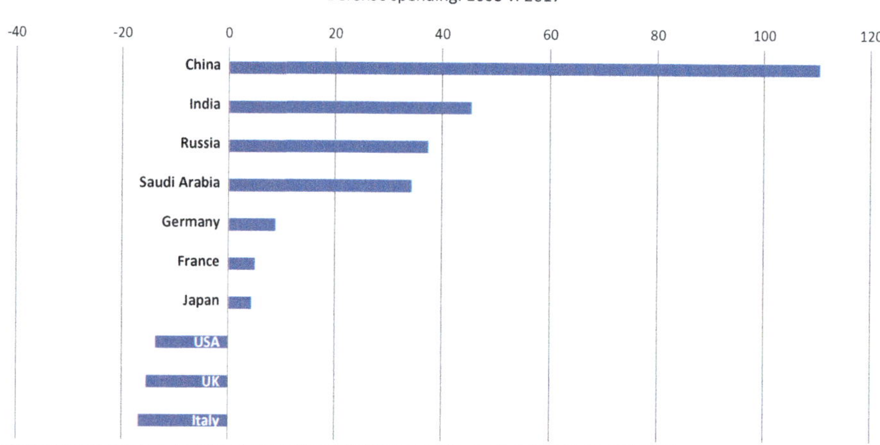

Figures represent percentage of military expenditures
Source: SIPRI Military Expenditure Database (https://www.sipri.org/databases/milex)
Defense spending dynamics reveal a different story than the one suggested by current levels of defense spending. This graph lists the top ten spenders on defense in 2008 and illustrates the evolution of spending over the past decade. Dynamics point to momentum that snapshot pictures of spending fail to illustrate: while the United States cut its spending, more revisionist powers like China dramatically increased it.

years, accelerated their defense spending are not those that were traditionally the top defense spenders. Similarly, the widely documented notion of "emerging economies" suggests that faster-growing economies are usually not the largest economies.[3]

China is a very special case from this standpoint: the growth of its defense spending has almost matched the growth of its economy[4]—a fact that offers a unique insight on what China's rise has meant: an accelerated development on two key fronts of power, a rise that is often depicted as being to the detriment of old, traditional powers like the United States and European countries. Both absolute volumes and dynamics matter in understanding the reality of today's and tomorrow's power distribution and the potential for geopolitical tensions between nations.

In addition, some analysts have also come to question the relevance of any form of power analysis that considers states exclusively, thus ignoring non-state actors. These analysts often put the emphasis on how big businesses are setting technological standards and are seeking to influence norms and regulation through lobbying. But perhaps more profoundly, these big businesses will increasingly need to fill in the void that states with fewer financial means and less legitimacy are leaving, not necessarily because they seek to adopt an altruistic approach towards the rest of the world but because in doing so, they take care of negative externalities that they could suffer from *themselves*. Their interests need not be contradictory with the rest of society: they may overlap, leading the value these big businesses create to be shared among that wide range of other stakeholders. But their interests may also come collide with the rest of society, leading to calls for regulation whose success varies greatly across countries and cases. The instance of tech firms is illustrative of this paradox: while they rely on a broader ecosystem as they particularly benefit from a well-educated and healthy workforce, and while they may increasingly play the role that public entities played in the past, their behavior, especially in terms of private data collection and in terms of antitrust standards, are a source of concern for public opinions and policymakers. Europeans may have failed to generate meaningful tech giants, but one of their key institutions, the European Union, has proved to be an effective regulator and standard-setter. The debate over the showdown between firms and states may not be new—but is not a closed one either.

Similarly, analysts should not overlook the role of non-governmental institutions and watch dogs that bring to the public debate alternative ideas and approaches to governance and to doing business. They can be substitutes to failing states or the generator of ideas shaping the public debate in a way that pressures companies and states to act differently. Their power stems from their ability to bring to the table a credible set of alternatives to the (at times failing) status quo.

The Power Play of Smaller Players

It is also important to remember that even smaller and weaker actors can become power players thanks to a perfect mix of circumstances placing them in a unique position (even compared to stronger actors) to exert short-term but decisive influence at a given moment in time or on a given outcome. For instance, it is striking that, the unmatched size of its military notwithstanding, the United States has not fared very well in theaters like Iraq and Afghanistan, where insurgency groups relying on asymmetric warfare tactics have frustrated American efforts. Asymmetric warfare tactics require that traditional powers rethink drastically their approach to a war theater: as two authors put it, "Instead of being undermined by disorder, military commanders turn friction, uncertainty, and fluidity against the enemy to generate disorder in his ranks, ideally creating a situation in which the opposition simply can't cope."[5] The power of smaller players, in other words, lies in imposing such new dynamics to the global environment that even the strongest must adapt in ways that defy intuition and logic, and that can be surprising to the too-naïve observer that architects of change cannot be.

American political scientist Bruce Bueno de Mesquita offers another thought experiment to illustrate this point: two rival coalitions, a blue and a red one, are made up of three countries each, with a clear identifiable leader in each and a clear weak player in each. The blue coalition enjoys an edge thanks to the joint capacities of its members (Fig. 3.2).

Two coalitions are opposed in a war. Their overall power can be summed up with a single number: the power index. Which are the most powerful countries in each coalition? Which is the most powerful coalition?

Coalition Blue	Power Index	Coalition Red	Power Index
A	60	D	55
B	50	E	50
C	5	F	3

Fig. 3.2 Two coalitions face-to-face. Source: Adapted from Bruce Bueno de Mesquita, Principles of International Politics, 2007

But here is the catch: not every player is as "blue" as its leader—that is, not every player adheres as much as the most powerful actor of the coalition to blue values. And if its weakest member, who is the least "blue" of the entire coalition, ever decided to flip to the rival coalition, the blue team would lose its edge to the red one. This configuration provides that weakest member with some unexpected power. This thought experiment explains why, for instance, a country like France was able to exit from NATO's (North Atlantic Treaty Organization) integrated military command in the middle of the Cold War without retaliation from the strongest member of the coalition, namely the United States. Alienating the French presented the risk of pushing France closer to Moscow, which would have been a definite blow to the western camp in the Cold War. Though Europe and France had depended on US efforts to rebuild in the aftermath of World War II (WWII), the strategic configuration gave the country's president, Charles de Gaulle, an unlikely source of power at that given moment (Fig. 3.3).

The coalition that unites D, E, and F, as well as C, is potentially the strongest coalition. If C ever decides to switch sides, it transforms the landscape. It is therefore the "swing vote."

As a result, the power that a country wields is rarely unidimensional. When seeking to understand how the rules governing the business environment may evolve over time, it is important for architects of change to not lack imagination when it comes to identifying the power players susceptible of making a difference and shaping the global landscape.

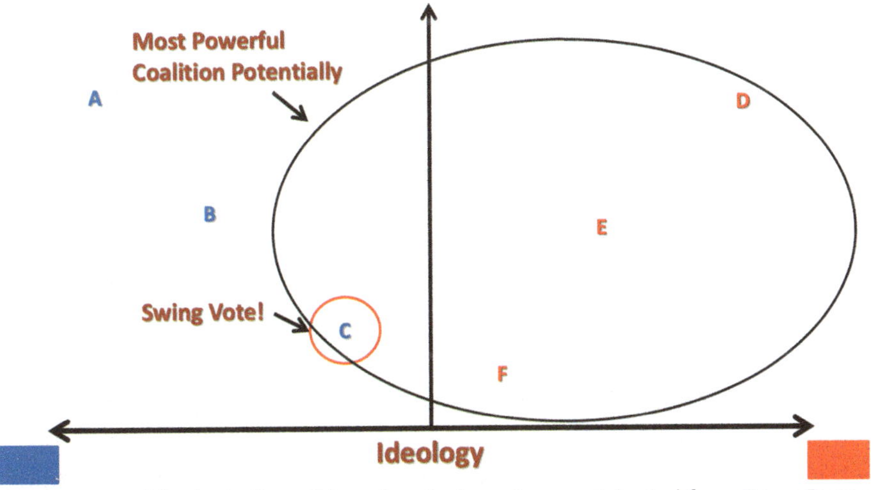

Fig. 3.3 Two (ideological) coalitions face-to-face. Source: Adapted from Bruce Bueno de Mesquita, Principles of International Politics, 2007

Moving Beyond Coercion

Furthermore, power may not only be about the ability to *coerce* but also about the ability to *convince*. That means that some actors that are relatively weaker on paper when it comes to military and/or economic power may in fact have, in practice, a greater ability to influence outcomes because of their greater ability to convince other actors.

Starting in the late 1980s, American political scientist Joseph Nye challenged the notion that power was only about coercion and suggested that it could also be a factor of a country's ability to convince (rather than to force) other actors so as to favor some outcomes over others. This is what the political scientist called "soft power," arguing that coercion is not the only source of influence powers can exert and that they should not underestimate the value of attraction. The ability to uphold norms and values, to be a beacon of stability that others seek to emulate, and to embody a model that others seek to follow is a source of soft power as a result. The influence that the United States and the European Union have exerted on other countries, conditioning their assistance on reforms those countries needed to undertake, has often been given as examples of soft power.

But in recent years, the apparent inability of democracies to function properly, with increasing discontent across public opinions in continental Europe, the significant difficulties the British political system experienced to find an orderly path to Brexit, and repeated and sometimes protracted shutdowns of the federal government in the United States, is an undeniable dent in those countries' soft power.

These difficulties have also triggered a discussion over the existence of an alternative form of power that some, like former US presidential candidate Hillary Clinton, have called "smart power" that is often defined as the ability of a country to strike the proper balance between hard and soft power. An alternative way to define the concept lies in seeing the state as a conductor trying to coordinate a wide range of stakeholders and actors in a complex environment. The more effective the conductor, the easier it will be for the state to attract resources and goodwill from non-state actors who will have a clearer understanding of how they, as one piece of a puzzle, fit in the broader puzzle itself.

What Power and Rivalries Mean for Architects of Change

Surviving in a world of geopolitical rivalries, tensions, and possible compromises requires a good understanding of power dynamics: who has, and who will have in the future, the ability to influence standards?

If great power rivalries are unavoidable, it is critical to consider geopolitical rivalries as a force shaping the business environment because doing so can shed light on who is shaping the landscape and thus who could be able to set the rules, define international standards and norms in the future—relying on its influence as well as on its tools of power, like state-owned enterprises that engage in activities that privately owned companies may never engage in, because they are independent and/or because they would lose money. The example of Chinese firms or national airline companies who can rely on excess capital to invest in unprofitable routes come to mind. A world dominated by one single hegemon who has the power to impose its standards to the rest of the world provides the clarity that architects of change value (even though they may have reservations about the hegemon's behavior). But history tells us that while not uncommon, hegemons are not eternal. Architects of change must therefore be attentive to disruptive moments when challengers successfully defy the status quo and bring about a whole new set of standards and rules.

For instance, the expectation has long been that the United States played that role given the size of its economy (and the influence of the dollar) and of its military. At the same time, the view that the United States is both losing influence and not willing to play the same global role it has played in the past is increasingly consensual. Other powers, like the European Union, are also setting influential regulatory standards and are inflicting fines on companies that do not respect them. Other powers, still, like China in particular, may have significant potential to do so in the future.

But even more critically, the potential of these powers often means that they will attract resources—especially human resources—in the future. In fact, it can also help an actor identify the countries that have the most resources and/or the ability to attract resources in the future and thus better anticipate the outcomes of power struggles and international dynamics. This seems to be the central point in conversation over emerging economic powers: to the extent that this is where growth potential lies, these economies have attracted a lot of attention, for their political aims in particular. This means that with their economic emergence comes political clout that they did not have in the past.

Geopolitical rivalries can also shape an individual country's strategy, as it tries to differentiate itself from others internally and/or as it seeks to offer alternative models. Actors considering these dynamics can be better placed to assess the prospects of countries who do this (or fail to do this), and the promise of the strategy it has adopted. Architects of change, in particular, need to consider how the piece of the puzzle they represent fits into the broader strategy of a country and whether they can appropriately fit in there.

A World of Cooperation

An additional limit of the world view that places geopolitical rivalries and power struggles at the heart of analysis of business environment is that it overlooks opportunities for mutual gains. These opportunities may limit the extent of great power rivalries. For instance, when a challenger cannot overturn the status quo, or when a group of countries seek to preserve an international order that is their interest, the admission is that there can be more gains from cooperation than from outright confrontation. The existence of mutual benefits means the possibility of *positive*-sum games, resulting from complex processes of negotiation and trial and error, that means more opportunities to prosper for a wide range of actors. Those are opportunities that architects of change can leverage to drive transformations, relying on the global momentum that other forces bring about.

Avoiding Chaos

The arguments discussed above have made the assumption that there is always someone in charge of the business environment. This is a rather natural assumption, because where there is chaos, the human mind usually looks for an organizing principle. But it may also be, at times, a very wrong assumption: a leaderless world, with no governing standards or norms, is a viable alternative if no single actor is able or willing to leverage any kind of advantage. This is what economist Nouriel Roubini and political scientist Ian Bremmer call the G-Zero world, an environment in which "no single country or bloc of countries has the political and economic leverage—or the will—to drive a truly international agenda."[6]

Lack of visibility can undermine the stability of the business environment as a whole—as history shows. Perhaps the most striking illustration of this is the story of the 1930s Great Depression. Most people remember the 1929 stock market crash as a major trigger in one of the longest and most consequential economic depressions of all time. But in fact, the combination of limited consultation among economic powers, the process through which countries imposed tariffs and retaliatory tariffs against each other and extensively relied on currency devaluations was what transformed the stock market crash into a durable depression. The experience of the 1930s, and the multiple policy mistakes that were later well-recognized, were at the heart of the liberal order building efforts that the victors of the Second World War undertook, betting that the benefits of international cooperation would help avoid the configuration of the past.

It now seems that some world leaders, including western ones, are not making those bets as enthusiastically as they may have in the past. In fact, today, the threat of a G-Zero world is the threat of durable instability and continuous disruption in the business environment. This is a business environment in which the state is likely to have less financial firepower and less ability to influence outcomes—both in absolute terms, and in relative terms compared to private actors, especially corporations. For architects of change, the burden is far more significant because it will require that either they complement the role of a less efficient state or they constantly adapt to a jungle-like environment that knows no rules.

Establishing Reciprocity

In fact, the possibility of mutual benefits opens up the possibility of informal and formal forums in which actors, finding conflict to be too costly, would one day find it more worthwhile to establish reciprocity in order to reap the benefits of cooperation and stability. Because they do not know what the future will be made up of, and because there is no guarantee that they will remain powerful in tomorrow's environment, great powers prefer to cooperate to hedge against future uncertainty. This preference is a source of stability for the business environment when powers durably commit to adhering to a common set of norms, values, and governing principles that provide actors with visibility about the future.

This view is also documented historically.

Looking to Create a Predictable Business Environment

For all of its flaws, the European Union is arguably one of the most illustrative examples of great powers, who, in spite of being geopolitical rivals for centuries, were able to successfully organize their peaceful coexistence (Fig. 3.4). As a recent white paper of the European Union argued,

Fig. 3.4 Europe's contribution to regional and global cooperation. Source: European Commission, 2017. http://europa.eu/rapid/press-release_IP-17-385_en.htm

> our troubled past has given way to a peace spanning seven decades and to an enlarged Union of 500 million citizens living in freedom in one of the world's most prosperous economies. The images of battles in trenches and fields in Verdun, or of a continent separated by the Iron Curtain and the Berlin Wall, have been replaced by a Union standing out as a beacon of peace and stability.[7]

The visibility that this peace and this stability has provided actors in the European theater has made the European Union a key theater for initiatives—not only profit-driven ones but also some resulting from citizen efforts and social innovation.

The evolution of free trade since the end of the Second World War tells a very similar story. The collective recollection of the trade and currency wars of the 1930s which amplified the effects of the depression on the global economy led Western powers (who were later joined by others) to organize trade relationships so as to avoid future tensions. The creation of the World Trade Organization (WTO) in 1995 helped further these efforts by requiring (with some exceptions) countries to treat their trading partners equally when it comes to goods—what is referred to as the most-favored nation principle. As a result, a country looking for new markets to export to is required to offer reciprocity in return, thereby accelerating the integration of local and regional markets and increasing opportunities for everyone. Until recently, these efforts have been fruitful. The total number of regional trade agreements signed since 1958 has constantly grown and at a faster rate in average since 1995 (Fig. 3.5).

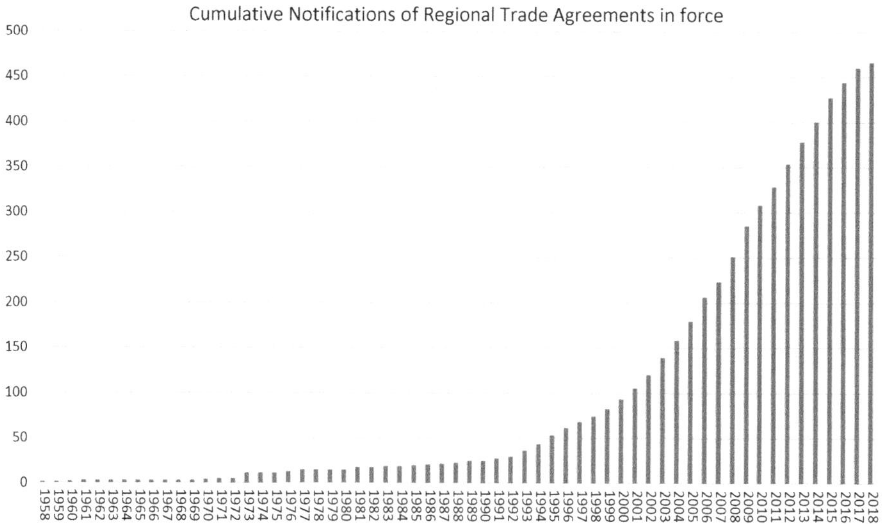

Fig. 3.5 Number of regional trade agreements in force. Source: WTO, Regional Trade Agreements Information System (RTA-IS)

Managing the Shadow of the Future

A very similar logic applies to military alliances—long-lasting ones in particular. The instance of the North Atlantic Treaty Organization (NATO) is revealing. Article V of the organization's charter states that members

> agree that an armed attack against one or more of them in Europe or North America shall be considered an attack against them all and consequently they agree that, if such an armed attack occurs, each of them … will assist the Party or Parties so attacked by taking forthwith, individually and in concert with the other Parties, such action as it deems necessary, including the use of armed force, to restore and maintain the security of the North Atlantic area.

The logic of the shadow of the future is omnipresent in this article: because of global uncertainty, the commitment of one member towards all the others serves as a policy insurance on all the risks that member may also face and that may require the assistance of fellow members. The irony of this article is that it was conceived to protect European nations from a Soviet attack, and that the only time it was invoked was in the aftermath of the 9/11 attacks on the United States. The irony of NATO as a whole is that, in spite of the fact that the threat from the Soviet Union has disappeared, the organization remains and is still attracting new members, seeking to build a "safe, stable and predictable business environment … since only this kind of business climate guarantees retaining existing and attracting new foreign investors," as one public official recently put it.[8]

Architects of Change: Seizing the Opportunities of Cooperation

Architects of change cannot be dogmatic about their worldviews—especially considering that it is more likely than not the case that they will not have the ability to force cooperation over rivalries (or vice-versa). On the contrary, architects of change are able to shape outcomes by understanding the forces that influence their business environment and the rules that constrain their action. And the key to this exercise that this conversation has uncovered lies in determining how much visibility there is in any given business environment.

Like a world dominated by a single hegemon, a world in which power is more diffuse can lead powers, looking to hedge against the uncertainty of the business environment, to cooperate—thereby providing the business environment as a whole with the same clarity a hegemon can. In fact, cooperation can lead to the integration of standards and the development of shared values that generate the stability a wide range of actors need in order to prosper. But history also teaches us that cooperation may not be eternal either.

Architects of change must also be mindful of one, ultimate option—namely one in which there is no real actor shaping outcomes and in which disorder and the absence of rules is the standard. This is not the natural scenario the human brain is wired to process. But, as the discussion above has shown, it is a prospect for the business environment that actors looking to have impact cannot ignore. The lack of visibility this option entails constrains their action but may also generate opportunities for social innovation and for the transformation of societies that are not functioning the way they should.

The Overriding Threats and Opportunities

The discussion on geopolitical tensions and opportunities for cooperation is critical. But it often assumes that the state is the actor with the ability to act and to shape the business environment—and thus, that it should be the only concern of the architect of change. This is an assumption we discussed above. In addition, it overlooks the potential for overriding threats to challenge the ability of states to continue to shape the business environment and, even more significantly, to shape the agenda of states regardless of what their initial priorities were.

Unrest at home, resulting from popular discontent with a dysfunctional political system, and overhauling a political agenda and a government's priorities, or even more existential threats, like climate change, are two examples of alternative forces shaping the business environment. Both are sources of instability for the global business environment. Both should also attract our attention to the potential for architects of change to make a difference.

Since optimism is a qualifying condition for being an architect of change, we must not overlook the potential of overriding opportunities that can increase, in some cases exponentially, the ability of actors to shape the business environment in a favorable way.

In particular, it seems hard for architects of change to overlook how technology is changing our lives and empowering us in ways past generations never enjoyed. But it is, at the same time, very easy to overstate the potential of technology in a world in which citizens and consumers seem to have increasing concerns about data and privacy. The challenge lies in understanding the degree to which technology can indeed help us solve the problem we have set out to tackle without ignoring (or being excessively obsessed with, for that matter) its limitations as a tool.

This section discusses these threats and opportunities shaping the business environment.

Dysfunctional Societies

Growing inequalities—not only in terms of wealth but in terms of status and prospects—combined with increasing political polarization between mainstream parties have gone hand in hand, in recent years, with rising social discontent with (mostly democratic) political systems that appear unable to accomplish yesterday's most basic tasks—like passing a budget or reforming the tax system. The inability of political systems to function has weakened social pacts across the globe and has questioned the actual efficiency and legitimacy of democratic and free-market based approaches.

The Changing Nature of Inequalities

And it is striking to note how the debate over inequalities has evolved over a very short time span. Traditionally, this was a debate that focused on economic differences between countries, and within countries. At the turn of the millennium in particular, the United Nations Development Programme (UNDP) defined accordingly its Millennium Development Goals to tackle extreme poverty, to prevent deadly diseases and to expand education for children. But barely a decade later, noting that it had reached many of its targets, the UNDP defined the Sustainable Development Goals (SDGs), which encompass a wider and more complex set of objectives: in addition to poverty, hunger and inequalities, the SDGs also incorporate a wide range of environmental concerns related to water, energy, health, cities, and climate change—that is to say indicators that are not the exclusive concern of poor and developing economies but that are preoccupations shared by virtually every country on the planet. This debate over inequalities has become, as a result, one that focuses more on welfare and on empowerment of individuals rather than on survival only.

Because the debate has shifted away from survival, towards welfare and longer-term prospects, the question of inequalities is also becoming increasingly complex. Economic differences are not the only determinant of inequalities: two individuals with similar economic conditions may feel very different about their prospects, and perhaps more critically about their children's prospects—thus placing them in very different states of mind. Inequalities in status and in prospects, which fuel fears of social demotion, are now increasingly at the heart of public debates. Populations that have historically considered themselves as middle classes and that have been persuaded by the political establishment to vote in favor of the conservation of the status quo: in doing so, went the usual promise, they preserved not only their own interests but those of their children as well. They would have everything to lose from the end of the system.

What is commonly referred to as the "populist wave" that has swept across western democracies and beyond results from the fact that those same middle classes feel that this very promise of the ability to maintain one's status and to empower one's children to improve their own status is profoundly broken. This is particularly true for those populations who fear for their status and who may not have as much resources to invest in their children as those whose future prospects are far brighter. These discrepancies tend to increase these inequalities.

The benefits associated with preserving the system seemed grossly overstated in the eyes of those middle classes who do not fear as much its demise because they do not feel that they have anything to lose if it ever disappeared. This fear of social demotion is arguably the central preoccupation in the debate over inequalities.

The Advent of Tribal Societies

The fact that societies are also becoming increasingly tribal in nature has not allayed these anxieties in any way. Tribalism results from the increasing polarization of politics and societies on which individual loyalty to one's social group or tribe trumps all other relationships and interactions. The truth of the tribe is the only one that matters, even if it is contradicted by facts on the ground.

A tribal world is one ruled by ideology and dogma, rather than by facts and analysis. On key issues that define a society like immigration as well as economic policies and in particular those designed to fight inequalities and help the least well-off, the likelihood for a strong consensus is very low as views are more influenced by the ideology of one's group, rather than by facts. Those key issues that once contributed to strengthening social pacts are becoming increasingly divisive, and societies increasingly divided as a result.

Political polarization is relatively easy to measure, though it is contingent on a country's political system. In the United States, a country founded upon the very notion of bipartisanship in which compromises between the two opposing parties is at the heart of the political system, polarization is measured by the size of the electorate which "holds consistent ideological positions."[9] The size of that electorate has been growing over time, as fewer people show mixed liberal and conservative positions on any given issues. The trend in Congress is similar: voting patterns show that the overlap between the two parties is increasingly small and potentially non-existent, making political compromises all the more so difficult.

In Europe, results in parliamentary elections show that the share of the vote of the winning party has dropped significantly since the 1950s from 38 to below 32%, whereas the number of parties obtaining more than 1% of the vote has increased from less than six to nine. This fragmentation of the political landscape makes coalitions in parliaments harder to build and harder to sustain over time, leading to more instability.[10]

The development of social media has accelerated polarization, as some studies have argued: because social media platforms act like an echo chamber providing individuals with confirmation of their pre-existing views and not challenging their preconceptions, they can contribute to increased divisions within societies. As one entrepreneur and observer of these platforms eloquently put it,

> The global village that was once the internet was has [sic.] been replaced by digital islands of isolation that are drifting further apart each day. From your Facebook feed to your Google Search, as your experience online grows increasingly personalized, the internet's islands keep getting more segregated and sound proofed.[11]

Tribal societies represent a challenge to the very notion of architects of change: unless the latter recognize the existence of the former, they may very well be preaching in the desert. The likelihood that they will fail in their quest for transformation because they will have convinced only those who already believed is significant. The combination of inequality—and the anxieties they entail—and both political and social polarization creates threats that can undermine even the best designed enterprises. What is perhaps even more paradoxical is that these dysfunctional and fragmented societies create opportunities for change and transformation, especially for those actors looking for impact.

Climate Change

And yet, for all the talk about dysfunctional societies and increasing inequalities, there may be one overriding threat that commands even more transformational change, not only in our daily lives but also in our *ways* of life, including consumption and living habits. In fact, the threat of climate change, once it materializes, may override any other threat to the business environment particularly because it is existential in nature: this may be a unique example in history in which a species—the *human* species—destroys its own habitat and, ultimately, autodestructs, perhaps without looking back.

The Climate Change Paradox

Climate change differs as a threat from the issues set by dysfunctional societies in the sense that as impressive and as worrying as the trend may be, it often seems more intangible and abstract in nature. This may explain why the headlines about global warming may be extremely alarming but the action on the part of governments and other actors surprisingly modest under these circumstances.

This paradox stems from the fact that for the general public, the nature of the threat is not entirely clear: what will climate change mean for me, in my daily life? It stems from the fact that the timing is not entirely clear either to the general public which often displays what psychologists refer to as disaster myopia—an inability to correctly grasp the likelihood of disaster, especially considering that this is not a threat we expect to materialize tomorrow morning. In addition, populations across the globe are most likely going to be unequally threatened by climate change: within a country, populations in coastal regions are more vulnerable than people inland; and populations from countries with weaker infrastructure are likely to be more vulnerable than populations from more developed countries.

As a result, as in any international bargaining process, the negotiation on climate change efforts has often about who should actually pay the price ultimately. Moreover, the significance of the efforts needed to contain the threat also adds to the paradox. The efforts are sizeable, in particular because they demand that we fundamentally change our way of life, the ways we consume and the ways we behave. It is not entirely clear that all populations across the globe have the means to do so quickly enough.

Unequal in the Face of Climate Change?

Until very recently, emerging economies also made it very clear that richer countries did not face the same environmental constraints when they were developing. Any attempt to force emerging economies to take into account these same constraints would be akin to protectionism to the extent that it would impede their ability to grow out of poverty. As Economics Nobel Prize recipient Thomas Schelling once observed more than a decade ago,

> There is no likelihood that China, India, Indonesia, Brazil, or Nigeria will fully participate in any greenhouse-gas regime for the next few decades. They have done their best to make that point clear, and it serves no purpose to disbelieve them. … Constrained by poverty and technological backwardness, their ability to adapt to climate change is limited. The best way for developing countries to mitigate global warming, therefore, is through economic growth.[12]

And yet, as the threat has become increasingly more tangible and concrete and as scientists have been able to document the consequences of climate change on the planet, efforts have accelerated with the support of those very same countries that had made it clear, barely a decade ago, that they would not participate in any greenhouse-gas regime. This evolution is not anecdotal. It suggests that the focus on geopolitical rivalries and threats emanating from other actors may become deeply misguided in a world in which the menace is directed to the business environment as a whole. As a result, as one scholar put it,

> the disruption to the earth's climate will ultimately command more attention and resources and have a greater influence on the global economy and international relations than other forces visible in the world today. Climate change will cease to be a faraway threat and become one whose effects require immediate action.[13]

The Significance of the Paris Agreement

The evidence of the threat that climate change sets is actually indisputable. A 2019 report by the US National Aeronautics and Space Administration (NASA) and the National Oceanic and Atmospheric Administration (NOAA) found in early 2019 that "globally, 2018's temperatures rank behind those of 2016, 2017 and 2015.[14] The past five years are, collectively, the warmest years in the modern record." A UN agency report published in November 2018 found that the total cost of climate change related catastrophes between 1998 and 2017 was 251% greater than between the previous 20 years. The cost is nearly 3 trillion dollars and is the consequence of increasingly extreme climatic events.[15]

Today, the consensus in the international scientific community is that our collective goal should be to limit the rise in global temperatures by 1.5°C. The 21st meeting of the Conference of the Parties of the United Nations Framework Convention on Climate Change (UNFCCC) in Paris, also known as the COP 21 summit that took place in December 2015 and that led to the Paris Agreement has provided a roadmap for countries and other stakeholders who agreed to strengthen their efforts to contain global temperature increases at a level significantly lower than 2 degrees Celsius—aiming at containing the rise at 1.5 degrees.

The motivation behind this objective is that, as a 2018 Intergovernmental Panel on Climate Change (IPCC) report has shown,[16] the differences in outcome expected between a 1.5- and a 2-degree increase are significant in terms of risk and impact. In fact, as the report explains, humanity can retain the ability to manage the consequences of climate change if we stay below the 1.5 degree mark, especially because climate-related risks are likely to be higher when temperatures increase by 1.5°C compared to today, but lower than if temperatures increase by 2°C. In particular, sea level rise may be lower by 10 centimeters with a 1.5°C temperature increase, potentially enabling "greater opportunities for adaptation in the human and ecological systems of small islands, low-lying coastal areas and deltas," and, more generally, lower needs in terms of adaptation. The report also adds that limiting temperature rises to 1.5 degrees instead of 2 will limit "impacts on biodiversity and ecosystems, including species loss and extinction," as well as "lower the impacts on terrestrial, freshwater and coastal ecosystems and to retain more of their services to humans."[17] Such efforts would also "reduce risks to marine biodiversity, fisheries, and ecosystems, and their functions and services to humans."[18] The report expects the risks associated with a 1.5°C temperature rise to increase risks for humans, in particular in terms of health, food security, human security, and economic growth—but these risks would be even greater with a 2°C temperature. As a result, though a difference of 0.5°C temperature may be hard to grasp for the naked eye, efforts to contain the rise of global temperatures at 1.5 degrees are meaningful.

The sort of changes that are needed to keep global temperatures from rising beyond 1.5 degrees are transformational, be they social, business or technological in nature. They rely on a transformation of either how we consume or how we produce—or a combination thereof—and therefore require that we explore our social organization and our business models, and that we innovate on both fronts, relying on technological change as well. The transformative nature of the coming change, and the stakes and sizeable opportunities, are not what is open to question. This is more about our very *ability* to carry out those changes and for actors, architects of change in particular, to seize them.[19]

What is more, the report notes that these efforts are not all contradictory with reaching the SDGs, as the number of synergies across the SDGs exceeds the number of trade-offs: efforts in terms of health, clean energy, cities and communities, responsible consumption and production, and oceans will also contribute to containing climate change, while tackling the challenges of poverty, hunger, water, and energy access can have potential trade-offs with temperature increase containment efforts.

The challenge lies in managing those synergies and those trade-offs. Architects of change looking to gain greater consciousness about the world they live in and a better grasp of the topics that are likely to attract resources and goodwill in the future need not look further than climate change in this perspective as the key force shaping the world. Climate change is an undeniable threat for humanity, but it also presents humanity with a wide range of opportunities to transform the way we eat and we develop. Those are the opportunities that architects of change are usually aware of.

Technology

It is difficult to overlook the driving role that technology has played historically in transforming the business environment in what it is today. As one columnist argues, the most important geopolitical feature of the nineteenth century is obvious:

> [I]t was the era of the Industrial Revolution. Without it, there's no rising middle class and no real pressure for democracy. There's no capitalist revolution because agrarian states don't need one. There's no colonization at scale because there's a hard limit to a non-industrial economy's appetite for raw materials. There's no total war without cheap steel and precision manufacturing. And with the world still stuck largely in a culture and an economy based on traditional subsistence agriculture, there's quite possibly no end to slavery and no beginning of feminism.[20]

Put differently, any given political, societal, social, or business transformation that humanity goes through arguably finds its roots in a technological change that made it possible, according to this view.

An Ability Accelerator

This argument has significant consequences on the way we view the business environment: it potentially sets all previous discussions over rivalries, cooperation, dysfunctional societies, and *even* climate change aside in favor of a broader conversation about how technological change can help us improve our business environment. By allowing for more efficiency, through greater productivity, a better allocation of financial and human resources, and by improving access to information, technology can ameliorate every actor's ability to thrive in a business environment.

Artificial intelligence (AI) today is a case in point that some have dubbed the "electricity of the Fourth Industrial Revolution."[21] Artificial intelligence is accelerating our ability to adjust to information about the changing environment and to adapt accordingly. As two experts put it, artificial intelligence is "a system's ability to correctly interpret external data, to learn from such data, and to use those learnings to achieve specific goals and tasks through flexible adaptation."[22] Another report defines artificial intelligence as "computer systems that can sense their environment, think, learn, and act in response to what they sense and their programmed objectives."[23]

As a result, this form of intelligence is only different than that of a human in the sense that it is enhanced and allows making calculations that individuals could not make in limited time or with limited resources. In fact, as the amount of available data and the flow of instant information that we have access to and that is incomparable to any other period in time, the ability of humans to analyze, understand, process, and act on what they know is increasingly limited. Faster and more effective computers mean the ability to make calculations and design strategies that are far more efficient and that may profoundly transform the landscape in a way that makes yesterday's concerns moot and that sheds light on new geopolitical rivalries.

New Solutions to Old, Current, and Tomorrow's Problems

In fact, as our ability to calculate probabilities and improve our responses increases significantly, artificial intelligence may have major effects on geopolitical rivalries and on dysfunctional societies and our ability to fix—and heal—them, as well as on how we frame issues such as climate change and sustainability. Here are two significant examples that are illustrative of these changes.

AI Against Climate Change, for Sustainable Development Goals

The notion that artificial intelligence (AI) can be a force for good, in particular for the planet, is now widely documented. As one report puts it, "AI can help transform traditional sectors and systems to address climate change, deliver food and water security, protect biodiversity and bolster human well-being."[24]

The report argues that artificial intelligence can help humanity meet the climate change challenge by unlocking new solutions in terms of clean energy (thanks to optimized systems and smart grids for example), smart cities and homes (affecting traffic and building design for instance), sustainable land-use (through better monitoring and forecasting), sustainable production and consumption (with smarter and more integrated systems), and smart transport systems (with better-suited transport solutions).

The report also contends that artificial intelligence could unlock other meaningful solutions to five other critical challenges that have placed "Earth systems under unprecedented stress," namely: biodiversity and conservation, healthy oceans, water security, clean air and weather, and disaster resilience. These solutions revolve around our ability to track with greater precision, to develop early warning signals in order to avert the most negative phenomena and to plan ahead, to better integrate our supply chains in a wide range of industries and, more broadly, our systems such as connected cities.

As a force for good for the planet, artificial intelligence enhances our ability to tackle both climate change and sustainable development goals.

AI As a Fix to Dysfunctional Societies

Artificial intelligence may also help us narrow the divide between the different groups—or "tribes"—that make society up by increasing awareness of our own biases and distorted views.

The examples illustrating this ability are numerous, but few are as representative as a startup called Knowhere News is. Relying on artificial intelligence and on a wide range of sources, the company provides its readers with three different versions of a same news story: one left-leaning, one right-leaning, and one impartial. The latter version of the story is designed to go beyond partisan lines and peel off the political influence that could distort it. The left- and right-leaning versions show the reader how partisanship and political ideology can generate a potentially different narrative of the very same story. This initiative in the field of education and media is one that hints to how the intersection of technology and dysfunctional societies can open up doors to those who are the most curious—like architects of change.

Persisting Old (and New) Challenges

But it would be inaccurate to equate the rise of a tech world with the end of humanity's problems. In particular, it is worth noting that historically, the advent of technology has often made weaker chunks of the population, namely the labor force that is relatively less skilled or ageing, more vulnerable. It is also noteworthy that technology is not easing geopolitical tensions: quite to the contrary, technology and the race to securing long-term hegemony in artificial intelligence are arguably driving geopolitical rivalries today. It should come as no surprise that China's massive investments in artificial intelligence place the nation on top of spending in this realm today. These massive investments, in turn, could profoundly shape the map of global influence.

Fear the Machine

During the first industrial revolution, the legend goes, Ned Ludd (or John, depending on the version of the legend), a British worker in the textile industry, allegedly broke two machines that he believed had stolen his job. He gave his name to the Luddite movement which protested throughout the eighteenth century against automation in the textile industry by destroying machinery in the industry. Today, the term "Luddite" is used to depict the fear or the rejection of machines and new technologies—and, more often than not, in a derogatory way to denounce the notion that technological progress can be the source of economic harm.

We should not take those reservations lightly though: while societies as a whole are likely to benefit from increased automation and technological progress, more vulnerable populations, in particular the unskilled workforce, are likely to bear a disproportionate burden of the cost. Political efforts, combined with all forms of social innovation, designed to contain the risk of durable unemployment and social marginalization, are two of many indispensable tools that should accompany automation. Unless they do, political and social backlash leading to greater instability in the business environment may be unavoidable.

But some fears about automation run even deeper: if artificial intelligence makes exponential progress, it may outperform humans who may lose their ability to control the very machines they put together. Though this modern Frankenstein-like story is not one that is widely shared among experts of artificial intelligence, it is one that entrepreneur Elon Musk, who arguably owes his success to scientific breakthroughs, firmly believes in. This shows the extent to which fears of automation are not just the product of uninformed masses that we should take lightly but a useful reminder of the actual mission of technology: making the life of humans easier.

The story of a fast-food chain CEO is telling from this perspective. In 2012, this CEO wanted to innovate on two fronts in his restaurants. While he was very enthusiastic about the first innovation—that triggered little reaction from reporters however—he was far more circumspect about promoting the other. The first innovation was service at the table. The second was a smartphone application that would allow anyone to order from home in order to get food even faster. As one reporter argued, through this app, the CEO was giving fast food a whole new dimension—implicitly arguing that service at the table was not the disruptive change the introduction of technology in this industry could ever represent. The CEO begged to differ: the rate at which technology changes, he argued, is always faster than the rate at which we, as human beings, accept that change. The challenge lies far more in understanding the incentives humans have to embrace technology rather than in improving their ability to ameliorate technology. And unless we do understand those incentives, we should be fearful of a backlash given how out-of-sync technology is with the rest of society. As American academic Andrew McAfee put it, "We have Stone Age mental processes, medieval institutions, and science fiction technologies. And that is a really uneasy mix."[25]

As a result, the view that puts technology as the driving force of the business environment is any less accurate or more limited than all the other factors that this chapter previously explored. But it does present a paradox. With the advent of automation and artificial intelligence, we are asking devices to make decisions that can involve ethical trade-offs, such as who to sacrifice and who to save when saving all human lives is not possible. But, as Karen Hao, an artificial intelligence reporter, puts it,

> Algorithms were never designed to handle such tough choices. They are built to pursue a single mathematical goal, such as maximizing the number of soldiers' lives saved or minimizing the number of civilian deaths. When you start dealing with multiple, often competing, objectives or try to account for intangibles like 'freedom' and 'wellbeing,' a satisfactory mathematical solution doesn't always exist.[26]

Put differently, these technologies are all based on algorithms that seek to solve human dilemmas, but that ultimately tend to reflect human contradictions stemming from the fact that our different aims are not all reconcilable with each other.

The ultimate solution may be surprising: instead of seeking impossible perfection for the algorithm, it may instead lie in replicating human imperfection and unpredictability. Instead of trying to make ethical principles concrete and precise (they never are in practice), the director of research for the Partnership on AI, Peter Eckersley, suggests designing algorithms that use "uncertain objectives, represented for instance as partially ordered preferences, or as probability distributions over total orders."[27] In doing so, instead of colliding with incompatible human preferences, the algorithm is able to offer different options that all display trade-offs. It is up to the decision-maker to take the ultimate decision.

In this sense, technology is part of a broader system in which the human component will be ultimately hard to erase.

AI As the New Terrain for Geopolitical Rivalries

Finally, it is noteworthy that technology has not done away with geopolitical rivalries. To the contrary, it may actually accelerate geopolitical dynamics.

In particular, the geopolitical consequences of the growing rivalries between global tech giants are hard to overlook: the actors that are able to get a strategic edge in artificial intelligence and in other key computing technologies are those that are likely to shape—and perhaps control—the future critical industries such as telecommunications and networks. In yesterday's world, it seemed as if the American tech giants—Google, Amazon, Facebook, and Apple, or GAFAs, in particular—had that upper hand in the industry and would be in a position to durably shape the business environment as a result.

But the GAFAs have met their match in the Chinese BATX—for Baidu, Alibaba, Tencent, and Xiaomi. The first three have heavily invested in AI and are applying the technology to an ever-greater set of industries. More broadly, other Chinese companies like telecommunications equipment and systems companies Huawei and ZTE, are playing an increasingly central and critical role in the industry of telecommunication equipment, giving them potential influence and control over individual and company data, as well as data flows. Controlling telecommunication networks is not just a business issue but potentially one of power and influence over the business environment as a whole. Strikingly, the rest of the world does not seem to have a single answer to China's rise in this realm: while some, like the United States and Australia, are taking drastic measures to avoid relying on companies like Huawei, others, like in continental Europe, are looking to hedge against risks rather than to take definitive measures. These contradictory responses increase the ambiguity around policies and standards that private decision-makers usually look to anticipate.

As a result, it is hard to disassociate the advent of the tech world from the discussion over power and influence that this chapter opened up with. These interactions are critical in understanding the world we live in—as well as the likely challenges and opportunities any actor looking to drive change is likely to face.

This is a Change-Maker's World

The idea that this business environment is complex is not new, nor is the statement that it is increasingly uncertain, volatile and fast-changing, or even cruel. These observations are even commonplace.

The implications these observations have for decision-makers are less trivial and documented. What this exploration has looked to put the emphasis on is the need to be open-minded and as pragmatic as possible in a world in which what may be true today may prove absolutely false tomorrow. As a result, the very assumptions you relied on to develop a vision, a mission, and a purpose to bring about change may be proven dramatically wrong—even in a very short time span. The effort to understand the business environment may be costly, but it must be a perpetual one, in particular for actors looking to remain relevant and to have impact.

This chapter discussed six mega-forces that have the potential to profoundly shape the business environment: geopolitical rivalries, global cooperation, identity politics, inequalities, global warming, and technology. To repeat the objective of this discussion, the rule of the game is not to choose which one of these forces is definitively shaping the business environment contrary to the five others. Instead, the real challenge lies in understanding which combination is likely to matter most at a given moment in time, in particular when it comes to your ability to drive change in this business environment and to execute your strategy.

Addressing that issue should shape the way you tackle the problem you are trying to tackle: once you can associate a meaningful explanation with their surroundings (as ever-changing as they may be), you will be in a better position to state what you are trying to achieve. This ability will be key for architects of change.

Alastair Newton was a former career diplomat before moving to the City, where he became one of the private sector's top political analysts globally. Helping both public and private-sector decision-makers understand the global landscape has been one of his central professional missions. In this testimonial, he explains how he came to play this role, the professional environment in which he exercised it, as well as the best practices he drew from his experiences. In the second part of his testimonial, he underscores the political, social, and technical factors that should matter most to private sector decision-makers today in this changing business environment.

The Role of a Senior Political Analyst, by Alastair Newton

Summary
Even today, when politics is clearly such an important driver of financial markets, there are very few specialist political analysts on the payroll of either brokers or fund managers. This note considers why this is and what it takes to try to break into this sort of role?

How I Got Started

I first took on the role of "Senior Political Analyst" on secondment from the United Kingdom's Foreign & Commonwealth Office (FCO) to Lehman Brothers in London in March 2000, originally for one year but extended to a second.

The idea of the secondment was born out of the 1998 Russian debt default which morphed the 1997 "Asian Financial Crisis" into the "Global Economic Crisis." At that time, I had very recently been appointed head of the FCO's Economic Relations Department and, as such, had day-to-day responsibility for running Tony Blair's G7/G8 team during a year when the United Kingdom held the group's presidency. Clearly (to my mind at least), the City had a key role to play if we were to avoid a complete economic crash; but I quickly discovered that there was no liaison mechanism between Whitehall and the City (the Treasury having devolved this role to the Bank of England (BoE) some years previously and Gordon Brown having made the BoE operationally independent the previous year!).

I had, however, a number of personal contacts in the City including Dr John Llewellyn, who had been a senior member of the OECD's (Organization for Economic Cooperation and Development) Secretariat while I was a member of the UK delegation there earlier in the 90s and who, by 1998, had become Chief Global Economist at Lehman. I contacted John immediately. Although the relationship between the FCO and Lehman was never formalized, the mutual benefit from this quickly became apparent and out of this, to cut quite a long story short, the idea of the secondment was born.[28]

My title arose from two strands of thought. The "Political Analyst" bit was obvious—that is what I was there to do even though none of us was quite sure what it meant in practice. The "Senior" bit was John's idea simply to give me more heft with Lehman's clients. As I used to quip, as the only individual occupying this sort of role, I was also the "Junior."

Others in the Field In-House

This being said, there were others at Lehman whose role predominantly revolved around what I at least would call "politics." Notable among them were the following.

- The New York-based Sovereign Risk team with whom I worked closely throughout, i.e., including when I went back to the firm as an employee from August 2005 until its crash in September 2008 (as I did with Sovereign Risk team in Tokyo during my tenure with Nomura from 2008 to 2015).
- Various board members who had retired from successful careers which had involved "politics" had been appointed to open policymakers' doors at a very senior level and advise the board. For example, at Lehman I worked closely with my former FCO colleague Sir Graham Boyce; and at Nomura with Lord Tugendhat. The key difference between such individuals and me was that they were very largely not "client facing" but internal advisory.
- There was a government relations team in Washington; but I never really had a good working relationship there despite—or, perhaps, because of—obvious overlap. Nomura too had a similarly responsible Washington office with which my relations were much better, confirming my belief that the distant relationship of my Lehman days was characteristic of the general attitude of colleagues in the United States to their "junior" brethren in Europe and Asia.

Nevertheless, when it came to what could be called "turf disputes" the biggest potential dog in the manger was the economist. In big banks at least, they have long regarded politics as falling within their remit, and the authority which chief economists wield accounts largely, in my view, for why there are so few dedicated and specialist political analysts in the financial sector.

To be fair, I have come across several economists in the financial sector who do make a decent fist of political analysis; but the interesting thing is that, pretty much without exception, those who do are quick to recognize the value-add which a specialist can (and should) bring to the table. For the most part, however, economists are not especially skilled in this field. At the risk of upsetting more than a few, I think this is because their discipline encourages them to think largely in linear terms whereas politics tends to be more multidimensional, often requiring what I have frequently referred to as "quantum jump" thinking—see also footnote 6 below. In this respect in particular, I was very fortunate in that I came to Lehman with the full backing of the firm's Chief Global Economist, Dr Llewellyn, who made it clear that he expected his team to work with me and use my expertise to the full, which is exactly what happened to the benefit of all concerned.[29]

External Expertise

The other challenger I faced at Lehman at the outset was the political risk consultancy Eurasia Group which had been hired by Lehman New York, essentially to come up with a quantitative model aimed at accurately forecasting the next rouble crisis or equivalent. I have never made any secret of my general distrust of quantitative modeling as a tool in political analysis, not because I am not by nature a "quants" person (I am not) but because when I was in the FCO's Policy Planning Staff during the Asian Financial Crisis I spent a great deal of time looking at models then in existence to see if there were any which would be useful to the FCO; there were—the *Economist Intelligence Unit's* notably—but, in my assessment, all had (and have) their limitations and were never alone going to give you "the answer."

This being said, there is a plethora of "expertise" (of varying degrees of quality) out there in the wider world, much more so in this current "social media" era even than there was back in the noughties. Much of it is also either free at the point of access or very cheap compared to the payroll cost of even an average City analyst—more on which below. Given this, I have always regarded a key part of my role as sorting out the wheat from the chaff for my clients (in-house and external alike) and getting them to focus on what really matters.

Defining My Role

It was amid all this "clutter" that I was charged with carving out a role with the single guideline that whatever I was going to do had to be "client facing" and therefore revenue generating—a key differentiator with other parties in the bank, excepting the economists, with at least a finger (often a whole fist) in the politics "pie."

It took a while to come up with a succinct definition of what I do but, in the end, I settled for the ludicrously ambitious:

> Anything, anywhere in the world definable as 'political' and likely to impact on financial markets, my job is to anticipate it, analyse it and explain it.

What was patently a soundbite-type definition clearly required some qualification, my main ones being:

- I try as far as possible to steer clear of regulatory etc. issues and stick to what I term "macro-politics."[30]
- I do not profess to expertise on smaller LatAm countries and am even cautious about some of the bigger ones.
- Similarly, the likes of the Central Asian Republics and the domestic politics of some of the smaller Central and Eastern Europeans.

The important point here is that if I am asked about such topics I do know people who can help me come up with answers if I am given 48 hours (again, more on which below).

Networks Are Key

Right from the outset, it was clear to me that, although the internal competition was not negligible, the external was, if anything, even greater, i.e., that I had to be able to add real value relative to the media, consultancies like Eurasia Group etc. This meant using the network of contacts I had built up at the FCO to the full to get behind the scenes and find out what policymakers were really thinking, to a large extent the flip side of the way in which I had interacted between the FCO and the City, Lehman especially, for the previous 18 months or so.[31] It is no coincidence when asked about how I do my job that I describe myself first and foremost not as an analyst but as someone who builds and nurtures networks, underlining that I could not possibly have succeeded in the City without my 20 years of networking in the FCO behind me.[32]

Twelve "Rules of Thumb"

But garnering information is not, of itself, sufficient. It then has to be presented in a form which is easily digested by the intended audience. Acknowledging that there are some differences in how to deal with financial versus corporate sector decision-makers, in all cases the following 12 rules of thumb are worth bearing firmly in mind.

- Bottom line first. In the end even for firms with impressive ESG (environmental, social and governance) credentials, it really is all about the bottom line. So, getting that out at the outset is usually a good idea.
- You should never assume this but it is a reasonable bet that your audience probably already has some knowledge (or, at least, prejudices) on the topic in question. City traders in particular are voracious consumers of both information and opinion on which they draw to form the view on which they base their bets. So, if you know your audience has a decent grasp of the subject and you subscribe to the "conventional wisdom" say so straight away—after all, it very often proves to be correct.
- But if you have an unconventional view, be sure to make that clear at the outset too.
- With the investment community in particular (especially FX traders), thereafter you probably have about the length of an elevator pitch in a mid-sized high-rise block to support your bottom line.[33] Less is indeed often more.
- If, and only if, you can grab your audience's full attention in that time with something new and different, you will get more time—and questions.
- Never ever ever try to bluff it with a question you do not know the answer to. Admit it, promise to look into it and get back to the questioner—and make sure you do just that ... quickly.

- If you use PowerPoint (and I accept that it has its uses) make sure the slides are clearly readable from the back of the room, easy to understand and total as few as possible.[34] And always remember that it you are reading a PPT you are NOT "reading" the client.
- In the case of client meetings, it is very often a good idea to offer to send your interlocutors something relevant to the discussion (but adding to it in some way) after the meeting. Just make sure that, if your offer is accepted, you follow up promptly.
- If you publish written analyses, it is difficult to avoid getting sucked in to a regular routine, i.e., dailies, weeklies or whatever. I have avoided this, allowing me to use as a promo line *"I only write when I have something to say which I think you'll want to read."*
- Always have an executive summary at the top of whatever you publish. Three bullets is good; one short sentence (if it can be done) is better still in the "age of Twitter!"[35]
- Hone your communications skills, written and oral, including through formal training. Great content is often undermined by poor delivery.
- Don't be afraid of making mistakes. If you voice opinions, you are bound to get it wrong sometimes.[36] Provided it is well-argued and you don't get it wrong too often, you will get away with it.

And one final piece of advice. Track record clearly counts. But always remember that, when push comes to shove, you are only as good as your next call.

Private Sector Decision-Making in an Evolving Global Context: The Factors That Matter Most

Political Factors

- The continuing shift in the global economic center of gravity from west to east.
- The related return of nationalism and the breaking down of the post-WWII global order leading to the re-emergence of "great power politics" and necessitating, in some instances, choosing between China and the United States.

"Social" Factors

- The unrelenting pressure of social media (for better or worse).
- Ageing populations in the West especially.
- A swelling wealth gap between rich and poor countries and rich and poor elements and individuals within individual countries.

"Technical" Factors

- The use of "big data."
- Artificial intelligence.
- The continuing destruction of low wage, low skill manufacturing jobs thanks to robotics.

- Shortening supply chains better to meet "local" demand.
- (Hopefully) the decarbonization of the global economy; or, failing that, catastrophic climate change.
- Increased use of genetic engineering of plants, animals and, possibly, humans.
- One or more "disruptive technology" we haven't even thought of yet.

Economic

- Central bank decisions on monetary policy.

Alastair Newton, March 2019

Notes

1. Dominic Barton et al., "Where Companies with a Long-Term View Outperform Their Peers | McKinsey" (McKinsey Global Institute, February 2017), https://www.mckinsey.com/featured-insights/long-term-capitalism/where-companies-with-a-long-term-view-outperform-their-peers.
2. Those were the six dimensions that the July/August 2018 issue of Foreign Affairs explored. This chapter presents an alternative reading and a different interpretation for most of these dimensions.
3. Geopolitical rivalries are also about the changing distribution of economic power and influence. The emergence of new, non-Western economic powers that do not belong to the Organization for Economic Cooperation and Development (OECD) has demonstrated that old industrialized powers have lost influence in the global landscape in relative terms. This is the very idea Goldman Sachs Economist Jim O'Neill sought to capture when he invented the BRIC (Brazil, Russia, India, and China) acronym and when he argued that those four economies would become dominant by 2050 and outweigh the traditional economic powers of the G7. Admittedly, the rise of these new economic powers need not necessarily mean increased rivalries—especially considering that with the notable exception of Russia, they are all embracing in one form or another the capitalist system. But it is hard to disassociate the group's economic power with the existence of a changing political reality. As Jim O'Neill argued, "What 9/11 told me was that there was no way that globalization was going to be Americanization in the future—nor should it be. In order for globalization to advance, it had to be accepted by more people … but not by imposing the dominant American social and philosophical beliefs and structures." Furthermore, BRIC nations seem to have given their acronym a political existence of its own by creating their own summit in 2009—a summit designed to explore the reform of the global political and financial architecture in the aftermath of the 2008 financial crisis. The group also sought additional legitimacy through enlargement to a leading African nation,

South Africa, which was formally included in the BRICS in 2010—even though the size of South Africa's economy does not match in any way that of other BRIC nations. The economic rise of BRIC nations has turned into a global forum offering alternatives to the Western created and dominated global order.

4. Richard A. Bitzinger, "China's Double-Digit Defense Growth," *Foreign Affairs*, March 19, 2015, https://www.foreignaffairs.com/articles/china/2015-03-19/chinas-double-digit-defense-growth.
5. Eric K. Clemons and Jason A. Santamaria, "Maneuver Warfare: Can Modern Military Strategy Lead You to Victory?," *Harvard Business Review*, April 1, 2002, https://hbr.org/2002/04/maneuver-warfare-can-modern-military-strategy-lead-you-to-victory.
6. Ian Bremmer and Nouriel Roubini, "A G-Zero World," *Foreign Affairs*, March 1, 2011, https://www.foreignaffairs.com/articles/2011-01-31/g-zero-world.
7. "White Paper on the Future of Europe: Reflections and Scenarios for the EU27 by 2025" (Brussels, Belgium: European Union, March 1, 2017).
8. AmCham Montenegro, "NATO Membership, an Opportunity for the Economy and Business," accessed January 16, 2019, http://www.amcham.me/2016/07/nato-membership-an-opportunity-for-the-economy-and-business/.
9. "Political Polarization in the American Public," *Pew Research Center* (blog), June 12, 2014, http://www.people-press.org/2014/06/12/political-polarization-in-the-american-public/.
10. "Europeans Are Splitting Their Votes among Ever More Parties," *The Economist*, January 12, 2017, https://www.economist.com/europe/2017/01/12/europeans-are-splitting-their-votes-among-ever-more-parties.
11. Mostafa M. El-Bermawy, "Your Filter Bubble Is Destroying Democracy," *Wired*, November 18, 2016, https://www.wired.com/2016/11/filter-bubble-destroying-democracy/.
12. Thomas C. Schelling, "What Makes Greenhouse Sense?," *Foreign Affairs*, May 1, 2002, https://www.foreignaffairs.com/articles/2002-05-01/what-makes-greenhouse-sense.
13. Joshua Busby, "Warming World," *Foreign Affairs*, June 14, 2018, https://www.foreignaffairs.com/articles/2018-06-14/warming-world.
14. "2018 Fourth Warmest Year in Continued Warming Trend, According to NASA, NOAA," National Aeronautics and Space Administration, February 6, 2019, https://climate.nasa.gov/news/2841/2018-fourth-warmest-year-in-continued-warming-trend-according-to-nasa-noaa.
15. Pascaline Wallemacq and Rowena House, "Economic Losses, Poverty & Disasters, 1998–2017." (Geneva, Switzerland: United Nations Office for Disaster Risk Reduction, 2018).
16. IPCC, "Global Warming of 1.5°C. An IPCC Special Report on the Impacts of Global Warming of 1.5°C above Pre-Industrial Levels and Related Global

Greenhouse Gas Emission Pathways, in the Context of Strengthening the Global Response to the Threat of Climate Change, Sustainable Development, and Efforts to Eradicate Poverty," Summary (Geneva, Switzerland: World Meteorological Organization, 2018), https://www.ipcc.ch/sr15/.
17. IPCC.
18. IPCC.
19. See in particular: "World Employment and Social Outlook 2018—Greening with Jobs," Publication (International Labor Organization, May 14, 2018), http://www.ilo.org/global/research/global-reports/weso/greening-with-jobs/WCMS_628708/lang%2D%2Den/index.htm.
20. Kevin Drum, "Tech World," *Foreign Affairs*, June 14, 2018, https://www.foreignaffairs.com/articles/world/2018-06-14/tech-world.
21. Celine Herweijer and Dominic Waughray, "Fourth Industrial Revolution for the Earth" (PricewaterhouseCoopers, 2018), https://www.pwc.com/gx/en/sustainability/assets/ai-for-the-earth-jan-2018.pdf.
22. Andreas Kaplan and Michael Haenlein, "Siri, Siri, in My Hand: Who's the Fairest in the Land? On the Interpretations, Illustrations, and Implications of Artificial Intelligence," *Business Horizons* 62, no. 1 (January 1, 2019): 15–25, https://doi.org/10.1016/j.bushor.2018.08.004.
23. Herweijer and Waughray, "Fourth Industrial Revolution for the Earth."
24. Herweijer and Waughray.
25. Steve LeVine, "One Fun Thing: We're All Luddites," *Axios*, June 11, 2017, https://www.axios.com/newsletters/axios-future-e8bdf7f3-3092-4b18-bb48-cb663a050f89.html?chunk=5#story5.
26. Karen Hao, "Giving Algorithms a Sense of Uncertainty Could Make Them More Ethical," *MIT Technology Review*, January 18, 2019, https://www.technologyreview.com/s/612764/giving-algorithms-a-sense-of-uncertainty-could-make-them-more-ethical/.
27. Peter Eckersley, "Impossibility and Uncertainty Theorems in AI Value Alignment (or Why Your AGI Should Not Have a Utility Function)," *ArXiv:1901.00064 [Cs]*, December 31, 2018, 13.
28. It did not die completely after Newton went back to the FCO in 2002; but his successor, who was at Lehman for a year, turned out to be the second and last second.
29. As far as it is known, the only other individual thriving in a similar role in London today is Tina Fordham (who was a member of the Eurasia Group team attached to Lehman in 2000–2001) at Citigroup.

    This may or may not be supported by the experience of the third person known to occupy a similar role during the past decade or so, an ex-Treasury economist who can "do" politics and who joined big US investment bank in London as government liaison. The eurozone crisis allowed him to cross over into a role something like Newton's, which was what he really wanted to do. However, he lasted less than two years before a powerful faction in the bank which regarded politics (at least as far as emerging markets were concerned) as its rightful domain got him axed.

30. This being said, where Newton does have relevant expertise and/or contacts he will get stuck in—trade policy being a notable (and highly topical) example, since he has relevant background there.
31. Newton has frequently been described as an interpreter between two sides, that is, investors/brokers on the one hand and policymakers on the other, whose relationships are all too frequently dogged by mutual misunderstanding. Notably, he lost count of the number of times during the height of the Greek debt crisis that someone in markets said to him "Surely Merkel must understand that…." Similarly, policymakers in Berlin in particular were generally totally bemused by what they saw as investors' failure to grasp the political realities. From their own perspective the arguments of each side were, in Newton's view, equally valid.

    And that is indicative of a very important part of being a successful political analyst, that is, being able to see the world through the eyes of top policymakers and anticipate how they will respond to a given set of circumstances.
32. Newton was once asked by a senior Lehman person how he had managed to get a meeting with a particular politician in India with whom he had not previously had any dealings. He explained that there were three ways in which he got people to see me. First, he knew them from a previous "incarnation." Second, he knew someone who knew the individual in question and who opened the door for Newton (in this case, it was actually twice removed but the principle still applies). Third, and failing the above, he would try to talk his way into the person's presence relying on "boyish charm and good looks"!
33. Newton was once asked by a top City FX trader what made a good political analyst. After a few seconds, he came up with "the same as makes a top trader, i.e. 'gut instinct.'" When asked (understandably) what he meant by "gut instinct," he replied: "Gut instinct is the conscious manifestation of your subconscious grinding through your collected knowledge".

    He stands by that to this day, often finding that he comes up with "the answer" then has to "retro-engineer" the argumentation in order to justify it to others. One's gut instinct is not always correct, of course. But he often quotes the great South African golfer of his youth Gary Player who famously remarked that he had always considered himself to be a lucky golfer and that "the harder I practice the luckier I get". In other words, work hard at acquiring information from all the quarters one can; and be sure to process it putting one's own personal prejudices to one side in favor of those of the policymaker(s) who will actually make the decisions.
34. To paraphrase Winston Churchill (talking about one of his fellow parliamentarian's use of statistics), too many presenters use PowerPoint "like a drunk uses a lamp-post, for support not illumination."
35. Bullets. Newton still sticks to the hard and fast FCO rule for submissions to ministers when he was starting out his diplomatic career that bullets should

be no more than three lines each. And it is worth adding that, at that time at least, submissions had to be no more than three pages—with anything else which was needed in support pushed into annexes.

36. There was a classic instance of this in 2001 when Newton and a senior economist, at a morning meeting, insisted that the ECB would not intervene to support the ailing euro at the end of the week before the IMF annual meeting. Two hours later, the ECB intervened. He felt gutted. It was another couple of hours before he ventured out onto the trading floor where he was asked what he was doing there. As he tried to apologize for a wrong call, he was told not to worry as the traders hadn't believed him at the morning meeting anyway! At that point, not knowing quite what to feel, he duly came down on "philosophical"! This being said, Newton recalls one economist who was patently wrong much more often than he was right, at least as far as politics was concerned. Newton asked the traders why they tolerated him to which he got the (ex-post) obvious answer, that is, that the trader was a great contrary indicator!

4

Case Study: The Change-Maker Game

Welcome to a world to come. We are 20 years into the future.

Imagine that you are sitting at the table of a café, reading the *Wall Street Journal*. The daily is running the following profile on its front page:

> *This person of the year (POY) is shaping the world in a dramatic, unprecedented, and wonderful way. POY has always been relentless when it comes to bringing change to how business is done in POY's industry. We are just starting to realize how transformative this change is, not only for the industry, but for the global economy as a whole. This all started years ago, with a modest set of goals, when POY clearly identified the industry's problem and became committed to fixing it with all available resources.*
>
> *But it was not* really *a problem for POY; it was an opportunity to have an impact, to provide solutions to an industry that so desperately needed it, to train local actors to respond to those needs durably. And ultimately, the solution set off a real revolution in this industry. Step by step, but relentlessly: the revolution did not happen overnight. The solution POY offered improved progressively, with close examination of results every step of the way in the arduous trial and error process. And before POY knew it, the solution became global and influential.*
>
> *Many people argue today that this story is about compassion: POY was acting to make the world a better place and to empower a wide range of actors by helping them achieve their mission more easily.*
>
> *But this story is also about empathy: the set of incentives shaping the interactions between actors was so complex, and the intentions, at times, so contradictory, that POY needed to constantly play devil's advocate to clearly understand the dynamics. It would have been hard otherwise for POY to bring about change that would have been truly meaningful for a wide range of actors. POY has always argued that one cannot ask vulnerable people, living day by day, without any real possibility to imagine what*

J. Ghez, *Architects of Change*, https://doi.org/10.1007/978-3-030-20684-0_4

their future might look like or might be about—let alone invite them to think about the greater good. POY is convinced that people respond to incentives, and unless we understand the world as they see it, we will fail to find a sustainable and scalable solution. This is why POY often likes to quote Atticus Finch, the famous fictional character from Harper Lee's novel, To Kill a Mockingbird: *"You never really understand a person until you consider things from his point of view, until you climb into his skin and walk around it." The "other" is the person I am negotiating the future with, POY concludes. If we remain hostages of the past, it is game over, POY contends. For all of us. This conversation has always been about the future. In POY's own words: "I need to understand my counterparts, appreciate their motives and their purpose, and get a good grasp of their psychology, their pride, their temper and their habits. That is how one can bring change to a whole community* and *to a whole industry."*[1]

This is how POY was able to measure the impact of the change brought about by this revolution: this revolution is not just about goodwill, or about survival in a world ripe for disruption. It was also about a person utterly convinced that without goodwill, local communities would not survive. Someone had to step up and empower local actors around the globe to act and maintain that ability to act over time. And unless we understand that this story was, most of all, about impact, about seizing the opportunity of fixing a long-term problem and creating value for a wide range of stakeholders—including for POY, who openly and happily admits it—we will not grasp the full, transformative nature of this revolution.

Who Is POY?

This story strikes you as illustrative of the times we live in, on the type of people who manage to have a meaningful impact in spite of impressive and even scary megatrends and exogenous forces. POY will be the most influential game-changer of tomorrow, undoubtedly. But this story is purposefully very vague, because the future is still to be written—so consider the following questions:

Who is POY? Is it really a person, or "something" else?
What is POY actually doing that is so game-changing? In what industry?
How did POY get there? With what skills? What personal qualities?

Food for Thought for Architects of Change

This is an exercise architects of change do regularly: it is the kind of mental gymnastics that can enlighten them on the real nature of the impact they are likely to have given the changing business environment and given how the states of mind of the people surrounding them are evolving.

Mental Gymnastics

Who will make it on the front page of the *Wall Street Journal* and why is one way of addressing this challenge—but it is not the only way. They may also wonder for instance why they may be invited back to their alma mater or their home community, and what type of impact they would like to be known for having.

One goal of this exercise lies in keeping an open mind about how the target problem they defined in the past is evolving over time and to remain pragmatic about their goals. This is why understanding the world they live in plays such a critical role in the life of an architect of change.

A second lies in understanding the transformational process *they* need to go through in order to remain relevant. A changing business environment means that the skills necessary to thrive are also shifting. The World Economic Forum's report on this topic is quite revealing as it predicts by 2020 an increasing significance of skills such as complex problem solving, analytical and critical thinking, creativity, and emotional intelligence, relative to people and financial management.[2]

One can always argue about the value of rankings especially for architects of change who will likely need to master a combination of these skills rather than a single one. But the study does show that successful actors of change will know how to adjust and shift focus away from some skills that may be getting relatively less critical, in favor of others. Architects of change also know how to change themselves.

But in doing so, they face two major pitfalls.

When and How the Environment Is Changing

The first lies in failing to see how fast their environment is changing and how these changes may make their approach, their tools, or even the very problem they are looking to tackle moot. Similarly, they may not always appreciate how fast the forces they are looking to leverage are actually accelerating, creating far more opportunities than they ever imagined. *New York Times* journalist Thomas Friedman offers a useful illustration of this phenomenon: in 2004, he argued in a book that the world was becoming increasingly "flat" as different forces were leveling the playing field for a wide range of actors and increasing competition in industries and in activities that once thought of themselves as immune to change.[3]

More than a decade later, he observed in a later book:

> When I was running around in 2004 declaring that the world was flat, Facebook didn't even exist yet, Twitter was still a sound, the cloud was still in the sky, 4G was a parking space, 'applications' were what you sent to college, LinkedIn was barely known and most people thought it was a prison, Big Data was a good name for a rap star, and Skype, for most people, was a typographical error. All of those technologies blossomed after I wrote *The World Is Flat*—most of them around 2007.[4]

In other words, we may make mistakes not only by identifying a trend that is not real or that might go into reverse mode at some point, but also by failing to understand at times, that they may actually accelerate. The difference can be in terms of degree and nature that may affect a wide range of positions, industries, and markets that may empower[5] individuals far more than what we initially believed.

Taken Hostage by Today's World

A second pitfall lies in failing to recognize that the most meaningful and impactful strategies of the day may fail dramatically in tomorrow's fundamentally different environment. As humans, we are prone to give excessive importance to the present, to what is around us—if anything because it is information that is easy to access. As a result, because of limited information about the future and limited ability to process trends that are shaping the future business environment, we tend to reason under the logic that all things *will* remain equal in the future. We excessively depend on the key numbers and concepts of the day without considering how our assumptions should change in the future. This is what psychologists refer to as anchoring.

Architects of change need to go beyond that natural reflex and design a robust action plan with the goal that it remains as relevant as possible in time. They cannot be influenced by the controversy of the day or the popular cause of the moment and disregard how mega-forces are shaping the future. In other words, to borrow a term from psychology again, they cannot jump on the bandwagon and take key aspects of the current business environment for granted—thus failing to see that what they are counting on to guarantee their success may not be there tomorrow. Conversely, they may also overlook opportunities for change: it is not because a product, a service, a market, or a particular position inside a company does not exist today that it will not exist tomorrow. Architects of change need to be willing to invent and even reinvent the system they evolve in so as to create the ideal ecosystem they need to thrive.

Expecting "others" to do it—the state in particular—is rarely a winning option. Instead, the architects of change need to learn and process the new information they collect, include it in their thinking and their strategy in the broader business environment, and make the changes that these new pieces of information demand. The ability to embrace this evolutionary process is, arguably, one of the most critical skills architects of change have.

Changing the System

American educator Daniela Papi Thornton makes a very eloquent argument about social entrepreneurs today who do not "just" run a social business but actually look to fix a broken system in order to create value for themselves and a whole lot of other people while they are at it.[6] This definition is what corresponds best to architects of change: they are not necessarily running a business but acting like what Thornton calls systems change leaders to solve the most pressing issues that society faces.

These solutions can involve a business, but are often more hybrid in nature, as they look for support within government and the non-profit sector. These solutions are not short-term fixes that seek to develop existing products to society but rather concentrate on why some chunks of the populations have been unable or barred from using those very products. Architects of change, as systems change leaders, understand the problem so well because they have worked in the sector and because they are aware of what has been tried; and because they have seen the issue with their own eyes, they understand why it is so persisting. By solving the problem, they can change the system.

An architect of change need not look for the status of a hero—though one may suspect some will, and it is their right to do so. Instead, having a local impact, just as POY did initially in this thought experiment, is a meaningful way to test the viability of a proposed change and to allow time and space for readjustment. The process of trial and error is central in the day-to-day activity of architects of change. This process is about failing forward, and fast, as the popular saying goes.

The Basic Qualities of the Architect of Change

This thought experiment suggests that architects of change display three fundamental qualities that they can leverage for transformative change.

The first is that architects of change are analytical, as they understand the complexities of their business environment and what this demands from them. In particular, they cannot reason only in linear terms and expect their environment to change in incremental ways. They must not only be able to survive disruptive moments like Brexit or the 2016 election of Donald Trump; they should also be able to anticipate them and to even leverage them as a force of potential change.

The second quality, as a result, is that architects of change are transformational in nature. The risk of stating the obvious here may seem great, but it is important to note that comfort zones should not be what architects of change look for as they recognize a striking paradox of business activity: in order to stay on top and to remain a leader—let alone to remain relevant!—one must keep on moving and embrace transformation.

Last but not least, the ultimate quality architects of change must display is the ability to mobilize. Because the nature of the change they push is like an invitation to leave one's comfort zone, their message is rarely reassuring, let alone a consoling one. Unless they exert a form of leadership that conveys the significance of the change they are looking to bring about and show the empathy to express this change in a way a wide range of stakeholders can understand, they are likely to fail in communicating with a broader audience. This is why architects of change will need to show imagination and creativity that will help them shape their idea and message for a broad audience.

Subsequent chapters explore these qualities in depth.

Notes

1. The language is drawn from British economist John Maynard Keynes' 1945 speech to British policymakers about the attitude they should adopt as they negotiated the global financial architecture with American officials after the end of World War II. See: "How Keynes Would Negotiate Brexit," *The Economist*, August 15, 2018, https://www.economist.com/open-future/2018/08/15/how-keynes-would-negotiate-brexit.
2. "The Future of Jobs Report 2018" (Geneva, Switzerland: World Economic Forum, September 17, 2018), https://www.weforum.org/reports/the-future-of-jobs-report-2018/.
3. Thomas Friedman, *The World Is Flat 3.0: A Brief History of the Twenty-first Century*, Updated, Expanded (New York: Picador, 2007).
4. Thomas L. Friedman, *Thank You for Being Late: An Optimist's Guide to Thriving in the Age of Accelerations* (New York: Farrar, Straus and Giroux, 2016).
5. As Friedman once put it in a radio show, empowering people means "enabling individuals to complete, connect and collaborate so much faster, farther cheaper and deeper."
6. Daniela Papi Thornton, "Reclaiming Social Entrepreneurship," (TEDx Talk, July 6, 2017), https://www.youtube.com/watch?v=RdrfMqBRfEQ.

5

The Road to Reinvention

When you constantly fight the flames of the day, it is rather difficult to take some distance with current fires and crises and look to the future. And yet, by doing so, you would broaden your horizons in a way that can help you overcome short-term stalemates and that can help you focus on the battles that may matter most tomorrow. In doing so, you would also be in a better position to transform your activity according to the long-term structural trends that are likely to matter in the future, not according to the short-term fads that current headlines are obsessed with and that are unlikely to matter.

This is what architects of change excel at doing: by refusing to be taken hostage by past and current trends, and thanks to their analytical skills, they understand how their business environment is changing, and perhaps more critically, how to surf on those changes in order to better transform their organizations and their activities—so as not to be passive observers of change but rather active players of reinvention.

This is the process through which their analytical skills become a springboard to meaningful transformation of businesses, activities, and even industries and broader organizations. This chapter shows how.

It starts with a brief discussion of the Red Queen's race, a story that English writer Lewis Carroll tells in *Through the Looking-Glass*, the 1871 sequel to *Alice in Wonderland*, a story which serves as a powerful reminder of the paradox of reinvention: in order to remain on top *and* stay true to yourself, you may need to constantly change.

The second section of this chapter is an exploration of the market, that is, the theater where reinvention occurs. The way we define today's market is fairly straightforward and sets fairly simple questions about day-to-day

J. Ghez, *Architects of Change*, https://doi.org/10.1007/978-3-030-20684-0_5

business dilemmas. But in a longer run perspective, the evolution of the market sets broader challenges for reinvention. This second section will show why.

The third section focuses on the role of competition in shaping the market and the reinvention process. We are often tempted to consider "competition" as a nuisance that we must circumvent in order to maximize benefits. And yet, this definition of competition is based on a very short-term perspective. Adopting it can lead you to allocate an excessive amount of energy and resources to today's battles, to the detriment of tomorrow's battles. This section will help us consider a more complex definition of competition that can help actors broaden their horizons and effectively overcome short-term stalemates—and be, ultimately, in a better position to reinvent.

The chapter concludes with what architects of change, on the road to reinvention, must remember to lead their transformation effectively.

The Red Queen's Race (and Its Implications for Reinvention)

In *Through the Looking-Glass*, the 1871 sequel to *Alice in Wonderland*, Carroll tells the story of how Alice enters, once again, an extraordinary world by climbing through a mirror of her house.

A Different Kind of World

This world is one that defies Alice's—and human—logic and intuition as everything seems to be in reverse, as her reflection was in the mirror. In fact, when she spots the Red Queen, whom she had already met in the past, her attempts to meet her fail because the Red Queen vanishes mysteriously. It is only when she walks in the opposite direction of the Red Queen that she finally succeeds in meeting her.

Alice tells the Queen that she wants to see the garden, up the hill, but—perhaps not so surprisingly—she cannot seem to find her way. After a strange conversation in which the Queen questions Alice's definition of gardens, hills, and even ways to a particular place, the two protagonists finally get on top of the hill. Alice realizes that the world she is in is actually divided up into many different chess boards and wishes she could be one of the chess pieces. The Queen offers her to be the White Queen's pawn.

And then, after this brief conversation, without any warning, they start running, very fast. The Red Queen keeps on demanding that Alice run faster, though the little girl states she cannot go any faster. And the race stops, as suddenly as it started. But to Alice's astonishment, the whole time of the race, they stayed under the same tree. In her own words, in her country, "you'd generally get to somewhere else—if you ran very fast for a long time, as we've been doing." But the Queen is unimpressed, calling her country "slow sort of country," because in hers, "see, it takes all the running YOU can do, to keep in the same place. If you want to get somewhere else, you must run at least twice as fast as that." And after giving Alice a few cryptic pieces of advice on how to play the game of chess she is about the play—including a more straightforward one, "Remember who you are!"—the Red Queen vanishes. How? Alice is not sure, though she remembers the Queen does run very fast; but she concludes there is no real way of knowing where she went. Alice then remembers it is her turn to play, and quickly forgets about this mystery.

Many Metaphors and Interpretations in a Single Story

Physicists and biologists have relied on this episode in Lewis Carroll's book to explore the paradoxes of time, evolution, and survival. American professor of biochemistry and science-fiction writer Isaac Asimov called this episode "The Red Queen's Race" in a short story that bears the same name and in which he explores the paradoxes of what determines history and any effort to go back in time, through time travel, to rewrite history: no matter how hard you try, you will end up in the same place as you are today, namely because attempts to shape history have already happened.[1]

As a result, "The Red Queen's Race" may not be a story about the past, but an invitation to think about the future and about our ability to leave our comfort zone—the type of environment the Red Queen would call a "slow sort of country." As Alice admits it, she (and many of *us*) would be quite content to stay where we are. But in thinking in such way, we are making an implicit assumption, namely that this place where we are will remain the same, durably. This assumption is responsible for the many analytical mistakes we make: we yearn for the "good old days," for some glorious past that corresponds to our ideal, but that either never really existed the way we remember it, or that will never be a reality ever again. This story is, in this way, about the sacred cows we excessively appreciate, even beyond their actual value.

This interpretation of "The Red Queen's Race" is perhaps the most meaningful lesson architects of change can draw: truly influential, dominant and/or impactful actors are not lazy stakeholders, resting on their laurels and appreciating their competitive edge; instead, they are more likely to be involved in a constant quest for reinvention, designed in a way that lets them *maintain* that edge. In other words, unless they constantly reinvent, they are likely to be blindsided. This is at the heart of the principle of creative destruction that Austrian economist Joseph Schumpeter elaborated on in his 1942 book, *Capitalism, Socialism and Democracy*.[2]

Schumpeter argues that some economists "accept the data of the momentary situation as if there were no past or future to it and think that they have understood what there is to understand if they interpret the behavior of those firms by means of the principle of maximizing profits with reference to those data." In fact, he adds that too often, the type of competition among actors that "monopolizes attention" is the one "within a rigid pattern of invariant conditions, methods of production and forms of industrial organization in particular." The analysis of competition is therefore overly focused on current dynamics and realities, leading market observers and players to overlook the coming transformations that could shape tomorrow's business environment. As a result, the competition that really matters is the one

> from the new commodity, the new technology, the new source of supply, the new type of organization (the largest-scale unit of control for instance)—competition which commands a decisive cost or quality advantage and which strikes not at the margins of the profits and the outputs of the existing firms but at their foundations and their very lives.[3]

It is the form of competition that drives the transformation of actors, including the most dominant ones, looking to maintain a competitive edge.

The Red Queen's race serves as a powerful reminder that ultimately change must be transformative and require that we run twice as fast, if the objective that we really seek to achieve is getting "somewhere else." But as the Queen tells Alice, this also requires that we not forget who we are: moving in space may not be contradictory with remaining true to ourselves; in fact, the two may be very complementary when we seek stability in an environment that constantly evolves.

The next section analyzes the theater of reinvention for many actors of change, namely the market. The following section focuses on how competition can drive reinvention.

The Market: Where Reinvention Takes Place

Thinking about what your market is today is a straightforward question: you think about who is selling and who is buying. The picture you come up with is simple because it is static. Trying to define the future market is a more speculative and no less critical exercise, because it points to the likely

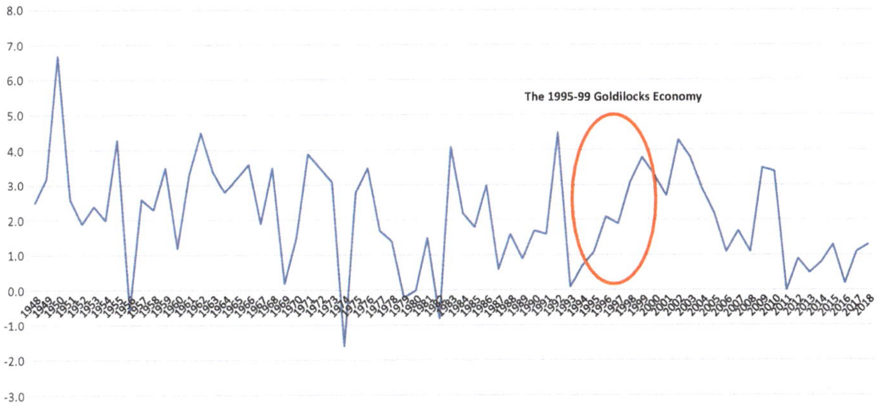

Fig. 5.1 Labor productivity in the United States since 1948. Source: Division of Major Sector Productivity, Bureau of Labor Statistics. Data reflects press release of March 7, 2019. Full report: www.bls.gov/news.release/prod2.nr0.htm
Between 1995 and 1999, productivity increase was quite robust compared to the longer period before that. Over the 1995–2005 decade, productivity experienced an even more substantial growth before declining and stagnating since then.

challenges you need to get geared up for as well as the opportunities you will be able to seize—or, in other words, the reinvention process you'll need to go through in order to survive in the coming economy. The story of the new emergence of a global market in the early 1990s, and how it has evolved since, is a telling example of how actors have reinvented and will need to reinvent, both their organizations and themselves. The US economy of the 1990s was characterized by a combination of high growth, dropping unemployment and low inflation—a combination that came to be known as the "Goldilocks economy."[4] In this economy, productivity, which, in broad terms, measures how efficient the production processes are, jumped up after having stagnated for quite some time—from 1.4% annual rate between 1973 and 1994 to 2.4% between 1995 and 1999 (Fig. 5.1).

The (First) New Economy

Different hypotheses sought to explain this phenomenon. Two are particularly noteworthy. The first focuses on the US economic actors reaping the first dividends of the information technology revolution. It was a period at which firms substantially increased their IT spending. But as some studies have argued, not all firms and not all industries enjoyed the same levels of productivity growth—some experiencing little or no growth at all, perhaps because the so-called IT revolution was not immediate. Because of this lack of correlation between spending and productivity gains, these studies have questioned the significance of the IT revolution. As a result, a second hypothesis is noteworthy here: increasing competition forced firms to innovate, in technology, but also in products, business, and management practices. In addition, workers lost bargaining power as supply chains became increasingly global and outsourcing increasingly easier to achieve in a post-Cold War world.[5] (Admittedly, though, these two hypotheses describe two intertwined realities and the role of technology is not absent in the second hypothesis).

This new reality—an increasingly single, integrated and global market that became even more obvious in 2001 when China joined the World Trade Organization (WTO)—explained the coexistence of dropping unemployment and high growth on the one hand (the result of increased worldwide opportunities) and low inflation on the other (the result of lower bargaining power of workers). It is what we have come to call quite commonly globalization, a process that accelerated right about that time and that has substantially augmented the number of opportunities but that has also made players compete for them in a way that was fiercer than in the past.

This reality meant that actors knew where to look for new opportunities, namely on the global stage. Changes in the global reality—for instance enthusiasm for new products and services, or consumer preferences and tastes—drove the reinvention of global actors in this set-up.

A Changing Reality

But the recipe for reinvention started to shift, especially with the 2008 Great Recession which placed the capitalist system as a whole under surveillance: a system that could blow up so easily did not deserve the legitimacy it had previously enjoyed. In particular, the degree to which this system, which was in theory designed to meet the needs and the wants of consumers, performed poorly when it came to meeting the needs of society was striking. In addition, it seemed as if companies had already picked the low-hanging fruits and it was time to grow differently, perhaps in new markets or by targeting less wealthy consumers. Ultimately, the challenge was in seeking productivity gains elsewhere.

As renowned academic Michael Porter and social business consultant Mark Kramer put it summarizing their seminal work on creating shared value,

> Society's needs are huge—health, better housing, improved nutrition, help for the aging, greater financial security, less environmental damage. Arguably, they are the greatest unmet needs in the global economy. In business we have spent

> decades learning how to parse and manufacture demand while missing the most important demand of all. Too many companies have lost sight of that most basic of questions: Is our product good for our customers? Or for our customers' customers?[6]

In fact, argue Porter and Kramer, traditional economic models have always assumed that there was a natural contradiction between economic and business efficiency on the one hand and social welfare on the other. The only way to get businesses to account for the social cost of their action was to rein in on them by taxing them or constraining what they could and could not do. And yet, the two authors observe, firms *are* able to bridge societal needs with conventional economic needs through innovations and new business approaches (by developing new procurement practices or new local clusters of activity) that allow them to address societal harms and constraints, and to create a bigger pie that a wide range of stakeholders can benefit from—the firms included. Porter and Kramer contend that shared value stems from the fact that "no company is self-contained," and that its successes and failures are conditioned by their location and its other stakeholders and infrastructure.

As globalization accelerated in the mid-1990s, actors may have overlooked the significance of this local ecosystem. As the authors argue, "Companies have failed to grasp the importance of the broader business environment surrounding their major operations."[7] As a result, investing in local clusters of activity and redesigning products to meet the expectations of local stakeholders will play a key role in success. The authors provide some examples suggesting that in the realm of cocoa for instance, the shared value model is far more effective than fair trade. In addition, in this author's experience, those who have defended the idea of shared value best usually argue that by adopting this mindset, you are able to become a piece of the puzzle in the broader economy—a feat none of your competitors will manage to achieve by free riding. The idea may still be controversial currently because the research evaluating its impact is still nascent. What is striking, though, is that neither charity nor altruism is driving this shift in mindset; instead, the need to address a wider range of societal needs will require actors to reconsider the parameters of their profit equation. Rather than focusing on a far too narrow set of firm-centric parameters, it may be time to rewrite—and even reinvent—that equation in order to enlarge the total pool of value.

The Difficult Transition

But this shift in mindset will require a delicate transition: resources, and human ones in particular, will need to evolve in ways that may not make any of us comfortable, considering the transformations we will need to go through in order to adapt to the changing demands of firms and of the labor markets. For this reinvention process to be complete, we, individuals, all have to go through a process of creative destruction of our own. This transition is filled with opportunities for those who have the means to adapt, but may further weaken the most vulnerable chunks of populations. Two examples illustrate this story well.

Dealing with the Skills Mismatch

The first is the skills mismatch that has been widely documented. This mismatch results from a situation in which the demand for low-skilled labor is significantly lower than its supply, and in which, conversely, the demand for low-skilled labor is significantly higher than its supply. This mismatch between demand and supply of skills represents a substantial obstacle to a smooth transition, in particular because our economies lack the human resources that such a transition would require.

The McKinsey Global Institute estimates that between 2016 and 2030, the demand for technological and other complex skills will accelerate while demand for more basic skills will drop substantially: they expect demand for physical and manual skills to drop by 14% and for basic cognitive skills by 15%, whereas the need for social and emotional skills and for technological skills to increase by 24 and 55% respectively (measured in terms of total hours worked in the United States and in Europe).

This is true in banking and in insurance for instance, an industry that will require far less "data input and processing, basic literacy, and basic numeracy" as opposed to a greater number of technology experts able to run forecasting models on risk. We can expect a similar trend in retail, in which automated vehicles and processes will replace traditional jobs in this industry that will require far more people with interpersonal skills, empathy, and creativity.[8]

This transformation will require organizations to be far more agile in incorporating a wide range of profiles that we likely know very little about currently. It will also require that organizations, governments, and leaders rethink the meaning of education and training in a business environment in which the skills required are increasingly complex and in constant need to be up to date.

The Transition Towards a Greener Economy

The second example—which is most likely telling a very similar story, one just more focused on the stake of ecological transition—is the expected amount of jobs created and destroyed by new opportunities in the "green industry." One International Labor Organization report found that

> Measures taken in the production and use of energy, for example, will lead to job losses of around 6 million as well as the creation of some 24 million jobs. The net increase of approximately 18 million jobs across the world will be the result of the adoption of sustainable practices, including changes in the energy mix, the projected growth in the use of electric vehicles, and increases in energy efficiency in existing and future buildings.[9]

This is a transition filled with opportunities as a result: achieving this transition into a new, greener economy will lead to an outcome with far more jobs than what pessimists on growth and employment suggest.

But this is by no means an easy transition, in particular for those that currently do not have the skills or the means to get the education and the training they need to strive in this new economy. As the International Labor Organization report argues, "In order to ensure a just transition, efforts to promote the green economy must be accompanied by policies that facilitate the reallocation of workers, advance decent work, offer local solutions and support displaced workers."[10]

As it is often the case, a transition usually entails large diffuse gains and very specific and limited costs; but the costs are more often than not concentrated on the weakest chunks of the population who bear a disproportionate part of the burden. The real challenge lies in identifying these populations and showing enough political courage and determination to develop the right retraining programs.

Ultimately, the process of creative destruction that Joseph Schumpeter described captures quite well the nature of the transformation individuals must go through in order to adapt and make an impact in this business environment. Like Alice, it often feels uncomfortable leaving the places we know, but it is equally deceiving to believe that those places will remain as they are forever. Embracing transformation of oneself in particular, is therefore a key feature of the road to reinvention that an architect of change is likely to choose.

Competition: The *raison d'être* for Reinvention

In addition to changes in the business environment that require us to rethink our most basic business equations and skills, competition can also drive reinvention. But the very concept of competition is far more ambiguous than it appears at first sight.

More often than not, the usual audiences the author of this book interacts with will happily say that it wants to crush and kill all competition. This view is in itself not illegitimate: the idea of competition suggests a form of contest that the human brain is well-wired to want to win. But the moment we explore the concrete meaning of competition, the question becomes more complex suddenly: is competition what you face today? Or tomorrow? Depending on the time horizon you chose, the list of competitors you come up with is likely to be extremely different. And we can push this logic one step further: will competition necessarily come from another specific product or service, or will the transformation of your industry (and others) ultimately make your product completely obsolete? You may not be facing any real "competition" down the line in an environment in which there is no actual demand for what you are offering; but that will not put you in a position of dominance, most obviously.

A key challenge when considering competition therefore lies in avoiding fighting yesterday's battles that are likely to tie up and mobilize an excessive amount of resources compared to the stake they actually represent. If you do not avoid those battles, you are likely to compromise your ability to reinvent, being stuck in yesterday's wars. It may be a trivial point to say that reinvention is a forward-looking process; and yet, those actors who cannot carry it out (and thus fail to become architects of change) are usually unable to do so because they are hostages of the present. That is the state that we must escape.

Another debate lies in considering the type of change we need to go through in order to meet the standards of reinvention: are incremental adaptations enough? Or is deep transformation the high bar we must set for reinvention? Though we may be tempted by an incremental approach, this section will show that ultimately, lasting competition will command deep transformation for any actor looking to make a durable impact. In order to achieve this goal, we must explore different market structures, ranging from those presenting a high degree of competition to those presenting no competition at all.

Competition—and Even Lack Thereof—Drives Reinvention

Anyone who has ever traveled to Paris is likely to know about *Rue des Rosiers*—the Street of Rose Bushes. The street is in the heart of the Jewish Quarter of the French capital. Tourists can enjoy falafel and shawarma sandwiches in the many little restaurants they will find there. But most of them may not wonder though how these little restaurants compete.

A Market in Which Competition Is High?

Imagine, for the sake of discussion, that there is, in fact, a very great number of players supplying tourists with sandwiches in this street that is the theater of significant competition among actors.

Economic theory calls this set-up pure and perfect competition, a set-up that meets a set of conditions that ensures a high degree of competition. In particular, in this set-up, no single actor can have any real influence on price, even by producing a little more or a little less. All of the actors are price-takers as a result. In addition, all goods must be homogeneous in the sense that consumers cannot distinguish between the different options they are offered, even if different firms are supplying these options. As a result, branding and differentiation either do not occur or have no real influence on consumer preferences. Furthermore, there are no barriers to entry (or to exit in fact): firms can come into an industry and are free to leave at any time. This is critical, because, if it is not respected, a firm can be left unchallenged and therefore have pricing power—which would contradict the notion of no actor having any influence on market outcomes. Finally, a high level of competition requires a high level of transparency, so that all actors have access to the same information about each other, about market conditions and consumer preferences in particular. It also requires that factors of production, labor, and capital in particular, be mobile across industries and across regions (and countries).

This definition of competition may seem highly ambitious—and quite unrealistic when we look for real-life examples. And yet, a close inspection of this definition shows how influential it has been historically and legally. The notion that no single actor can be big enough to have influence on prices is at the heart of antitrust legislation in the United States and in Europe. The idea that transparency is critical for a market to function is also one that is widely shared among regulators, considering their concerns regarding insider trading for instance. Similarly, while movements of capital have been guaranteed for quite some time around the planet, the free movement of people is still in the making; but an institution like the European Union, through the Schengen Treaty, which guarantees the free flow of people, has sought to make this a reality. As a result, as unrealistic as this definition may be, the influence it has had is quite striking.

In addition to this influence, this definition can also help us replicate what actually happens on this sandwich market in which there is a high degree of competition. Imagine that at some point in time, these shops are making a profit. Because capital and labor are mobile, and because there are no barriers to entry in this market, other shops will be attracted to the market, leading overall supply to increase and prices to drop as far they can. Each individual falafel shop will have little leverage since all of them are price takers. Ultimately, they will not be able to make any substantial profits on this market in the long run and remain passive victim of market forces, in particular because their consumers will only consider price when making choices in this environment in which goods are undifferentiated. The consumer, who will pay the lowest price possible, is the winner who takes all.

The only solution firms may have in this setting lies in differentiation: if all goods are not homogeneous, that is, if consumers must make a choice between two sandwiches that are not the same because of differences in terms of quality or branding for instance, the sandwich shops that succeed in differentiating their food can attract new clients by putting forward the unique selling propositions they offer. As a result, clients may pay attention to factors other than price and the sandwich shops, by differentiating, may not be bound by market prices anymore.

Differentiation is one way to think about the reinvention process a firm needs to go through in a highly competitive landscape: Rethinking the features of what you sell, the way you sell it, and the message you sell it with can help you escape the most vicious forces of the market—even if this often entails running twice as fast as the Red Queen suggests.

A Market in Which Competition Is Inexistent?

The incentive for a firm in a highly competitive landscape to reinvent is clear: the objective lies in remaining immune to the most challenging market forces and not being bound by the low price of that market. Does this mean that a very dominant firm, or even a monopoly, has no incentive to reinvent because it is already immune from market forces? The answer is no, and this section explains why.

Imagine now that *Rue des Rosiers* is dominated by one, dominant sandwich shop, which is recommended by famous actors and musicians and by all tourist guides. This very dominant restaurant has undoubtedly more pricing power; but that power is not infinite. If it decides to sell its sandwiches at a very high price, very few people will buy them. If it decides to sell them at a low price, it may attract a lot of consumers but may lose revenue—in addition to the aura it may have enjoyed by charging higher prices. This reasoning suggests that this dominant firm must find a sweet spot in the short run, one that allows it to sell sufficiently while not foregoing revenue. But once it finds that spot, will it be able to remain eternally dominant?

As Schumpeter puts it, it will not, unless it understands that the competition that truly matters is the transformative one that provides the firm with a decisive advantage, be it in terms of cost or quality, and that redefines the way it operates. In Schumpeter's own words, this form of competition

> disciplines before it attacks. The businessman feels himself to be in a competitive situation even if he is alone in his field or if, though not alone, he holds a

> position such that investigating government experts fail to see any effective competition between him and any other firms in the same or a neighboring field and in consequence conclude that his talk, under examination, about his competitive sorrows is all make-believe. In many cases, though not in all, this will in the long run enforce behavior very similar to the perfectly competitive pattern.[11]

In other words, while other stakeholders, government, and regulator included, may fail to see it, what matters most to the dominant firm is not that it does not face any competition *today*, but that it may very well face competition *tomorrow*. That threat is what commands reinvention, even on the part of a firm that is dominant. Unless it does, it will fall to tomorrow's challengers that may be nimbler or that may blindside it when it did not expect it.

And here lies the paradox of competition: regardless of how much competition you face today (or tomorrow), reinvention is the unavoidable process for actors who seek to not only survive the rocky market forces but to strive in tomorrow's business environment.

Limited Competition … Still Drives Reinvention

Imagine now a different setting, one in which there is just a limited set of falafel shops competing with each other. There are not many restaurants, so each of the shops actually has *some* bargaining power. But there is no real dominant shop either, so the bargaining power of each is limited. The challenge lies in understanding how they might interact with each other. Answers may differ depending on your own experience and personal inclinations; but they usually come into three forms: the firms look to erase any sense of competition by colluding, or they look to compete by wrestling for extra market share, or they look to compete by lowering their prices. This section explores each of these three options and offers a somewhat unsurprising conclusion: it is likely that none of these options actually exempt any of these firms from reinventing.

Collusion, or Looking to Erase Competition

It seems that one natural inclination is to try to avoid competition all together. Many will voice legitimate concerns over the ethics and the legality of this approach, as collusion is illegal in most countries; but beyond those critical questions, it is worth remembering that collusion is actually hard to sustain over time anyway.

A Story of Two Prisoners

The famous story of the prisoner's dilemma reminds us why.

Mike and Joe are two burglars. They go to your homes and steal from you. But one day, they get arrested by a policeman, Daniel. He places the two burglars in separate cells and takes away any means of communication. He tells Mike that he is in trouble and is likely to spend his life in jail given what he did. But there is a twist to his interpretation: he believes Joe is that actual brains behind the operation, he tells Mike, so if he were to provide enough evidence to put Joe away, he would be willing to cooperate. He leaves the cell and joins Joe in his, and he—most obviously—tells Joe the very same story.

Consider Mike's and Joe's options. Each can decide either to denounce the other, or to just stay silent.

If one decides to denounce the other, while the other stays silent, Daniel will collect all of the information he needs to put away the one staying silent. The case will be closed, with one person convicted, and another burglar walking free. The person convicted does not get any payoff—meaning a payoff of 0. The person who walks free gets the best possible payoff—say 5.

If both denounce each other, Daniel will collect contradictory pieces of evidence that is likely to limit the extent to which he will be able to convict Joe and Mike. He may be able to put them away, but not as long as when he has clear evidence like in the case above. Mike and Joe will go to jail, but for far less time, and thus still collect a relatively small payoff—say of 1.

If both stay silent, Daniel will not collect the evidence he needs. Mike and Joe will be able to walk away; but Daniel is likely to be frustrated with this result, still convinced that Mike and Joe are up to no good. He is likely to keep an eye on both of them. As a result, even if they are not convicted and walk free, Mike and Joe are in a less favorable position than the one walking free when the other stayed silent, but they both get a relatively high payoff—say a 3 (Table 5.1).

Table 5.1 The prisoners' dilemma

		Joe's choices	
		Denounce	Silent
Mike's choices	Denounce	(1;1)	(5;0)
	Silent	(0;5)	(3;3)

What Could Possibly Happen

Those rooting for the prisoners in this game (the only players actually making a decision in this game) will be quick to point out that Mike and Joe could both agree to stay silent to save themselves. This collusion agreement would in fact be the most acceptable solution to both parties who would be able to maximize their joint gains.

And yet, this collusion agreement is likely to be difficult to sustain, in particular because Mike and Joe may both be attracted by the alternative option—even once they agree on colluding. By denouncing Joe, Mike would be able to get a greater payoff of 5 instead of 3. Likewise, by denouncing Mike, Joe would be able to get a greater payoff of 5 instead of 3. This collusion agreement, like all collusion agreements, is extremely *unstable* as a result: all involved parties do not actually have any incentive to respect it once it is in place.

This thought experiment, famously titled the prisoner's dilemma, does not suggest collusion is impossible. Instead, it shows how difficult it is to sustain: it is likely to take time and trust-building measures. Historically, this difficulty has affected Saudi Arabia's ability to sustain cooperation within the OPEC (Organization of the Petroleum Exporting Countries) cartel for instance. It is a striking reminder that unless actors are actually considering a time horizon that goes beyond immediate profit perspectives, unless they believe there are significant profits to be made in the future and unless they think they can trust their partners, market forces are likely to prevail and influence the ultimate choices of actors.

Believing collusion can help you avoid market dynamics *and* the need to reinvent is therefore likely to lead to disappointing outcomes.

Competing at the Margin, on Market Share or on Price

Of course, actors may try to differentiate when there are a limited set of players—just like when there were many of them, in the highly competitive market. Differentiation helps them not be taken hostage by market forces and charge the price they want. The process is the same as above. But suppose they cannot, and that collusion has failed.

An alternative to collusion lies in direct, frontal competition. This can come in two ways: these shops may look to eat away their competitors' market share; or they may try to drive them out of business by launching a price war. These two options do not lead to the same outcome.

The falafel shops may try to eat up the market share of others. They are not likely to succeed unless they have a cost advantage that they can exploit by producing more and reducing the potential production of other, weaker shops. As a result, they may try to eat away their competitors' market share; but they will only succeed by reducing their *current* costs. The battle is one focused on the very short-term, the issue of the day, rather than on the long-run transformation of the business.

If some have a cost advantage, those restaurants might also feel tempted to launch a price war and "clean up the market" to remain alone—and, hopefully, dominant. But in reality, the process can be far trickier than it seems. First, it assumes that the restaurant launching the price war can continue underbidding for a sustained period of time without harming its ability to survive. This outcome is akin to that of a market in which there is a high degree of competition—without needing too many actors. And even if it does and it drives out of the market other restaurants whose costs do not allow them to drop so low, the actor who waged the price war will be in a paradoxical situation: either it keeps its prices low and does not reap the benefits of being the only actor on the block, or it raises prices again, opening the prospect to a new comer on the market that will be attracted by higher profit opportunities. In either case, it is unlikely to get the benefits it may have initially expected when it launched the price war.

Ultimately, it appears that any option explored here can help actors avoid reinvention. Quite to the contrary, the fact that they lead to unsustainable outcomes suggest that reinvention, in the way it was explored in the first section of this chapter—that is, the form of reinvention that requires blowing up the tired to elaborate a whole new approach—is the only real path forward for an actor looking for impact.

Architects of Change, and Reinvention

Looking for logic and seeking to verify one's own intuition in a turbulent business environment is a very natural human reflex. And yet, managers and decision-makers often find themselves, like Alice, in situations that completely contradict what they know, or what they think they know. They then look to give sense to a situation that feels chaotic to them—failing to accept, in fact, that the situation warrants no real explanation and is actually absurd.

The real challenge in this turbulent business environment for an actor looking to make sense out of it lies in accepting that in order to achieve the goal of containing the chaos, you must transform—rapidly at times—so as to find greater congruence between your activity and the outside world. In fact, reinvention is the process that helps actors move forward in a changing business environment that is likely to undermine them if they do not make any efforts. This chapter has shown it ultimately comes down to creative destruction—the way influential actors reinvent in order to *preserve* their advantage—and to differentiation—the way relatively weaker actors reinvent in order to limit the number of substitutes they face, and to create *a world of their own*, in which there is no rival.

Architects of change embrace reinvention as much as out of taste as out of necessity: unless they move as fast as the business environment—faster would suggest the Red Queen—their actions and activities are unlikely to be impactful.

Pascal Picq is a paleoanthropologist at the very prestigious Collège de France, a research and education institution founded by Francois 1er in 1530. His research, initially focusing on the morphological and social evolution of humankind, led him to explore innovation and managerial processes. In this exchange, he tells us more about his research journey and what lessons he draws for the future of the business environment.

The opposition between two important figures of evolutionary theories, namely Lamarck and Darwin, plays an important role in the way you interpret the business environment and its evolution. Why?

Simply because we are dealing with the universal process of change in nature and in human societies. Lamarck's model is best explained with the giraffe parabola: the ancestor of the giraffe had a far shorter neck. As tree crowns grew, through a sort of vital force, giraffes stretched their necks and were able to reach higher up the tree. This characteristic was transmitted to the following generation. This approach wad dominant throughout the "first age of the machine," in other words, the two centuries of industrial era until the advent of the digital revolution.

This is a form of active innovation: the environment provides us with the incentive or pressures us and we react. When the market and businesses set problems and challenges, we mobilize our internal forces to make sure that the environment remains competitive for instance. This has a major consequence: when the environment does not change, *we* do not change. In Lamarck's world, the logic of demand dominates: we identify needs and we look for ways to address them.

The fall of the Berlin Wall and globalization in the 1990s gave us confidence that Lamarck's model best explained the "progress" that we were enjoying. But at the turn of the century, we also have this intuition that an upheaval is about to occur with digitalization. Classic models are still omnipresent, but they are challenged with the rise of the Internet and now forms of business organizations—and later, the astronomical amount of data available online and the advent of artificial intelligence. Why? Because natural resources are overwhelmed by artificial resources: data. Think that between 2008 and 2018, all the big oil companies which were among the top ten of the most valuable firms have been replaced by digital/platform companies!

This is where Darwin's model, that is fundamentally different than Lamarck's, comes in by shedding light on these evolutions. Products and services do not appear because we need them, but if they are supplied and they are selected, they can change the world. This is what we call the variation-selection process. New characters, new ideas, new processes arise with quite a few means. At this stage, we deal with inventions. If they are not selected, nothing is happening. If they are selected, it can change the world; the invention becomes an innovation. We are talking contingency. (Only a small percentage of apps and startups are succeeding, the Darwinian rule being: succeed rapidly or fail fast.) Why it can change the world rapidly: because of the "zero marginal cost" of part of the digital business. In evolutionary sciences, we call that the "Baldwin effect": a new character, if successful, changes the landscape of adaptations of a population of a given species, then populations of other species interacting with and, finally, the whole ecosystem.

One common example that everyone understands well is Twitter: the ability to write a message in 140 characters or less does not coincide with a fundamental consumer need; but the service is selected because of contingency and has the ability to shape the business environment as a result of its selection. Of course, young startups dream of developing the game-changing app that they imagined because they know someone who once expressed a need and they figured out a way to tackle it. But the way this app becomes successful is a process of variation-selection. Natural selection is not about elimination of others or about the law of the strongest, but about favoring the most advantageous variations at a given time that will allow the company to survive in the longer run and so one. We are talking about auto-adaptative firms which follow the rule of the red queen (a figure in Alice in the Wonderland): run as fast as you can in order to keep your position. We are not in the wonderland, but it true like never before in the Darwinian digital world.

The smartphone and the platform of apps that accompanied its rise follow a similar logic. When Steve Jobs presents the iPhone, he may not have fully grasped what was about to happen: it will take him a year to understand the importance of apps, in particular those that are not designed and developed by Apple. We are not yet in a platform economy, but in an ecosystem economy in which Apple develops products that the firm sells for a profit; but by distributing third-party apps, it makes more money and is able to expand. This was a profound economic change that no one foresaw. Then came the platform economy that allowed for the degree of disintermediation that we see everywhere today. In fact, this is the disintermediation of classical, linear business models overwhelmed by new digital networks of intermediations (BtoB, BtoC, CtoC, BtoBtoC ...). This movement which started from the bottom, with third-party actors developing at a very low cost apps that Apple would distribute, was fundamentally different from the model in which a company sold its products and its know-how. It disrupted the economy profoundly. This is when the world becomes Darwinian: the digital revolution has brought about an economy in which the processes of variation and selection are key, as, for instance, only 10% of Silicon Valley firms are really successful. Our understanding of these mechanisms are important—if anything because those taking risks by investing in this economy need to have a good grasp of why they might win or lose money ultimately. This disruption should affect our thinking on the processes of evaluation and understanding of the risks and the successes of entrepreneurial projects. It demands an alternative look and a solid understanding of human societies' dynamics.

You find this difference between the Lamarckian and the Darwinian models in artificial intelligence as well. There are two broad models of artificial intelligence. The first one is based on expert knowledge and on logical and mathematical reasoning. It starts from human intelligence and it seeks to reproduce it, albeit faster and more efficiently. The second, we call machine learning (ML) and deep learning (DL) and starts from the base: how can entities without any skill be capable of exchanging information with other entities, thereby creating intelligence, reasoning, and competence. It is based on inductive reasoning that generates hypotheses that we may have not thought about or that we may have overlooked (but that we still need to check). This form of artificial intelligence, deep learning, is definitely Darwinian in nature and represents a complete overhaul of the way we think about intelligence and how ideas are generated. It helps us understand patterns in the data beyond the noise and, moreover, make unexpected patterns of innovations, modeling, and predictions. We are entering the creative world of induction: how to extract patterns and rules from data sets.

Ultimately, I would say that we have entered into a Darwinian world in which Lamarckian processes have not disappeared but have been profoundly modified. Big companies are still very Lamarckian in their approach as they react to changes, but if they want to innovate, they need to be Darwinian and generate ideas, some of which might be selected while other will die out. In a Darwinian world you ought to be Darwinian: diversity, organization, and modularity (how to make diversities able to work together), and environment (CSR or Corporate Social Responsibility and CSV or Corporate Share Value).

What does this say about the business environment we can expect?

When an actor changes his behavior in a way that gives him advantages when it comes to accessing food or to reproduction, the likelihood that other actors in the same population will abide by the new standards and emulate the successful actor is high. This change affects the ecosystem as a whole, the species as well as the other species with which it interacts. We initially thought that species were changing by themselves and, except for special cases of co-adaptation between butterflies and orchids for example, the view was not ecosystemic.

Now we have come to realize that we have been propelled into a world in which if one actor moves, it is the ecosystem as a whole that shifts in a very complex process. In that world, you may be competing for the same market share but what is truly innovative and what profoundly shapes the environment: the first-movers that lead others to change and that modify all the interactions of the ecosystem create a new space that may be entrepreneurial, digital, and so on. This is the Baldwin effect and the best way to cope with this changing world is to imagine a set of possible scenarios.

The startup and entrepreneurship world is a Darwinian world. The innovation and invention world is a Darwinian world. And today, all societies are rocked by these artificial forms of intelligence that are Darwinian. This does not mean that this is a world in which there will be no solidarity, or one in which there will be more massacres. There can be opportunities for cooperation and mutual help in fact. Whether it is in the economy or in nature, when one player disappears in any ecosystem, the social fabric and the relationships between other actors all can weaken.

How does an anthropologist like you come to pay attention to the dynamics of businesses and to the business environment?

This may sound paradoxical. But this was not my idea initially. Twenty-five years ago, as it is often the case in management, there was a very fashionable word: adaptation. I had just written a book on the origins of humankind that explored the issue of human adaptation—I am an anthropologist after all! The Association for Management Progress (APM) contacted me and wanted to understand what I meant by "adaptation." They did not realize that these questions were some of the most complex ones in evolution theory, but the idea was very good. This gave me the opportunity to develop lectures about what adaptation meant in the theory of evolution.

Through these lectures and the conversations that came with them, I became acquainted with the private sector which I knew little about, but which I found absolutely captivating: the actors of the private sector face adaptation and competitive issues that resemble the Darwinian world that I knew so well. Of all these topics, innovation stood out in particular because the stakes are huge: in the field of evolution, innovation is like a new character. How does it appear? How is it selected? How can it modify the life of people, or even the ecosystem and the human species as a whole? All of these questions were relevant for the private sector which required insights from anthropology and the theory of evolution.

The task is not that easy. During the 1990s, several scholars proposed a renewal of evolutionary economics and tried to make working analogies between species and firms. As a matter of fact, and according to Ronald Coase, firms are the great oblivion of general theories of economics. Despite some biased assumptions, we need to develop new theories based on experimental and behavioral economics, similar to the work of Daniel Kahneman, with studies on human, monkey, and ape comparative ethology, for example. We are not talking with "monkey business" but with universal patterns of economics. For example, the field of "biological business" or how species are dealing in nature. My purpose is not to claim that we have solved all these questions in my field. We have simply encountered the same theoretical and epistemological problems. Some advances in my field could be useful for firms and economics in our new world while, on the other hand, some key concepts which were more or less abandoned in my field are reactivated, like the Baldwin effect.

As a researcher, the stake for me was to identify consiliences: what universal realities can come out of the study of two different realms (humankind and business) facing similar questions but that do not concentrate on the same objects? This effort is not about identifying laws akin to laws of physics of biology but to understand human and social mechanisms.

At that time, I also rediscovered the works of Joseph Schumpeter who was profoundly influenced by Darwin's book on the evolution of species. There are two key themes in Schumpeter's work: there is the question of innovation and entrepreneurship, and there is the question of competition, where his focus is on big companies and monopolies. So, what I found striking is that his perspectives and the way he tackles both of those themes are extremely different. Schumpeter espoused the Darwinian view of the world when it came to his description of the entrepreneur and innovation. The major consequence of that is creative destruction that focused on the process through which new products and ideas emerged. But when he discussed competition, Schumpeter espoused a Lamarckian view of the world: he focused on big industries and big companies and did not really consider the variation-selection processes.

By the turn of the millennium, I was also very invested in the questions of racism and sexism that repel me. In my research, I keep on finding references to the same group of people that founded the Lunar Society that regularly met in Birmingham in the United Kingdom between 1765 and 1813. This was a diverse set of people who all adhered to a common vision based on the Enlightenment. At the end of the eighteenth century, during the Industrial Revolution and the beginning of the French Revolution, they understood that changing modes of production and distribution would trigger societal changes—as Karl Marx explained it years later. They were the first to tie economic, natural, and societal changes. This will lead them to fight racism and sexism. I found this intellectual consistency remarkable: at the onset of the Industrial Revolution, they argued that there was link between production modes, society and nature. We are rediscovering that link today with the discussion on corporate social responsibility. Then, from the very beginning of the industrial revolution, there is fundamental link between economics and evolutionary theories. One of the most outstanding members of the Lunar Society was Erasmus Darwin—Charles' grandfather; Joseph Schumpeter was inspired by Charles Darwin for the process variation/selection or invention/innovation and evolutionary economics in the Darwinian digital ecosystem.

This was at the heart of the synthesis I put together to better understand the different dynamics inside a company and inside a business environment. This synthesis was the beginning of my work on the intersection between businesses and anthropology. I realized then that we had completely neglected the role of techniques in the changes of human societies, not only as means of actions but as our way of thinking about social interactions, society, and our place in nature and evolution. And I linked this question to the issue of transhumanism, that is, the idea that human evolution has come to an end and that humankind has shown the most of its potentialities. Since we can't do any better, we need technical procedures to extend human life, something nature cannot do, even in better environmental and social conditions (that are not met anyway). In this perspective, tools are an extension of human activity: tools help us become stronger and more efficient, but are ultimately an extrapolation of human capacities. But this view completely overlooks the question of anthropology, which does not only focus on archaic societies but can also enlighten us on the questions of corporate social responsibility, discriminations, and values. It becomes increasingly hard to ignore these topics when studying the business environment.

We are entering in the era of the third coevolution. The first coevolution describes the complex interactions in-between species in an ecosystem (for example, our microbiote). The second coevolution is exclusively human: how our technical innovations and uses—what we call General Purpose Technologies or GPT—have changed our biology (for example our physiology with cooking two million years ago; our morphology with better education and social advances after the Second World War and our cognition with writing and reading six millenaries ago). The third coevolution begins with new hybridizations between humans and machines in all aspects of our life. Transhumanist fans are making a wrong assumption when claiming that evolution is over and that our future is only in the hand of technologies. But if, in agreement, tools and technologies are very specific to human evolution, we do not escape from evolution simply because the tree coevolution are interacting, meshing like between the real facilities and their digital twins or, very soon, our digital avatars, hopefully for a sustainable future of humanity.

Notes

1. Isaac Asimov, "The Red Queen's Race," *Astounding Science Fiction*, January 1949.
2. Joseph Alois Schumpeter, *Capitalism, Socialism, and Democracy*, 2nd edition (Harper & brothers, 1947).
3. Joseph Alois Schumpeter, *Capitalism, Socialism, and Democracy*, 2nd edition (Harper & brothers, 1947), p. 84.
4. Robert Gordon, "Foundations of the Goldilocks Economy: Supply Shocks and the Time-Varying NAIRU," *Brookings Papers on Economic Activity* 29, no. 2 (1998): 297–346.
5. Bill Lewis et al., "Whatever Happened to the New Economy?" (McKinsey Global Institute, November 2002), https://www.mckinsey.com/featured-insights/employment-and-growth/whatever-happened-to-the-new-economy; International Monetary Fund, "Global Trade: What's Behind the Slowdown," in *World Economic Outlook*, 2016, 63–87, http://www.imf.org/external/pubs/ft/weo/2016/02/.
6. Michael E. Porter and Mark R. Kramer, "Creating Shared Value," *Harvard Business Review*, January 1, 2011, https://hbr.org/2011/01/the-big-idea-creating-shared-value.
7. Porter and Kramer.
8. Jacques Bughin et al., "Automation and the Workforce of the Future" (McKinsey & Company, May 2018), https://www.mckinsey.com/featured-insights/future-of-work/skill-shift-automation-and-the-future-of-the-workforce.
9. "World Employment and Social Outlook 2018—Greening with Jobs," Publication (International Labor Organization, May 14, 2018), http://www.ilo.org/global/research/global-reports/weso/greening-with-jobs/WCMS_628708/lang%2D%2Den/index.htm.
10. "World Employment and Social Outlook 2018—Greening with Jobs."
11. Schumpeter, *Capitalism, Socialism, and Democracy*.

6

Case Study: Founding a Popular Pizza Place in Paris

Emilie was having a good day. She finally got the loan she desperately needed to secure the very trendy location of her future Italian restaurant, Popular Pizza. It was a unique place, right in the center of Paris, through which professionals and tourists pass every day. She wanted to become the new story in town, as quickly as possible. Now she just needed a strategy to achieve her goal.

The Restaurant and the Market

Emilie knew that over the course of one night, she would not be able to host more than Q^* people overall, across all the services: Q^* is the maximum number of clients she would be able to accommodate; beyond that there would not be enough space to move around! So she was clear on how much she could supply.

Bella, Emilie's marketing genius, was able to determine how much typical customers, professionals and tourists included, would be willing to pay for a menu (that includes a pizza, a drink, and a desert). As expected, the number of people that would be willing to go to this Popular Pizza would be limited if the price of the menu was set high but would increase linearly as price decreased. This was no surprise, but Bella was happy to offer a visual of what demand looked like on the following graph (Fig. 6.1).

The result was very instructive to Emilie who clearly saw her options when it came to choosing prices. The challenge now lies in understanding what objectives each of these prices entailed.

J. Ghez, *Architects of Change*, https://doi.org/10.1007/978-3-030-20684-0_6

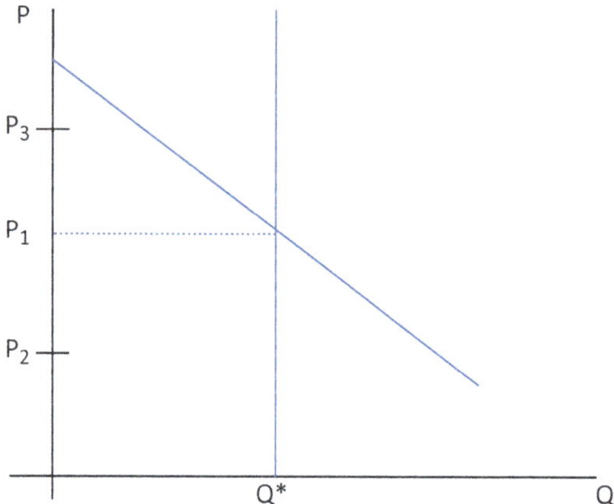

Fig. 6.1 Popular pizza's market

Choosing a Price

Adrien, her associate, felt that the analysis led to one, unique conclusion: the right price was P_1. It was the maximum price they could charge to fill the restaurant up. The price was good for revenues, and it was good for publicity as well. It was a no-brainer to Adrien. And yet, Emilie had her doubts. Was it not worth exploring another option?

Pricing for the Premium

It was not clear whether revenues would actually decrease at P_3, Adrien said: depending on how sensitive customers were to price (that is, on the slope of the demand curve), it was possible to make more money at P_3 than at P_1. But that was beyond the point, Emilie observed. Making money was not the best way to have an impact, or even to be the new story in town. She was looking for something else. In particular, she wondered, what message would she be sending out at P_3? Would she be able to convey the notion that if you wanted to come to Popular Pizza, you needed to pay the price *and* make a reservation?

But that, in turn, customers would expect a unique, premium experience that they would not be getting anywhere else. And she could always make up for the smaller number of clients by leaving more room between the tables and creating a more intimate atmosphere, right here, in the center of Paris. That would certainly be an experience that customers would be willing to pay for (and plan ahead for, by making reservations).

Pricing for the Buzz

While Adrien accepted Emilie's logic, he went on to argue that never would P_2 make any sense and that the team should exclude it immediately from the panel of options to choose from. But Bella, the marketing genius, had a different point of view on that question: what if we tried to create a major hype around the restaurant by doing the exact opposite, namely by refusing reservations and pricing the menu well-below the maximum price to pack the restaurant? By pricing at P_2, not only would you fill up the restaurant quickly; you would also be able to get a long line of people waiting outside the restaurant and attracting new comers. That is the buzz we need to be the new story in town, she said!

Adrien was still skeptical though. This meant a substantial loss of revenues in the name of creating the hype. But Bella fought back: you are only losing revenue today to create a bigger base of clients tomorrow. In doing so, you are able to put Popular Pizza, our restaurant, right at the center of the radar screen of professionals, locals, or tourists looking for a great experience and for great food. And who knows, relying on this buzz, you might be able to open up new places throughout Paris—and throughout Europe?

One Strategy, One Price

Emilie had to make a decision.

But it was clear to her that all three prices had their merit: they would all help Popular Pizza build up its brand in one way or another—P_3 by making the experience at the restaurant a premium experience and P_2 by bringing this experience on many people's radar screens. And ultimately, there was a trade-off to make: did I want to be the next story in town because of the premium I offered or because of the buzz I triggered?

Ultimately, what was the most impactful way to reinvent people's experience dining out?

The New Experience

What also struck Emilie was the fact that, overall, the restaurant experience had remained pretty stable for ages. It had consisted of going to the restaurant, sitting at a table, ordering from the menu and enjoying good food and a night out. Who (and how) would ever disrupt this industry? In particular, what would be the "the new commodity, the new technology, the new source of supply, (or) the new type of organization" that Joseph Schumpeter talked about in general terms—that would creatively disrupt but that would redefine what the restaurant experience would look like?

Of course, online food delivery companies had changed the landscape, by allowing clients to enjoy the food in other places, and at home in particular. But if every actor rushed to this option to broaden its consumer base, was that not the exact trap that would push everyone down the path of undifferentiation? And Emilie wondered whether this was really a form of impactful disruption. The same way, others were trying to disrupt vending machines by offering free access to microwaves. But Emilie knew it: the food was distasteful at best and stomach-turning at worse; and anyone who thought differently would never appreciate her efforts anyway.

Was automation the new route, then? Relying on artificial intelligence to predict how traffic, the weather, or even ongoing sports or entertainment events would affect client tastes in the short run as well as demand for tables on a particular night felt like a fad to Emilie: these tools could obviously play a role that is all the more so useful that competitors would rely on them to adjust and allocate resources more efficiently; but that was a management problem and not a factor that would really influence customer experience. Emilie was somewhat more sensitive to a point J. Stephen Sadler, the Founder and CEO of The Techmar Group, a developer of unique restaurant concepts, made on Quora:

> How about placing your smart phone next to a tap and placing your order for any drink you want, all perfectly blended exactly the way you want, without ever talking to a bartender. Or watching a robot cook hundreds of hamburgers, without any line cook intervention. Maybe you would like to place your order, make additions and pay for your order, without ever seeing a server. How about walking into your favourite restaurant and instantly, everyone knows who you are, what food you prefer and your favourite table.[1]

But as Sadler had argued, there was nothing futuristic about this, as these trends were shaping the industry already. So had that ship not sailed already? If so, surfing on these trends would never make Popular Pizza unique. What was worse, in Emilie's mind, was that she was sure people came to bars to *talk* to the bartender, and to restaurants to *interact* with waiters who would take care of *them* specifically—not to have some dehumanized experience. This was definitely *not* the experience she wanted to give to *her* consumers.

This question is one that she pondered, in particular because she did not want to be blindsided after having invested so much effort into putting together what she thought was a unique experience for her clients. Now was not the time to rest on her laurels. She needed to identify her options.

Architects of Change Are in for Business

Admittedly, this brief case study opens up more questions than it provides answers. But this is by design: Emilie's problem lies less in identifying *the* correct answers to her challenges, namely pricing and putting together the next experience, than in deciding the type of impact *she* wants to have with her restaurant and on her industry. In particular, wanting to be *unique* is a wish that all entrepreneurs seem to share.

What distinguishes architects of change from others is their ability to understand market forces well enough to see them as factors to harness, rather than obstacles to cope with. This is what the debate between Adrien and Emilie is really about: for Adrien, what you can and cannot do is dictated by the market, whereas for Emilie, market constraints are not really constraints but waves that you can ride to get to places that are fundamentally different. The problem lies in choosing the place where you want to end up, not coping with a constraint. In a competitive and/or unfriendly environment, that is, in an environment in which you are not the undisputed leader, it is unlikely that you will be able to bring change all by yourself. It is therefore useful to stop seeing every constraint as a headwind and to start identifying tailwinds that will help you reach your objectives faster.

Architects of change are also deeply skeptical of small, short-term fixes that will probably not help them be as transformational as they want. When you feel your business model is obsolete, or that your industry is ripe for disruption, you may look for temporary fixes through incremental change. But you may also look to overhaul the way you do business because you see an opportunity to create new value for a wide range of actors, including yourself. This is what will ultimately make you an architect of change: not looking for a one-size-fits-all solution to a well-known problem but a unique fix, that you perhaps develop through a grueling process of failing fast and failing forward, and that people will value for the difference it brings to the table.

Note

1. J Stephen Sadler, "How Might the Restaurant Industry Be Disrupted?," *Quora*, April 11, 2018, https://www.quora.com/How-might-the-restaurant-industry-be-disrupted.

7

The Power of Analysis

We live in strange times. For all the talk about economic stagnation, political instability, and social unrest, humanity has never been wealthier nor healthier than today. As individuals, it is hard to remember a time at which we have been more connected, let alone more empowered than today. What is challenging is to put the daunting challenges we face in perspective, without understating their significance and without undervaluing our ability to tackle them successfully. And as the thought experiment of the previous chapter illustrated, with just enough awareness about the business environment and enough imagination about faint signals of what the future could hold, architects of change are well placed to have impact in this world.

Their starting point lies in a solid understanding of the world they live in, that is, in analysis grounded in facts and reality rather than in wishful thinking or in dogma. Recognizing the power of analysis is what will help architects of change maximize their impact as they correctly identify levers of action rather than rely on existing consensus (or dogma) and acting without any clearly identified target.

This is by no means an easy task in this business environment. It feels as if human brains are very well wired to grasp linear trends and understand the effects of incremental changes. But linearity increasingly feels like only a part of the story of this business environment, if it is not an exception: Exponential trends and complex causal links can generate disruptive moments that linear thinking is ill-equipped to deal with. Architects of change need to go beyond linearity and embrace chaos in order to have impact in this business environment. This chapter explores how to do so.

J. Ghez, *Architects of Change*, https://doi.org/10.1007/978-3-030-20684-0_7

It starts with an exploration of the traditional approaches that shed light on the forces shaping the business environment—namely the PESTLE (for Political, Economic, Social, Technological, Legal, and Environmental) and its recent adaptations. As insightful as the results it generates may be, the PESTLE may not be enough though, as a tool, to survive in a chaotic world, in which deep, global instabilities can transform the business environment into a radically different landscape with a new set of rules. In that environment, in which industries are ripe for disruption or going through transformational changes, and in which complexity tends to blur causal links, architects of change need to complement their analysis with additional tools—tools that can help them embrace complexity and make sense out of the business environment's chaos.

This chapter concludes on the key analytical qualities architects of change need to survive in this business environment.

Scanning Your environment

In this business environment, traditional analytical, managerial and decision-making tools will be useful to understand threats and opportunities of the strategic landscape. The most illustrative example of those tools is PESTLE, an analytical framework that helps them understand how individual exogenous forces are shaping the business environment. This exercise can be particularly insightful in a stable environment: would-be architects of change can rely on this framework to identify levers of action.

Understanding Your Business Environment with PESTLE

PESTLE analysis was first offered as an analytical tool by Harvard professor Francis Aguilar in 1967, when he offered in his book *Scanning the Business Environment*[1] a framework to understand economic, technical, political, and social forces influenced an organization's external environment—and leading him to call this framework initially ETPS (for economic, technical, political, and social). The framework is meant to help actors understand their business environment, its evolution over time, and how different business environments compared, so as to better identify the threats and opportunities of a wide array of operational theaters. In particular, the most critical objective of the framework was to identify external threats for an organization and especially those that are beyond its control but likely candidates to make its projects fail or to create opportunities for success.

As the name suggests, PESTLE explores six dimensions of the business environment: the political, economic, social, technological, legal, and environmental dimensions that shape the landscape.

Politics

Without political stability in their business environment, decision-makers will have a hard time formulating long-term and meaningful strategies. In order to achieve that goal, they need visibility and transparency. Visibility comes with a stable political system in which policy does not undergo repeated and erratic changes. Transparency comes with policymaking processes that are clear to stakeholders and that allow for changes when necessary without undermining the stability of the system as a whole.

The political dimension of the PESTLE framework is meant to assess how much visibility and transparency decision-makers can count on. Strikingly, the level of each depends less on how democratic the system is than how much institutional stability it enjoys—though that institutional stability is also a factor of economic freedom and the consent of the governed. In a business environment in which decision-makers enjoy visibility and transparency, they may be better able to plan ahead but cannot count on radical changes in the policies that are the most misguided and detrimental to their activity. On the contrary, in a business environment in which there is little visibility and transparency, day-to-day tactics will trump long-term strategies; but policy instability also means the potential for changes.

Economics

Decision-makers are also likely to have their eyes set on key economic variables that are shaping their business environment. Their success may depend on the overall vitality of the economy that may drive their revenues, or on how much consumers may have to spend on the products and services they offer. Their success may also depend on the cost of key commodities, such as energy or real estate.

The economic dimension of the PESTLE framework helps decision-makers determine the extent to which they are facing economic headwinds making their objectives harder to reach, or, to the contrary, the extent to which they may be able to ride on the overall economic momentum of their business environment. What can be challenging in assessing this dimension is that both these headwinds and that momentum may depend on a wide range of national, regional, and global conditions. Decision-makers need to monitor all of them over time, in particular because economic activity is cyclical by nature, leading economic upturns and downturns to radically rock their boat if they do not do so.

Social

Social realities can also profoundly shape the business environment in a way decision-makers need to be mindful of. Changing behaviors and shifting cultural realities can also be key drivers of success or failure of a strategy. In particular, the key lies in understanding how these realties are shaping people's expectations in terms of what is acceptable or what is not. Those expectations are likely to evolve as societies open up, age, and/or develop over time.

The social dimension of the PESTLE framework helps decision-makers gauge the relevance of their strategy given those changing expectations that can shape consumer preferences, short-term fads, and long-term habits. It can also enable decision-makers to get a better grasp of what may undermine their image in the eyes of public opinion and, to the contrary, what may enhance it. Ultimately, it may also help them get a better grasp of what expectations are unfulfilled because traditional powers like the state are unable to fulfill them—or lack the legitimacy to do so. Thanks to the social dimension of this framework, decision-makers can reflect upon their changing social role within a community or a broader business environment.

Technology

Technology is not only a source of greater efficiency and lower costs when it comes to more reliable infrastructure for instance. It can also accelerate transformations at a pace that no one foresaw and extend the range of what is possible and what is not. What seemed like pure science-fiction to the generation of our grandparents, like taking a picture from your phone that lives in your pocket, is our reality.

This is why the technological axis of the PESTLE framework is critical, as it helps decision-makers determine the extent to which technological changes in the business environment can help them have a greater impact—or, to the contrary, help *others* increase their own influence by making yesterday's practices obsolete. It gives decision-makers the opportunity to measure the potential for disruption in a given business environment or landscape, and test how relevant (or out-of-date) their own products and services, as well as their overall strategy, may be. This dimension of the framework measures how fast stakeholders will (or should) change over time and assess the extent to which they are protected by barriers to entry.

Legal

As it is the case for technology, opportunities may expand or shrink under the influence of changing legal realities. For instance, increased regulation in a sector, designed to protect consumers or the economy from unwarranted effects of an activity, may limit business opportunities today and tomorrow—whether these regulations are driven by legitimate concerns or not. But to the contrary, when a state decides to eliminate what it considers burdensome and obsolete regulations, it may be able to create new opportunities and unleash new forces of growth.

The legal dimension of the PESTLE framework can help decision-makers determine how existing or future legal factors, including regulation, standards, and precedents, can impact their ability to reach their objectives over time. A regulator need not only be the one reducing opportunities but also be the one in a position to better protect copyrights and, more broadly, enforce the rule of law. The challenge lies in determining how, on balance, the legal dimension of the business environment, is shaping overall risks and opportunities.

Environmental

Increasing environmental concerns among policymakers and consumers arguably represent additional constraints that decision-makers must face. But those who do so may be in a better position to show creativity and to drive change by allocating resources and energy to the issue that may very well drive and dominate the future agenda. In particular, as it was the case with the technological and the legal axes of the business environment, environmental considerations may very well define what we can do and not do in an increasingly hotter world whose climate is more and more unstable.

Accounting for the environmental dimension of the PESTLE framework means considering the ultimate external force shaping the business environment—namely the climate in the first sense of the word. Depending on geographical location, the willingness of public authorities (and the private sector) to act and the existing legislation, this factor can be critical when seeking a better understanding of the business environment and the forces shaping it. But today's legitimate consensus is that it will be ultimately key in defining how our way of life and behavior, as humans, may change or be preserved in the future.

The Evolution of a Tool

The evolution of the acronym is also very telling. Aguilar's initial acronym, ETPS, was not the easiest to pronounce, leading some to modify it to PEST—thereby giving the political dimension a greater weight compared to others, and perhaps recognizing the increasing political nature of the business environment. Later iterations generated the PESTLE acronym which is the most widely used now and that accounts for the business environment's legal and environmental dimensions. More recent adaptations of the framework have also included new dimensions such as demographics and ethics. This increasing number of dimensions is a recognition of the growing complexity of the business environment.

The framework has the merit of offering a snapshot, at a given moment in time, of the business environment and provides an overview of key indicators to monitor. Actors looking to drive change and to transform their business environment can increase their awareness of the world surrounding them through this framework that can help them identify levers of action: any given problem you identify is unique in nature and a better understanding of the broader landscape can help you determine which one of its dimensions will be most influential in shaping the solution.

Architects of change should treat it with caution though, especially in a business environment characterized by chaos rather than by linearity: PESTLE and other traditional managerial tools will only get you so far in a complex landscape, in which these forces are interacting with each other to shape in additional, unprecedented, and unanticipated ways the business environment.

In fact, PESTLE does not provide any means to understand how these dimensions can interact with each other—as they often do, leading the business environment into a whole new degree of complexity. Deep global instabilities that are driven by a wide range of exogenous forces that all interact with each other can transform the business environment radically. Traditional management tools like PESTLE only provide one side of the story in this environment in which chaos, rather than linearity, captures the reality of the world you live in.

Grasp the Complexity of the Business Environment

Grasping the complexity of the business environment therefore requires additional efforts, as traditional tools will only get you so far. This is particularly true at a time at which we seem to approach topics that are difficult to discuss with the baggage of dogma and ideology, rather than in a more analytical way. As a result, and more often than not, we are taken hostage by the slogans, the images, the comparisons, and the sensational headlines that can easily shape our thinking to the detriment of more complex analysis and sophisticated thought processes. This leads us to experience difficulties in distinguishing between facts on the one hand and speculation and opinion on the other. It represents a challenge to our ability to fully grasp the complexity of a business environment, thereby undermining our ability to ultimately make a difference and to act like architects of change. (The testimonial at the end of the chapter discusses why.)

Three factors explain why the business environment finds itself in this state: truth decay, the unexpected convergence of trends, and the changing behavior of the consumer-citizen-activist figure. In order to deal with these issues, we need to embrace complexity by achieving a real comprehensive reading of the phenomena we are studying.

The Issue of Truth Decay

Western countries, and the United States, may be a case in point here. As one report, focused on the United States, suggests, this situation is leading to "the diminishing role of facts and analysis" as we increasingly disagree "about facts and analytical interpretations of facts and data," as the line between opinion and fact is increasingly blurry, as opinions and personal experiences gain in influence compared to facts, and as the trust "in formerly respected sources of facts" declines.[2]

(It is noteworthy that not only social media, but technology may also be accelerating this trend: it is one thing for a rumor to have great impact because of social media playing the role of an echo chamber that actually reinforces unfounded speculation; it is another to see a wide range of technologies helping ill-intentioned actors distort the truth. Deep Fake is a telling illustration here: like we can modify a picture using Photoshop, Deep Fake allows people to distort a video with sound to show public figures making statements they never actually made, in a way that is invisible to the naked eye. Fighting truth decay demands a healthy dose of skepticism and analysis—the very same we seem to have on April 1, and that we somehow forget all about the rest of the year.)

While the authors argue that their study applies to the case of the United States, the reality and the consequences of truth decay is one we see in many Western and non-Western economies, as this author has observed in his conversations with a wide range of audiences.

Truth decay, argues the report, results from confirmation bias: humans have always been vulnerable to—as they look for stories that confirm, rather than contradict—their initial thinking. It is a consequence of the changing "information system," as we rely increasingly more on social media and news channels that may favor partisanship over facts. It also results from the fact that we may not have the means anymore to train the younger generation, especially when it comes to "civic education, media literacy, and critical thinking," given the fiscal constraints we face. This makes the newer generation more prone to cognitive biases. Increased political and social polarization drive groups with different political and social affiliations further apart. As the report argues, "The groups on each side can become insular in their thinking and communication, creating a closed environment in which false information proliferates."

The consequences of truth decay are significant. It leads to the erosion of civil discourse, making it very hard for different political and social groups to debate and to find compromises, leading to political paralysis as a result. It may also increase the sense of disenfranchisement leading to a decline in trust of government action. It can also increase uncertainty at the national level, with all the costs this entails in terms of delayed decisions and lack of visibility.

Trend Convergence

Because of the narrow-mindedness that this situation entails, we may also fail to appreciate the potential for widely different trends, that appear completely disconnected on paper, to converge.

The example of the evolution of communications and entertainment illustrates this quite well. Imagine that you are a cab driver in 2007, in a city like New York, Paris, or Mumbai. You take a break and sip coffee, watching Apple CEO Steve Jobs introduce the iPhone on television. You may find this new product intriguing and appealing as an individual—or you may just be plain indifferent to it. But it would be very hard for you to imagine how that single product will completely upend your industry in the not-so-distant future by allowing connected individuals to easily get in touch with transportation network companies that you may know nothing about today, but that may be your direct competitors tomorrow.

More broadly, what the previous generation called a "phone" yesterday has no real connection with what we think of when we look for a new "phone." The same holds true when we think of an experience like "going to the movies," as 3D and even 4D technologies transforming the entertainment experience. A similar argument can be made about computers, once heavy and unhandy devices that now have the potential to be in every set of hands—or about game consoles, that are more powerful today than what we could have imagined less than two decades ago.

Each of these evolutions described above are in and of itself game changers transforming the way we communicate, enjoy entertainment, access content, and share information today. But the effects of these evolutions are compounded by their convergence: communicating, enjoying entertainment, accessing content, and sharing information increasingly rely on very similar devices—a tablet for instance—thereby redefining what we mean by each of those activities. This is by no means a linear process but a complex one in which a multitude of factors are driving transformation in a wide range of areas. Those who rely exclusively on unidimensional thinking are bound to be blindsided. Architects of change, on the contrary, need a more holistic understanding of these seemingly unrelated trends that are actually far more likely to interact and collide with each other than what linear thinking would suggest.

The Changing Nature of the Consumer-Citizen

The behavior of stakeholders we are likely to meet every day may be getting increasingly volatile in an environment in which immediacy and urgency are the new rules of the game. In many industries, worldwide, on-demand and customized experiences have become the norm and have created an expectation of continuous disruption: whichever actor is able to create the product or service that will allow it to get ever closer to clients and understand their changing preferences and demands is likely to win decisive battles. As a result, these increasingly "picky, impatient, distracted and demanding" as one report puts it,[3] are transforming industries such as entertainment, media, and advertising and upending industries such as retail and mobility.

The disruption might not stop to these industries, though, and may also affect political processes. The expectation of disruption has become central in politics as well to a large extent as public opinions worldwide have increasingly expressed their discontent with the business-as-usual approach favored by political establishments. These political establishments encouraged public opinions for years to vote for mainstream candidates, to make "obvious" choices when it came to referendums, and to raise future generations to respect and value the political systems we live in. For years, public opinions accepted the premise of political establishments, namely that they would have everything to lose from non-mainstream and extreme political choices and that it was their responsibility to support the status quo—until that very same status quo became unbearable and the perception was that those political establishments failed to deliver.

Disrupting the system seems to be the name of the game in politics as a result, making the business environment more volatile and erratic as politicians, old and new, try to outmaneuver each other to get as close at their electorates as possible, sometimes to the detriment of policy substance or priorities. This undermines the level of visibility in the system. But it does create opportunities for social innovation as well. In the words of French serial entrepreneur, Carlos Diaz,

> The America that voted for Trump does not own a Tesla, nor an iPhone and when it needs money, it does not ask business angels for help: it relies on bad credits. It is time to recognize that we need to develop technologies and businesses that will benefit the widest range of people possible, algorithms that do not divide but that bring together.[4]

Metaphorical Thinking As the New Tool?

Ultimately, the problem may lie in the fact that we may favor intellectual approaches, like comparisons and metaphors, that help us understand the world in a distinctive but partial way.

As British-Canadian organizational theorist Gareth Morgan puts it, metaphors highlight key interpretations of what we are trying to study. But in doing so, they tend to "force others in a background mode," even though these interpretations might be as critical to our understanding of the world. As Morgan puts it, "When we say 'the man is a lion,' we use the image to the lion-like aspects of the man, … drawing attention to the lionlike bravery, strength, or ferocity of the man," but perhaps overlooking that "the same person may also well be a chauvinist pig, a devil, a saint, a bore, or a recluse."[5]

The metaphor is helpful to convey simple—and even simplistic—messages in a world governed by urgency, but it fails to convey information about the very complexity of the phenomenon we are studying because it is not homogeneous, it presents multiple layers of reality, and it is not unidimensional. "Our ability to achieve a comprehensive 'reading' of the man depends on an ability to see how these different aspects of the person may coexist in a complementary way or even a paradoxical way."[6]

Slogans, images, comparisons, and sensational headlines rarely offer the opportunity to achieve this comprehensive reading. The solution to a more comprehensive reading lies in relying not on one metaphor but a series of metaphors as a result. As Morgan argues, when we think of an organization or a company, it is tempting to describe them as a highly structured machine, with well-defined processes and seeking rationality and efficiency. The image is very appealing given that it has generated a series of principles that have made organizations extremely efficient—Taylorism being an illustrative example of this. But it fails to explain why and how organizations and companies transform themselves over time to adapt to their business environment.

In fact, the organization can also be seen like an organism with "biological concerns."[7] For instance, organizations can help the people that compose them satisfy their needs, from the most basic ones in terms of survival to the most complex ones, in terms of ego and self-fulfillment, to borrow Abraham Maslow's terminology on hierarchy of needs. The metaphor also accounts for the selection process organizations can go through, leading them to differentiate and integrate as they look to adapt to their outside environment. But as Morgan underscores, this metaphor, too, is incomplete: it views "organizations and members dependent upon forces operating in an external world, rather than recognizing that they are active agents operating with others in construction of that world."[8] These organizations are not necessarily passive victims of outside forces, as they too can be actors of change. The metaphor may also lead us to overlook dynamics that are internal to organizations and thus ignore their contradictions and conflicts. Finally, it may also lead us to accept the success and failures of organizations as resulting from a law of nature, as social Darwinism would argue, thereby overlooking the "influence" and "choice" humans have in shaping their world.[9]

These limitations lead Morgan to offer a set of alternative metaphors, including three addressing them directly. Instead of adapting like an organism, the organization may be like a brain, as they not only adapt to the outside environment, generating ideas that can contribute to their agility and their ability to innovate. They may also be more of a political structure as the theater of power struggles in which outcomes are shaped by interactions between a wide range of actors with different functions and clout. They may also be like psychic prisons, in which individuals take for granted the meaning or meanings they gave to the world without questioning them over time.

What metaphorical thinking brings to the understanding of an environment is the notion that we must fear unidimensional explanations that overlook the multilayered reality of the organizations and actors that make up this environment. Complexity stems from the fact that there are a multitude of layers explaining how an organization behaves. Unless we seek a comprehensive reading of them, we may miss some subtleties that are critical to grasp what linear thinking ignores.

A Roadmap of the Architect of Change

You arguably become an architect of change the moment you embrace chaos and recognize the limits of merely scanning your business environment. Admittedly, change may feel more incremental than radical in nature when considered on a day-to-day basis. A well-developed radar screen, providing an overview of the key opportunities and challenges that you must be mindful of, can most definitely help from that standpoint by increasing awareness of the business environment.

But, at the same time, the possibility for disruptive moments, resulting from the fact that a wide range of mega forces can interact with each other or that key stakeholders are more volatile in the way they behave or the way they think about facts and fiction, may also rock the world of architects of change by radically transforming the business environment. Being one means recognizing that the radar screen actually represents your comfort zone from which you can be quickly pushed out if you are not careful about the complexity of the world that surrounds you. If that complexity and that chaos are indeed the new normal, as so many headlines predict they are, then architects of change will need to look for ways to circumvent them, or even embrace both in order to truly put their weight to drive change.

As a result, architects of change will need to show intellectual honesty to a degree that most likely outmatches what was demanded from previous generations: at the very moment at which we may be increasingly taken hostage by the truth of our tribe and our beliefs may be increasingly guided by our identity, surviving in this business environment demands that we pay far more attention to facts and to actual realities.

It also demands that we recognize our own analytical limits. Humans are paradoxical from this standpoint: while we generally do not have any issue admitting our physical limitations that lead us to design a world that can help us overcome them, we experience greater difficulties conceding our intellectual limitations, leading to well-known cognitive biases such as overconfidence for instance. And yet, the solutions to both types of limitations are very similar: they demand practice and training. Our analytical limits therefore require the type of (mental) training akin to the one running a marathon would demand. That type of mental gymnastics is what architects of change ultimately embrace as a means to better tame this business environment.

James A. Thomson is the former president and chief executive officer of the RAND Corporation, an American non-profit think tank that focuses on global policy. He has repeatedly underscored the challenges of partisan gridlock in America and in its capital, Washington D.C., which has become a less analytical and more ideological place. This polarized environment makes it hard for actors to develop robust and sound strategies because facts matter less than the politics of a problem. As he observed,

> We deal with this challenge daily at RAND. We're in the 'what works' business. We expect that decision-makers want first to get the facts on the table and then apply their political skill, which will certainly include their worldview, to finding solutions. But we've been seeing less and less of that over the past three and a half decades.[10]

In this interview, he talks about polarization, how the United States got this situation, and potential ways out that could include the private sector.

You have written a lot about political polarization in the United States. What is this phenomenon about in your opinion?

I looked at voting behaviors in roll call votes in the US Congress and observed that polarization between the two sides, the conservatives and the liberals, has grown substantially—meaning the overlap between the two parties is becoming smaller and smaller. Polarization has even accelerated over the past 20 years: conservatives and liberals are now perfectly well sorted into the parties that match their preferences. Each party votes as a single group and consistently—and in opposition to the other. This is a real difference from 40 years ago when politicians crossed the aisle to vote for the other party's proposed legislation. This made coalitions possible in the Congress. Now, coalitions block each other from passing legislation and make compromises hard.

There is a geographic component in the rise of polarization. There are many districts that are very conservative and others that are very liberal. A politician needs to be one or the other to win in those districts. In addition, very few districts are in the middle of the political spectrum. In practice, geographic polarization has grown rapidly and is well correlated with the rise of polarization in Congress in which increasingly concentrated clusters of partisans are represented.

There is also a demographic component to polarization. People want to live with people who are like themselves—share interests, have similar incomes and education, are family-oriented, and so on. Communities are increasingly homogeneous as a result. For instance, people that are married increasingly live in areas that have high marriage rates and people who are not live in areas that have a low marriage rate. And this trend is correlated with polarization. This is hard to prove, but the prevailing hypothesis is that adherence to traditional family values is higher and conservative leanings are more significant in areas with high marriage rates.

How has the United States become so polarized?

A popular explanation (that is largely wrong until recently) is political parties manipulating the boundaries of congressional districts (that can be redrawn every 10 years) are responsible for polarization. This is what is called "gerrymandering." But when we look at data by county (whose boundaries cannot be redrawn), we see the same phenomenon of partisan clustering. This could have become more significant after the 2010 Census when districts were redrawn, but before that, there is little sign that gerrymandering is a major driver of polarization.

Others blame the media and its conservative and liberal channels, driving wedges within the US population. This makes sense because we don't have real news channels in the United States anymore. In fact, the BBC is what comes closest to one if it is available on the local cable service. But it is hard to actually collect data that shows this correlation. We don't have any real data on exposure to these media.

How about the electorate itself? Voters have sorted themselves out: people who identify as conservatives are all in the Republican party, whereas those that identify as liberals are all in the Democratic party—especially those with high information and who are interested in politics (low information voters are more independent).

But ultimately, the first-past-the-post electoral system in the United States, in which the voter chooses one candidate, and the candidate with the most votes wins, is to blame for polarization ultimately. In this system, you need a plurality, not a majority. It forces people to vote for one of the two parties, and there is no room to voice a second preference. In this system, the message from the leadership of both parties is that we need to stick together and oppose others—and even hate others, as the tribal message gets increasingly extreme. This contest between the two groups leaves someone in the middle with no real option.

Do you see similar patterns in other countries?

There has often been a historical divide between rural and urban areas that has been the cause of polarization elsewhere.

The United Kingdom has been polarized because of the same first-past-the-post electoral system. But with Brexit, this may be crumbling: the two major parties have trouble positioning themselves because of their internal divisions, so this system may be breaking down. Australia is also very polarized because of the same system. But the country is moving towards rank-choice voting which lets voters express different preferences rather than just one.

In the end, I don't see a lot of polarization in other places.

What do you think would be the most meaningful response? From the private sector in particular?

This situation is very difficult for the private sector, especially for companies that are client focused: they can't take stances that would alienate half of their clients. This is particularly true for retailers and people who make products. They could see their sales hurt as a result. Keeping their heads down may be the only solution.

Another way to look at this would be electoral reform, with an emphasis on voting reform. This would require that redistricting is placed in the hands of a party-neutral organization. This would also entail getting rid of the first-past-the-post electoral system, so that people can run in the center, and so that membership in a party does not mean adherence to a tribe. Some US states are trying to implement this. For instance, Maine has tried rank-choice voting in its midterm elections and this had an impact on the outcome: the candidate that ran the least negative campaign was able to win it ultimately.

So if companies want to avoid polarization, electoral reform is something they can support. Up until now, both major parties in the United States agree to oppose such reform because it threatens them. This may be the only thing they agree on: when it comes to political power, it should not be in the hands of anyone but them. Companies could be a counterweight by supporting electoral reform as they would benefit from getting us out of this tribal behavior.

Notes

1. Francis Joseph Aguilar, *Scanning the Business Environment* (Macmillan, 1967).
2. Jennifer Kavanagh and Michael D. Rich, "Truth Decay: An Initial Exploration of the Diminishing Role of Facts and Analysis in American Public Life," (Santa Monica, CA: RAND Corporation, 2018), https://www.rand.org/pubs/research_reports/RR2314.html.
3. Sara Fischer, "How On-Demand Media Took over the World," *Axios*, May 22, 2018, https://www.axios.com/how-on-demand-media-took-over-the-world-1526912650-b13562ca-d88a-4158-a7db-bf60b356dce8.html.
4. Gilles Sengès, "Carlos Diaz: «Le Mur de Trump, c'est La Silicon Valley Qui l'a Construit»," *L'Opinion*, November 13, 2016, http://www.lopinion.fr/edition/international/carlos-diaz-mur-trump-c-est-silicon-valley-qui-l-a-construit-114167.
5. Gareth Morgan, *Images of Organization* (Beverly Hills: SAGE Publications Inc, 1986), pp. 12–13.
6. Gareth Morgan, *Images of Organization* (Beverly Hills: SAGE Publications Inc, 1986), p. 13.
7. Morgan, p.40.
8. Morgan, p.70.
9. Morgan, p.76.
10. James A. Thomson, "A House Divided: Polarization and Partisanship," *The RAND Blog* (blog), May 14, 2010, https://www.rand.org/blog/2010/05/a-house-divided-polarization-and-partisanship.html.

8

Case Study: Strategizing at Amazon When Globalization Comes Under Pressure

Looking through the window of his office in the Amazon headquarters in Seattle, Jeff Bezos watched people below hurry home on this Friday night. He liked this little moment of peace before the weekend, when the office had fallen silent and when he could think about longer-term issues that were on his mind and that daily urgencies prevented him from considering. It had been a tough week on a professional level, and a grueling one at a personal level. Now, it was time to move on and to think about the big picture and his firm's global market.

The issue was not trivial: was globalization, the process that guaranteed Amazon's access to a global market, coming to an end? A report in the British weekly, *The Economist*, warning against the risk of complacency when "globalization has given way to a new era of sluggishness," that Dutch trend-watcher Adjiedj Bakas once called "slowbalisation," caught his attention.[1]

He wondered: was he, like many others, taking globalization for granted? In fact, any given crisis around the globe that called into question either the future of free trade or democracy, the willingness of world leaders and global public opinions to pursue political and economic integration or the ability of world powers to cooperate on a global issue, would, of course, catch people's attention. In recent years, the decision of the United Kingdom to pull out of the European Union; the election of an unlikely candidate, Donald Trump, in the United States; and persisting protests in France were examples of how instability was not the monopoly of a few, weaker states, but the very nature of the global system. But once

J. Ghez, *Architects of Change*, https://doi.org/10.1007/978-3-030-20684-0_8

each of these crises is solved, world affairs usually proceed, in a "business-as-usual" manner. Yet, the repetition of these crises could also be interpreted, in a not so outlandish way, as a warning sign about globalization and about its resilience: The assumption about durably free, global markets is so central in the minds of so many business leaders, that it deserves some closer scrutiny.

Jeff Bezos's company had undoubtedly benefited from a single, integrated, and global market in the past. What did slowbalisation mean for a company like Amazon that relied on global markets to prosper? Could the company survive in a world in which globalization was not the dominant reality of an increasingly turbulent business environment? How would Amazon need to adapt? He pondered those questions as the sun was going down.

Too Many Actors with Too Much to Lose

Globalization results from the increasing degree of integration of national and regional economies through the free movement of capital, goods and services, and people, as well as from the acceleration of the internationalization of supply chains and corporate activities. As a concept, it captures the changing and expanding nature of opportunities in a world economy in which opportunities, in theory at least, should be growing.

An Impossible Reverse Mode

In fact, it is hard to believe that globalization could be thrown into reverse mode or to imagine any event that could lead to its demise. The internationalization of supply chains across industries meant that no wall could be viable, Bezos believed. Furthermore, it was far from clear that free trade was the culprit to blame for the West's economic woes: technological progress and automation in particular contributed far more to unemployment and outsourcing than globalization did.[2] In the end, too many powers had too much to lose and it was, after all, in the vested interest of today's economic powers, China and Western countries, to "maintain the dynamism of world trade."[3] Populists alone could not undermine by themselves that dynamism, both Asian and Western analysts agreed (Fig. 8.1).[4]

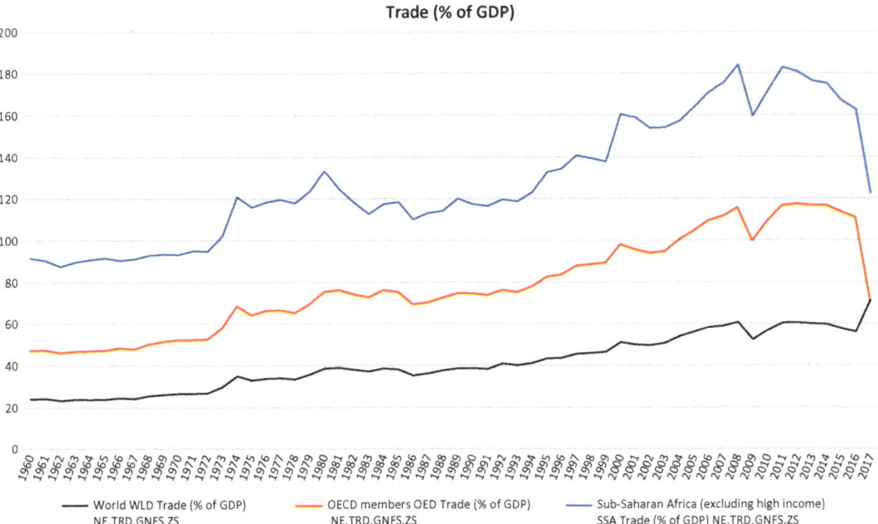

Fig. 8.1 The evolution of trade (as a percentage of GDP) since 1960. Source: World Development Indicators, 2019
Global trade increased a quasi-steady rise between 1960 and 2008. It took a hit in 2008 with the Great Recession before bouncing back in 2011, and yet experiencing a plateau through 2015 and a new drop in 2016. The increase in 2017 of world trade is not universal: OECD (Organisation for Economic Cooperation and Development) economies and sub-Saharan countries both experienced sharp drops. The future of free trade is in question as the steady rise of the second half of the twentieth century is not today's reality.

And by some measures, the world has never been this connected and interdependent.

Consider current levels of trade openness, especially how they compare to historical standards. As *The Economist* puts it,

> today's era sprang from America's sponsorship of a new world order in 1945, which allowed cross-border flows of goods and capital to recover after years of war and chaos. After 1990, this bout of globalisation went into warp speed as China rebounded, India and Russia abandoned autarky and the European single market came into its own. Containerising freight sent shipping costs plummeting. America signed NAFTA, helped create the World Trade Organisation and supported global tariff cuts. Financial liberalisation freed capital to roam the world in search of risk and reward. World trade rocketed as a result, from 39% of GDP in 1990 to 58% last year.[5]

Or consider the speed at which new products spread. As one report put it, it took nearly eight decades for the telephone, launched in 1878, to reach 100 million users worldwide and fifteen years for the mobile phone that first appeared in 1979. But it took the World Wide Web just seven years to reach the same level of users. Facebook reached it in less than five years. And the game Candy Crush in just over a year.[6] The extent to which these products and services are used on a daily basis is perhaps even more staggering: as another report stated, in one minute, 3.7 million searches are executed on Google; 481,000 tweets and 18 million text messages are sent; 38 million messages are shared on WhatsApp; $862,823 are spent online and 4.3 million videos are viewed on YouTube.[7] This is the image of how connected humanity is. It also illustrates the reach each and every one of us has in this business environment.

This seemed pretty irreversible to Bezos: this was, after all, the new reality of global interdependence. World powers and a wide range of economic actors would stand to lose so much from globalization-ending conflicts.

The notion that economically developed nations—and, moreover, an economically developed world—would never go to war because of trade and capital interdependence is not new, after all. The argument is actually quite straightforward: self-interest could only lead to global cooperation and to the conclusion that war is incompatible with wealth accumulation and economic development. And the argument seems even more cogent in this day and age, given how much powers participating in the global economy would have to lose from disruptive confrontation.[8]

The logics of escalation and war could not be those of the twenty-first century by this account.

And Yet, This Has Happened Before

How tempting is it to dismiss the scenario of the demise of globalization, as a result. And yet, for whoever paid attention to international dynamics and to history, warning lights seem to be blinking far more today than in the past two decades.

After all, World War I (WWI) caught most international investors by surprise, even though tensions were building across the continent since the beginning of the twentieth century. The assassination of Archduke Franz Ferdinand of Austria was the spark that put in motion a complex process that ultimately led to the world war and the end of the last period of globalization. Ultimately, despite the way it started, this last age of globalization "ended not with a whimper, but with a deafening bang, as the principal beneficiaries of

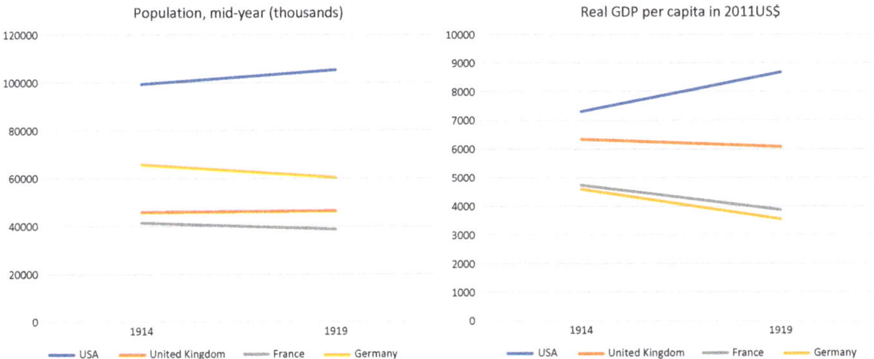

Fig. 8.2 The effects of WWI on the West. **(a)** Population, mid-year (thousands). **(b)** Real GDP per capita in 2011 US$

the globalized economy embarked on the most destructive war the world had ever witnessed," as one historian put it.[9] The seismic changes the war led to is a definite warning to the shortsighted of today, especially considering the transformational consequences WWI had on the world economy (Fig. 8.2).

But how reliable a guide can history really be? Comparisons, especially of different times, rarely lead to the truth. And yet, were there not striking similarities between then and now that served as a powerful reminder that today, too, sparks could lead to disruptive moments for globalization? As one political scientist put it,

> World War I offers a sobering reminder of man's capacity for folly. When we say that war is 'inconceivable,' is this a statement about what is possible in the world—or only about what our limited minds can conceive? In 1914, few could imagine slaughter on a scale that demanded a new category: world war. When war ended four years later, Europe lay in ruins: the kaiser gone, the Austro-Hungarian Empire dissolved, the Russian tsar overthrown by the Bolsheviks, France bled for a generation, and England shorn of its youth and treasure. A millennium in which Europe had been the political center of the world came to a crashing halt.[10]

Should that threat of potentially seismic losses not be enough in itself to deter global powers from entering such conflict, growing populist and protectionist sentiments in public opinions worldwide notwithstanding? Political discontent across Western economies and beyond could just be the noise of discomfort, not the rumblings of angry actors wanting the demise of globalization we are often tempted to convince ourselves. But as history suggests, it only takes a spark, one little spark, to disrupt the whole system. Those seeking impact, like Jeff Bezos, in this business environment, need to be attentive as a result.

Looking for Signs in the Calm but Uncertain Present

And yet, by some measures and some accounts, globalization may have already gone into reverse mode.

Free Trade Is Not the Rule

The fact that global trade was now slowing down at an alarming rate was undeniable. As one report summarized the alarming trend, "between 1985 and 2007 trade volumes shot up at around twice the rate of global GDP (gross domestic product); since 2012 the rate of growth has barely kept pace."[11] In early 2015, world trade plateaued, as global organizations such as the IMF (International Monetary Fund) and the WTO (World Trade Organization) expressed concerns about increasing protectionist measures across the globe.[12] In 2016, the pace of trade and output growth was the slowest since the financial crisis in 2008. It experienced a fast acceleration in 2017 thanks to growth that was stronger than expected in Asia and in North America. But the pace decelerated in 2018 again, as trade tensions between the United States and China surfaced and threatened global trade. It was expected to be at 3.9% in 2018 and 3.7% in 2019 compared to 4.7% in 2017.[13]

Weak global growth admittedly played a significant role in this slowdown. But as an annual IMF publication, the *World Economic Outlook*, pointed out, since 2012, the slowdown in trade initiatives and increasingly less global value chains also accounted for "a sizable share of the unpredicted shortfall in annual global trade growth."[14] This was not just a matter of sluggish economic activity: it was also the result of key policy and strategic choices on the part of economic actors. And the rising tensions between the United States and its traditional trading partners, China and the EU in particular, were not going to reverse the trend, quite to the contrary. It may be the time, Jeff Bezos thought, to stop taking globalization for granted.

In addition, increasing signals that governments worldwide, even those of developed economies, are not as attached to free trade as in the past are worrying. Jeff Bezos agreed with the *Wall Street Journal* columnist who observed that while "broad majorities of the public still think free trade and immigration are good things," "the bad news for globalizers is that the populists on the right and left who disagree are increasingly able to stop the process."[15] The inability of the G7 and the G20 forums to find a compromise on a strong defense for free trade and strong condemnation of protectionist measures was also unprecedented since the Second World War.[16] This was not about a mere economic cost-benefit analysis of the situation: the politics of the issue were also significant.

The 2017 World Economic Forum had been, perhaps, the most striking illustration of this new global reality. The leader of a global superpower who reminded the rest of the world of the importance of globalization and free trade was neither American nor European but Chinese. It was indeed president Xi Jinping of China who argued that globalization could not be a scapegoat. "Countries should view their own interest in the broader context and refrain from pursuing their own interests at the expense of others," he added, warning the rest of the world of trade and currency wars that could be destabilizing for all countries, in what has become a very influential speech about the future of globalization.[17] Donald Trump, the newly elected president of the United States, did not attend the Forum.

Global Tensions Are the New Rule

It seems as if fragmentation, not integration—both in the economic *and* political sense—characterized today's period. The relative stability of the second half of the twentieth century in the West, despite the ongoing Cold War, often represented in the minds of many the golden age of political and economic integration, as the European Union and free trade, under the aegis of the GATT (General Agreement on Tariffs and Trade), made substantial headway. Now, it is not only free trade that is in decline.

In addition, the crisis of the European Union, the institution that was supposed to put an end to geopolitical rivalries and to offer a stable regional business environment for yesterday's foes to prosper, is emblematic of the world's move towards more disintegration and fragmentation: whereas financial markets seemed in the past to welcome and legitimize economic integration of diverse European economies, the euro crisis and the inability of eurozone countries to quickly find a compromise made it look as if the convergence of European economies was over. And, in the eyes of the pessimists, with this reversal came the evidence that fragmentation, rather than integration, was the new normal—especially if the Europeans, who once championed regional integration, were not able to pull it off anymore.

Similarly, growing tensions in the Persian Gulf and in the Korean Peninsula did not necessarily mean that war was likely, but the possibility of miscalculation was growing. Miscalculation can make even the smallest spark sufficient to start a conflict—and the possible sequences leading to a conflict seem to get increasingly clear. An even greater risk of disintegration looms in the Middle East compared to the European Union: the possible collapse of Syria and Iraq as nation-states and the related geopolitical rivalries between global powers in the region thwart the prospects of integration at the regional and global level.

And beyond turmoil in Europe and in the Middle East, could the combination of the rise of China and the relative decline of the United States not lead to increased instability and chaos? As Graham Allison puts it,

> Most such contests have ended badly, often for both nations .... In 12 of 16 cases over the past 500 years, the result was war. When the parties avoided war, it required huge, painful adjustments in attitudes and actions on the part not just of the challenger but also the challenged.[18]

And this period does not seem to be an exception: troublesome signs that free trade was not the norm, either in the political discourse or in practice, shed additional doubt on the prospects of global economic integration. Increasing polarization in the United States and in the European Union, leading to substantial political divisions and, at times, to calls for secession, suggest that the logic of fragmentation, not that of integration, may have now taken over.

In addition, frail social pacts are a real threat to international stability, especially considering, if history is a guide to better understanding the present, that you only need one spark for a crisis to unravel. The rise of populist movements across the West was an obvious illustration of this. The rise of violence related to (ISIS) the Islamic State of Iraq and the Levant, beyond the borders of the Middle East, was additional evidence of these frail social pacts that could undermine the ability of globalization to move forward, amid a chaotic business and societal environment.

Finally, Bezos reminded himself, it was important not to forget that globalization remained in a relative concept that was not necessarily the reality of all regions of the world. As *The Economist* put it, "World trade can be split into tens of thousands of separate potential corridors between pairs of countries: America and China, say, or Gabon and Denmark. In a quarter of those corridors there was no recorded commerce at all."[19]

Current measures of volatility on financial markets, which are usually indicative of how fearful markets are, point to a relative level of calm, especially compared to previous peaks during the European crisis or during the 2008 Great Recession. Similarly, the sustained progress of confidence indices for business and consumers since 2008 suggest that the prospects of the global

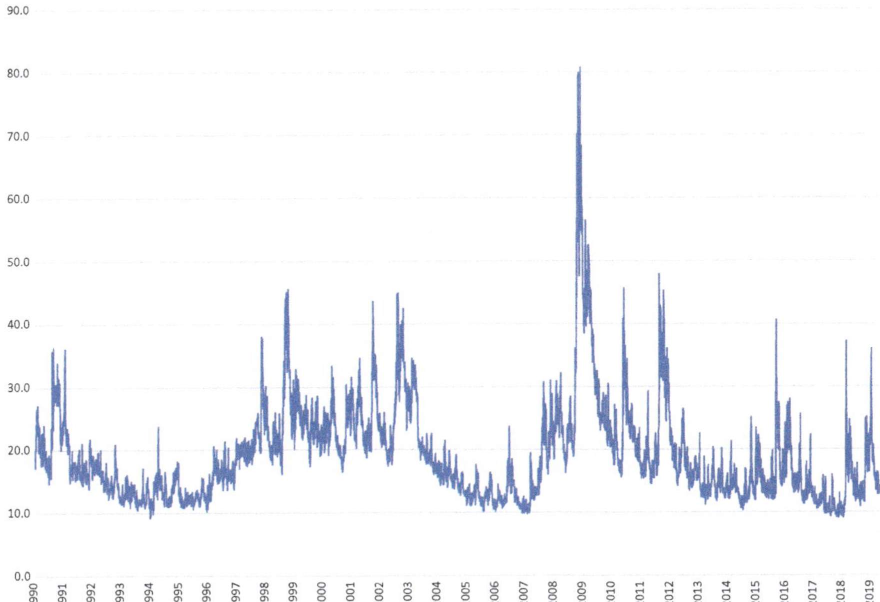

Fig. 8.3 The volatility of markets since 1990. Source: Yahoo Finance
The Chicago Board Options Exchange Volatility Index, also known as VIX, is a widely used indicator of volatility expectations of stock markets. It is commonly used to measure how nervous stock markets are. While the indicator has experienced a few peaks after the 2008 Great Depression when it hit it all time high level, it seemed to point to a remarkable calm between 2012 and 2015 and between 2016 and 2017. Since then, the indicator has experienced two peaks at the beginning and the end of 2018. Are these indicative of what is coming next?

economy are rather positive. But are these indicators of optimism or more measures of our collective shortsightedness (Fig. 8.3)?

"How Far Will the Pendulum Swing Against Globalization?"[20]

In fact, was "deglobalization" that surprising considering what populations in the region had gone through? Western middle classes may still be substantially richer than Asian ones. But they experienced very modest gains in real income between 1988 and 2008 (between 2 and 5%) when those of Asian middle classes grew between 60 and 70%, and those of the top 1% neared 60%. The global 1% and the Asian middle classes were the clear winners of globalization while Western middle classes were the clear losers.[21]

This trend explained the wariness of Western public opinions who seemed increasingly preoccupied with the risk of demotion—the sense of loss of social status and influence over political processes. After all, had they not played by the rules, by choosing to remain "mainstream" and accepting to make efforts to remain relevant economic actors? The dividends of these efforts did not amount to much in retrospect for someone who lost his or her job, and who believed that the future generation would live a significantly harder life than they did. In this political landscape, it was almost surprising that this rise in populism did not occur before, Bezos thought to himself. These populations believed that they had nothing to lose anymore and that no option was off the table. This made the political climate all the more so toxic.

The end of "hyper-globalization," as one influential Harvard professor put it, was one way out. He argued in particular that "A reassertion of the nation state may be inimical to hyper-globalization but as long as it is made in the service of social inclusion, robust economic growth and liberal democracy, it will serve the needs of an open world economy quite well."[22] While Bezos certainly understood the argument as a citizen, he was not convinced that curbing globalization, that brought so many newer products to the most remote areas of the planets, was really an answer. It was perhaps time for his company and the likes to engage with governments across the world in order to strive for better policies and better governance. But would that ultimately work? The corporate state had become a powerful social-political actor—perhaps as powerful as any nation state. This power came with strings attached nevertheless, given the fear it triggered among politicians and public opinion.

Dave McClure, of 500 startups, offered an alternative. He argued: "Instead of marching on Washington, where maybe a lot of people don't want to listen to you and don't really care, we should be marching on people and places that have an influence that we can control: Mountain View, Menlo Park, and Cupertino—and San Francisco."[23] And Jeff Bezos was even tempted to dig deeper: could his company not factor in as well a wide range of populations that were never able to benefit from more sophisticated products? He was reminded of the words of a French serial entrepreneur, Carlos Diaz, who argued that Donald Trump's election was the fault of the Silicon Valley:

> The America that voted for Trump does not own a Tesla, nor an iPhone and when it needs money, it does not ask business angels for help: it relies on bad credits. It is time to recognize that we need to develop technologies and businesses that will benefit the widest range of people possible, algorithms that do not divide but that bring together.[24]

This was not just about a new political reality: it was about what that reality meant for a company like Amazon. It was a call for action.

Time to Act for Architects of Change

Slowbalisation, argued *The Economist*, is not the same as globalization going into reverse though. This slowdown would not necessarily undermine living standards: slowbalisation is likely to entail "deeper links within regional blocks" whose sizes are significant enough for them to prosper. But the British weekly warns that the United States and its Federal Reserve are still likely to shape interest rates across the globe even if regional trading blocs were relatively more independent. In addition, in spite of the changing global reality, the problems that globalization generated would not go away: unskilled workers were still vulnerable and at the risk of losing their jobs, climate change was still a major threat and China's regional hegemony would only be greater.[25]

Acting on the Analysis

Amazon had already acted on the question of income inequality in the United States in the past. In a move to compete with its rival Walmart for low-income shoppers, Amazon offered a substantially reduced Amazon Prime monthly rate ($5.99, down from $10.99) to Americans on food stamps—a segment of the US population whose online purchases increased by 28% between 2009 and 2016.[26] Beyond that, by opening up physical stores and by acquiring the supermarket chain Whole Foods, Amazon looked as if it was trying to become omnipresent in an ever-growing range of consumer segments, in people's daily scenery. But was that enough?

Amazon's Asian rival, Alibaba, went one step ahead. Jack Ma, the company's CEO, designed an electronic world trade platform which makes it easier for ecommerce to prosper in Asia and for small- and medium-sized businesses to trade across borders—a "parallel World Trade Organization for SMEs, with business in the lead and governments playing a supporting role rather than being in the driving seat" in a nutshell.[27] In fact, this platform represented a real challenge for the global trade architecture which had been, until now, influenced by sovereign states. With this platform, Alibaba, not China, was able to sign a free-trade agreement with Malaysia in order to facilitate goods shipment by small businesses from both countries.[28] Again, the rise of the corporate state redefined the way business was done in this global environment.

Similarly, Jack Ma also committed to making it easier for US small businesses, farmers, and entrepreneurs to sell in China via Alibaba. There was, of course, a huge opportunity for Alibaba to increase imports of US consumer goods into China,[29] a country whose internal consumption was beginning to revitalize. But maintaining the free flow of trade also meant that globalization still had a chance to continue being the norm. If countries failed to deliver on free trade agreements, Alibaba was looking for a way to become a good substitute.

There was no shortage of creative thinking either though on the part of Amazon's rivals. Jeff Bezos, always staying true to himself, wanted to get an edge over his competitors and wanted to act quickly. He recognized that small, incremental innovations would not be enough in this business environment. He needed to know what was the next big idea—the new product or service, the new technological application, the new source of supply, and/or the new company organization—that would allow Amazon to adapt to this new global political reality of discontent, characterized by fear and rejection of yesterday's norms. What would represent a decisive and durable advantage for his firm?

Developing Agility and Awareness

Because decision-makers do not take a decision in a vacuum, they must be alert to changes in their business environment. Those changes can occur very rapidly, requiring them to be agile and resilient. It is hard to defend a "wait-and-see" attitude in this context: the challenge lies in developing a firm's situational and strategic awareness of the business environment. One way to achieve this is to determine the early warning signals that can help a company identify a real shift of globalization dynamics—and more generally to continuously improve one's awareness of the surroundings.

After all, it arguably "only" took one murder in the Balkans to trigger one of the bloodiest and geopolitically consequential wars of all time in Europe. History suggests that attention to potential abrupt changes is by no means a luxury.

Rethinking Globalization

Another challenge lies in going beyond the concept of globalization the way we have been considering it since the end of the cold war. Granted, without the existence of global market, the current business model of virtually all international companies, tech giants included, would lose their relevance. And yet, it is tempting to consider that these changes in the business environment, this phenomenon of "slowbalisation" can present opportunities to these companies. How would they go local? And why?

One idea would lie in considering technological developments like 3D printing. Global trade would not be about shipping and importing goods anymore but trading blue prints. Companies could compete on the user-friendliness and the quality of these blueprints, acting as platforms allowing consumers to access them rather than letting them buy actual physical goods.

Another idea would lie in reconsidering the nature of what is export- and import-worthy. If free trade is not the rule anymore, there could be a premium on products that are particularly authentic, original, and impossible to obtain outside of a particular place they are made in. This means that rather than looking to develop global supply chains, companies could look to offer consumers with products that are very country- or region-specific, goods that consumers would never be able to find elsewhere. That would be a transformation of globalization that is congruent with concerns regarding climate change and the respect of local cultures.

The architect of change may find convincing and less convincing ideas in these discussions. But what is most significant is the mental gymnastics that they entail: taking current trends for granted is not a viable option—and ignoring the potential for disruptive moments is not a winning strategy. What is required is considering what opportunities could emerge in changes in the business environment we knew. This is by no means a one-time effort.

Notes

1. "The Steam Has Gone out of Globalisation," *The Economist*, January 24, 2019, https://www.economist.com/leaders/2019/01/24/the-steam-has-gone-out-of-globalisation.
2. Martin Sandbu, "Three Reasons Why Globalisation Will Survive Protectionist Rebellions," *Financial Times*, March 9, 2017, https://www.ft.com/content/1a4e31ce-0333-11e7-aa5b-6bb07f5c8e12.
3. Martin Wolf, "Donald Trump Faces the Reality of World Trade," *Financial Times*, November 22, 2016, https://www.ft.com/content/064d51b0-aff4-11e6-9c37-5787335499a0.
4. See Wolf; Wen Wang, "Emerging Markets Are Set to Lead Globalisation," *Financial Times*, April 10, 2017, https://www.ft.com/content/f60d77a4-1ded-11e7-b7d3-163f5a7f229c.
5. "Globalisation Has Faltered," *The Economist*, January 24, 2019, https://www.economist.com/briefing/2019/01/24/globalisation-has-faltered?fsrc=scn/tw/te/rfd/pe.
6. Ralf Dreischmeier, Karalee Close, and Philippe Trichet, "The Digital Imperative," *The Boston Consulting Group* (blog), March 2, 2015, https://www.bcg.com/publications/2015/digital-imperative.aspx.

7. Jeff Desjardins, "This Is What Happens in an Internet Minute in 2018," *World Economic Forum* (blog), May 16, 2018, https://www.weforum.org/agenda/2018/05/what-happens-in-an-internet-minute-in-2018/.
8. New York Times journalist Tom Friedman called this the Dell Theory of Conflict Prevention which he stated this way: "No two countries that are both part of a major global supply chain, like Dell's, will ever fight a war against each other as long as they are both part of the same global supply chain."
9. Niall Ferguson, *The Ascent of Money: A Financial History of the World*, 1 edition (New York London: Penguin Books, 2009).
10. Graham Allison, "The Thucydides Trap: Are the U.S. and China Headed for War?," *The Atlantic*, September 24, 2015, http://www.theatlantic.com/international/archive/2015/09/united-states-china-war-thucydides-trap/406756/.
11. "Why Is World Trade Growth Slowing?," *The Economist*, October 12, 2016, http://www.economist.com/blogs/economist-explains/2016/10/economist-explains-5.
12. Shawn Donnan, "Global Trade Slowdown Worse than Thought," *Financial Times*, July 13, 2016, https://www.ft.com/content/97a10864-490b-11e6-8d68-72e9211e86ab.
13. World Trade Organization, "WTO Downgrades Outlook for Global Trade as Risks Accumulate," September 27, 2018, https://www.wto.org/english/news_e/pres18_e/pr822_e.htm.
14. International Monetary Fund, "Global Trade: What's Behind the Slowdown," in *World Economic Outlook*, 2016, 63–87, http://www.imf.org/external/pubs/ft/weo/2016/02/.
15. Greg Ip, "Can Globalization Be Salvaged?," *Wall Street Journal*, November 2, 2016, sec. Economy, http://www.wsj.com/articles/can-globalization-be-salvaged-1478102789.
16. See for instance Claire Jones, "G7 Signs off on Watered-down Free Trade Pledge," *Financial Times*, May 13, 2017, https://www.ft.com/content/6cdbdba6-37c9-11e7-821a-6027b8a20f23; Claire Jones and Sam Fleming, "G20 Drops Vow to Resist All Forms of Protectionism," *Financial Times*, March 18, 2017, https://www.ft.com/content/241cdf2a-0be9-11e7-a88c-50ba212dce4d.
17. Jinping Xi, "Speech to Davos" (January 17, 2017), https://www.weforum.org/agenda/2017/01/full-text-of-xi-jinping-keynote-at-the-world-economic-forum/.
18. Allison, "The Thucydides Trap."
19. "Globalisation Has Faltered."
20. You can find a summary of the debate here: Lorenzo Bini Smaghi, "How Far Will the Pendulum Swing against Globalisation?," *Financial Times* (blog), November 15, 2016, https://www.ft.com/content/0c777dda-bed4-326e-b130-2ab08079e5a9.

21. Branko Milanovic, "Why the Global 1% and the Asian Middle Class Have Gained the Most from Globalization," *Harvard Business Review* (blog), May 13, 2016, https://hbr.org/2016/05/why-the-global-1-and-the-asian-middle-class-have-gained-the-most-from-globalization.
22. Dani Rodrik, "There Is No Need to Fret about Deglobalisation," *Financial Times*, October 4, 2016, https://www.ft.com/content/d9a28a08-895c-11e6-8cb7-e7ada1d123b1.
23. Kim Hart, "Dave McClure's Investment Strategy for the Trump Era," *Axios*, March 16, 2017, https://www.axios.com/dave-mcclures-investment-strategy-for-the-trump-era-2316191240.html.
24. Gilles Sengès, "Carlos Diaz: «Le Mur de Trump, C'est La Silicon Valley Qui L'a Construit»," *L'Opinion*, November 13, 2016, http://www.lopinion.fr/edition/international/carlos-diaz-mur-trump-c-est-silicon-valley-qui-l-a-construit-114167.
25. "The Steam Has Gone out of Globalisation."
26. Laura Stevens and Sarah Nassauer, "Amazon Fights Wal-Mart for Low-Income Shoppers," *Wall Street Journal*, June 6, 2017, https://www.wsj.com/articles/amazon-fights-wal-mart-for-low-income-shoppers-1496732400.
27. Louise Lucas, "Alibaba Kicks off Ambitious Plan for Frontier-Free Global Trade," *Financial Times*, March 22, 2017, https://www.ft.com/content/590d815a-0ec6-11e7-a88c-50ba212dce4d.
28. Lucas.
29. Elizabeth Weise, "Alibaba Launches Program to Help 1 Million U.S. Businesses Sell to China," *USA Today*, April 25, 2017, https://www.usatoday.com/story/tech/news/2017/04/25/alibaba-launches-program-help-1-million-us-businesses-sell-china/100827290/.

9

The Significance of Anticipation

In a fast-changing business environment, the challenge lies as much in understanding the world you live in as in anticipating how it will evolve over time. Your analysis is likely to be incomplete in an environment in which you can become easily obsessed with your inbox, and be tempted to micromanage, isolate issues, and be excessively backward-looking in your analyses as a result. Broadening horizons requires adopting a longer time horizon in your analysis by locating your choices in a time stream and understanding how mega-forces can interact with each other. This is likely to make you and your organization or activity as elastic as possible in an environment in which you are likely to face significant sources of stress.

Anticipation should, as a result, be an integral and significant part of your analysis—and there are many historical examples that illustrate why.

Consider, in particular, the example of the African continent and the pace at which its prospects have changed over the years. In early 2000, Africa was dubbed "the hopeless continent" by the front cover of the British weekly *The Economist*. This view was widely shared at the time: the continent was marred by wars, corruption, poverty, and famine. International aid had failed to actually raise the standards of living of African countries. It was as if the international community had given up on nearly 15% of global population.

Yet, by the turn of the decade, the consensus shifted.

The very same British weekly revised its judgment, barely a decade later, noting, in 2011, that in the 2000s, "six of the world's ten fastest-growing countries were African," and that in all years over the period except two, "Africa has grown faster than East Asia, including Japan."[1] From the hopeless continent, Africa became the rising continent. And the movement continued,

J. Ghez, *Architects of Change*, https://doi.org/10.1007/978-3-030-20684-0_9

two years later, when the weekly called Africa the "aspiring continent," whose diverse populations are "embracing modern technology, voting in ever more elections and pressing their leaders to do better."[2] All of a sudden, the narrative about the continent is not one that focuses on the survival of its people but one that focuses on its welfare and well-being.

And this shift happened in *barely more than in a decade*. Had we been, in 2000, asked to formulate a judgment on the outlook of the continent, it is likely that we would have been quite grim about Africa's prospects.

This is why anticipation is so significant: it is an exercise that should help us broaden horizons and not be stuck in a linear view of the world, in which we solely extrapolate without any consideration for possible shifts in trends, leading to substantially different outcomes. The objective of anticipation is to generate a set of distinct, mutually exclusive scenarios—between three and five—that points to the major themes we should have on our radar screen. These scenarios make up the map of the future—or what is plausible to expect going down the line. They can help us determine the extent to which what we are doing today, whether our current strategies, will resist to tomorrow's stress. Will our current strategies let us be as relevant as possible in tomorrow's world?

As a result, anticipation is an important exercise that we should handle with care, in particular when we are looking to improve our ability to make a difference and to have an impact on outcomes: unless we understand the potential for these shifts and the potential for sensibly different scenarios, we are unlikely to be able to design strategies that will have an impact in this turbulent business environment.

This chapter shows how we can achieve this, using the future of the European Union as an illustration throughout. It starts with some key considerations about anticipation—what it is and what it is not. It then details the approach to generating meaningful scenarios and impactful analysis. This approach relies on three steps.

The first step lies in understanding the forces that shape the future. In order to achieve this, we can rely on three forms of analysis: historical analysis, feedback (or the study of current dynamics), and horizon scanning. The chapter discusses each of these forms, their objectives, and their limits, and applies them to the case of the European Union.

The second step lies in identifying the key dimensions of the future in order to generate scenarios. Again, this chapter discusses the approach and applies it to the instance of the European Union.

The last step lies in understanding the implications the exploration of the future has for the present. As one practitioner of strategic foresight once eloquently put it, unless you are revisiting what you are doing today, "If long-term thinking doesn't influence what you do today, it's only entertainment."[3] Scenario analysis is therefore an important part of the reinvention effort of architects of change.

What Anticipation Is (and Is Not)

It may be important to first emphasize that by *anticipation* we do not mean *prediction.*

Anticipation Versus Prediction

It is not only that the two concepts do not have the same meaning, as it will be clear by the end of this chapter; it is also noteworthy that we, humans, are not very good at predicting—even the most expert among us, as studies have illustrated. As American scholar Philipp Tetlock underscores, dogma plays, yet again, a significant role in undermining our ability to better understand our environment: we are unwilling "to change one's mind in a reasonably timely way in response to new evidence," and when asked to explain our predictions, we tend to "to generate only reasons that favor (our) preferred prediction and not to generate reasons opposed to it."[4]

This unwillingness to change our opinions results from the fact that we are usually very overconfident when it comes to making predictions. Nobel Prize recipient Daniel Kahneman tells the story of how, over a long period of time, researchers at Duke University collected chief financial officers' expectations of how the Standard & Poor's index would perform. Lessons of the study were two-fold. First, "the correlation between their estimates and the true value was slightly less than zero," suggesting that these expectations were completely wrong—and that these chief financial officers were most likely unaware of this troubling fact. Second, and worse, they were far more vulnerable to surprises than what they seemed to believe. As Kahneman puts it, "in addition to their best guess about S&P returns, the participants were provided two other estimates: a value that they were 90% sure would be too high, and one that they were 90% sure would be too low," thereby offering a confidence interval in which 80% of their predictions should fall, the rest being "surprises." But, "as frequently happens in such exercises, there were far too many surprises; their incidence was 67%, more than 3 times higher than expected." Overconfidence, as it is often the case, drives predictions in a way that makes them more biased and potentially worthless than we think: "when we estimate a quantity, we rely on information that comes to mind and construct a coherent story in which the estimate makes sense. Allowing for the information that does not come to mind—perhaps because one never knew it—is impossible."[5]

Another piece of research offers the same conclusion, suggesting that "experts who beat the odds are probably just lucky," in particular because those who make one correct prediction on a particular outcome tend to make wrong predictions in the longer run. This piece suggests that we may be giving too much credit to individuals who turned out to be correct on a specific prediction they made. If this is true, we may need to revisit the meaning we give to the notion of expertise and the implications this may have for the way we network.[6]

And even when predictions are grounded in facts and trends and result from intellectually honest analysis, it is not always entirely clear that we are well-wired to understand what they actually mean. In particular, a low likelihood of an outcome can lead us to ignore all together the possibility of this outcome actually materializing, when instead, we should be attentive to it in order to avoid surprises. We rarely understand likelihoods the way we should.

Anticipation Must Have Consequences

And ultimately, there is rarely any accountability associated to predicting. If you take a wild guess about any uncertain outcome, chances are that no one will really remember and hold you accountable if you turn out to be wrong. Conversely, if you are right, you may advertise this as much as you would like, but it will be hard to disassociate what results from luck from what results from actual and sound analysis. In the words of academic Philip Tetlock,

> More often forecasts are made and then … nothing. Accuracy is seldom determined after the fact and is almost never done with sufficient regularity and rigor that conclusions can be drawn. The reason? Mostly it's a demand-side problem: the consumers of forecasting—governments, business, and the public don't demand evidence of accuracy. So there is no measurement.[7]

Anticipation is not about predicting the future but about developing a better grasp of what the future might hold. The ultimate output of an anticipation exercise is two-fold. First, it consists of a set of mutual exclusive scenarios that each describes a possible reality in the future. Taken together, all of these scenarios should be able to capture a wide range of future possibilities. Second, it should lead to a consideration of the *implications* these scenarios have for current strategies: will these approaches to the business environment still be relevant, no matter what reality emerges tomorrow?

Three tools can help you generate these scenarios: historical analysis, feedback, and horizon scanning. The following three sections detail each of these tools and apply them to the case of the European Union, whose tumultuous recent history provides a good illustration of how scenario-analysis can help us see beyond the noise.

Historical Analysis

It may seem paradoxical that in an effort to explore the future, we would feel the need to explore the past. After all, it is hard to avoid the temptation of extrapolation when relying on history. And, as we know, the equation yesterday equals today equals tomorrow is seldom true in any realm shaped by human behavior.

Use with Caution

Disruptive moments and brutal reversal of fates of great historical figures or companies urge us to move with care: consider, for example, how some analysts believed, in the 1980s and the 1990s, that the United States and Japan would one day go to war again because of the past history and the growing economic tensions between the two countries (and arguably what some analysts are saying today about the United States and China);[8] or consider some analysts believed that dictators, like Hosni Mubarak of Egypt and Zine el-Abidine Ben Ali of Tunisia, would durably be part of the regional landscape.[9]

It is very tempting to use the lessons of history when it serves your point and to ignore them when they contradict your analysis. Ultimately, it never helps to drive only looking in the rearview mirror; and if you do, you are likely to crash, no matter how interesting the information you collect. Using historical analysis with care is therefore critical.

History Can Enlighten Us

Nevertheless, when carried out carefully, historical analysis can shed light on precedents, analogies, and historical comparisons that could be driving other people's behavior and that may be influencing future outcomes. By digging into collective memories, we can identify some keys to understanding how the business environment could evolve in time. Economist and Nobel Prize recipient Thomas Schelling calls these keys "focal points": in a seemingly complex situation, a wide range of stakeholders with different profiles and beliefs, may be able to coordinate their actions and converge to a natural outcome, that is, a focal point, that will appear straightforward to most, even in the absence of formal communication. Schelling provides a telling thought experiment: imagine that you are lost in a mall and you are trying to find the person who you came with and that the two of you know each other very well. While there may be a wide range of possible answers to that question, it is likely that two people who know each other well—or, more generally, two people who understand the power of symbols well—will have a greater chance of finding each other than two brilliant mathematicians looking to solve this equation with many unknowns and many possible outcomes. In Schelling's own words, finding a mutually recognized key for coordination "may depend on imagination more than on logic; it may depend on analogy, precedent, accidental arrangement, symmetry, aesthetic or geometric configuration, casuistic reasoning, and who the parties are and what they know about each other."[10]

Historical analysis serves a strikingly useful purpose by enlightening us on all of these elements: in particular, it can help us identify the benchmarks and the references that are shaping people's expectations and beliefs and that actors in a particular situation—as complex as it may seem—have in mind as they develop their strategy. Similarly, historical analysis can serve as a guide to human experience and as an analytical tool to inform current trends. In particular, history can be a guide to better understand continuities and ruptures in human history, that is, help us identify the conditions that make a game changer or a disruptive moment possible. In other words, history can help us address the question of what, in the past, transformed the strategic landscape in a durable way.

An Application: What the Story of the Euro Tells Us About the Future

The formal creation of the European Union on November 1, 1993, when the Maastricht Treaty came into effect in the old continent, is the culmination of a very long historical project that took a very concrete turn in the aftermath of the Second World War. Reconciling the two major European powers, France and Germany, whose rivalries had caused two bloody wars in less than 30 years, was a priority for a wide range of stakeholders. The consensus at the time was that it would be difficult to avoid another war unless European powers could find a way to integrate further the continent's economies and develop a common political narrative about the continent's future. There also was an implicit agreement that in order to truly rein in Germany's position of force inside the European Union and contain Berlin's long-term geopolitical aspirations, the country needed to be placed inside a broader network of countries that would ultimately dilute its geopolitical clout.

But while European officials took incremental steps towards integration, the division of Germany represented a significant impediment to real and meaningful integration. In 1989, the fall of the Berlin Wall presented other European leaders with a striking dilemma: accepting German reunification could help the European continent define its common and unifying political narrative at last. But it presented the project with a threat: while it was first designed as a way to contain geopolitical rivalries, would the reunification of Germany not create, once again, a geopolitical giant inside Europe?

François Mitterrand, the French president of the time and a key actor of the European project, knew that German reunification would be hard to avoid. But he also found in the idea of a common currency for the continent a way to strike a meaningful trade-off to solve this dilemma: Germany's European partners would accept the country's reunification if Berlin accepted to give up one of its major economic (and perhaps political) assets, its currency, the Deutschemark. The European project would survive German reunification by becoming the European Union and by getting Berlin to share the international clout it had developed thanks to its currency. This trade-off also came with a promise: because Germany was now sharing that international clout with the rest of Europe, other European nations could borrow with the same credibility as Berlin did. This meant that the cost of borrowing would drop substantially and allow the less developed economies like Spain or Greece to modernize quickly. This promise materialized quite quickly as the convergence occurred by the turn of the millennium, just before Euro notes and coins started to circulate—before the Euro crisis, beginning in 2009, undermined it substantially (Fig. 9.1).

What to Look for in History

Historical analysis can serve as a guide to lessons from the past, as this brief overview of the origins of the Euro suggests. In particular, it can help us identify past focal points and dynamics that have mattered. In the European case, as German historian Ludwig Dehio once put it,

> it is possible to imagine a history of the Western world that relates all events to the principles of unity and diversity. It could, after all, be said that for more than

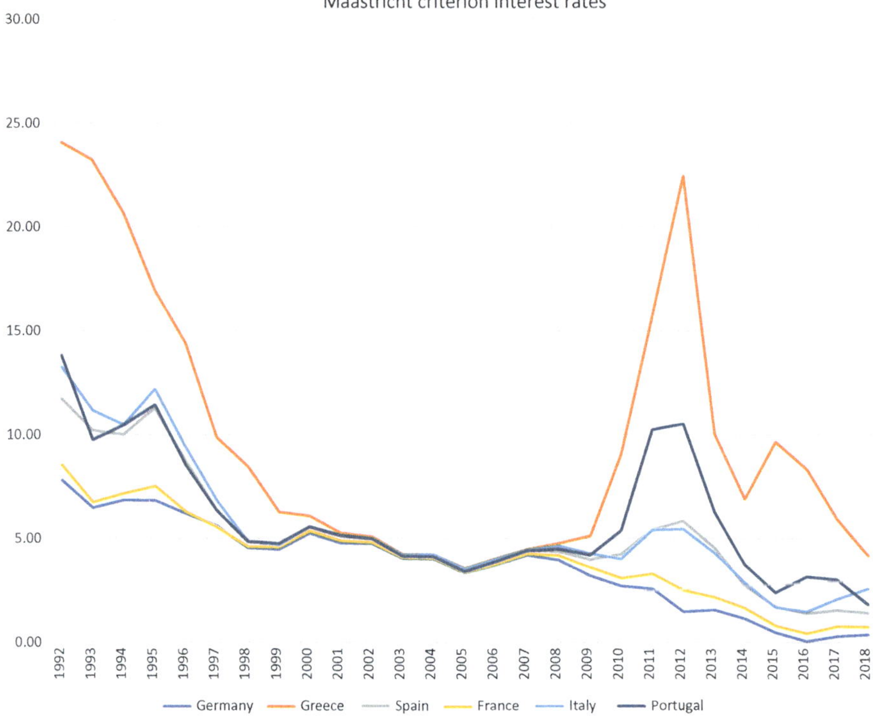

Fig. 9.1 Interest rates on long-term European government bonds (denominated in national currencies): 1992–2018. Source: Eurostat
As Eurostat, the official statistical body of the EU states,
The Maastricht Treaty EMU convergence criterion series relates to interest rates for long-term government bonds denominated in national currencies. Selection guidelines require data to be based on central government bond yields on the secondary market, gross of tax, with a residual maturity of around 10 years.
The long-term interest rate convergence that occurred by 2001 among economies as diverse as Germany and Greece was one of the most significant successes of the European Union. Yet, the Euro crisis, starting at the end of 2009, undermined this convergence.

> a thousand years the pendulum has swung back and forth between a tendency toward unification, which never led to total unity, and a divisive tendency, which never led to complete disintegration. In different epochs the two tendencies are linked with varying circumstances and forces.[11]

This observation is particularly relevant in the case of the European Union, the theater of what seems to be a long-lasting struggle between forces of reconciliation and geopolitical rivalries (that have led, more than once, to the total destruction of the continent). The particularly intriguing issue that this piece of historical analysis raises is whether the European Union has found a recipe to overcome the forces of division thanks to the euro that bears the promise of economic integration and all the political benefits it entails in terms of modernization. Those variables are likely to shape the future of the European Union as a result.

Feedback and the Analysis of Current Dynamics

The present can also offer many insights about the forces shaping the future, so long as we can correctly interpret the raw information it is providing us and adjust our strategies accordingly. In fact, if we pay sufficient attention to trends and to failed and successful approaches, we are in a better position to draw the appropriate feedback from the present.

A Matter of Interpretation

Two metaphors can clarify the objective. The first is when you drive a car and you rely on the dashboard that provides all the indicators you need to adjust your driving. The second is when you take a temperature (either literally or figuratively) with a thermometer (or any other tool in the figurative sense). The information that a thermometer provides is usually indicative of the situation you find yourself in and can thus help you adjust your current approach accordingly. It is noteworthy that in both instances—driving a car and taking the temperature—interpreting the result and making the necessary adjustments is critical. After all, driving at 100 km/h is not the same in a city or on a highway. And a very cool temperature might feel awfully cold after heat, or very agreeable after a long period of cold.

As a result, measuring reality requires understanding the relative value of your metrics. Drawing feedback from the realities and the trends you are seeing is therefore about transforming raw information and data, indicators and signposts into meaningful pieces of a bigger puzzle. There is a wide range of ways to accomplish this goal.

Facts and the Wisdom of the Crowds

The first lies in asking others when you do not have any certainty about facts. For instance, as a banker or a consultant, you may have stakes in the Middle East because of the clients or the assets you have in the region. You may be concerned about political instability in the region, but you may not have all the necessary tools to understand the reasons and the drivers of the instability. As a result, the network you may need to put together is likely to be far more diverse and multidisciplinary than what you imagined: historians, religious experts, or sociologists will never be able to give you the solution to your problem; but they will be able to enlighten you on those reasons and those drivers. It will be up to you to interpret the data they are offering.

Similarly, you may need to ask *groups* of people when you do not have any certainty about *trends*. In theory, this is the role that financial markets are supposed to fulfill: the prices of the assets they provide should be indicative of future cash flows.

The same way, the development over recent years of prediction markets, designed to provide a snapshot of the mood regarding a particular question, can help you identify the existing consensus and formulate expectations about what could happen in the future. Canadian-American academic Philip Tetlock's work on "superforecasters" is quite striking from this standpoint: after having observed that "the average expert was roughly as accurate as a dart-throwing chimpanzee," Tetlock, along with Barbara Mellers, launched the Good Judgment Project that relied on the judgment of "more than twenty thousand intellectually curious laypeople (who) tried to figure out if protests in Russia would spread, the price of gold would plummet, the Nikkei would close above 9,500, war would erupt on the Korean Peninsula, and many other questions about complex, challenging global issues." Researchers were able to identify the type of factors and tools that could help participants improve their foresight. The Good Judgment Project outperformed most expert groups trying to forecast the future, including a group of analysts who did this for a living and who had access to classified data. Tetlock argues that with proper training, a group of people can generate reliable expectations about the future: "Foresight isn't a mysterious gift bestowed at birth. It is the product of particular ways of thinking, of gathering information, of updating beliefs. These habits of thought can be learned and cultivated by any intelligent, thoughtful, determined person."[12]

Companies have also sought to harness the wisdom of crowds to uncover the new forms of thinking and the big ideas that could possibly shape the future. Through contests and experiences, and more recently, events like hackathons, companies can better understand the incentives of other stakeholders and identify new and meaningful ideas and confirm existing ones that were not yet public. These events help firms understand the most telling features of the landscape—that is, those features that may not be apparent on the surface but that are most likely to weigh in the future.[13]

An Application: The Roots of a Crisis Shaping the Future

The promise of the euro did materialize as the cost of borrowing substantially dropped, even for the weaker economies of the Euro area. This promise could have had substantial political consequences, in particular by allowing these economies to modernize.

But in practice, many governments did not try to leverage the benefits it generated: instead of helping countries truly invest in their economy, lower interest rates fueled high-risk lending and borrowing as well as real estate bubbles and made lax fiscal policy choices possible in some of the EU members. Modernization was relegated to a lower level of importance.

The problem became apparent by the end of 2009, in particular when the newly elected Greek government admitted that its debt had reached an unprecedented level in modern history, contrary to what previous official statistics suggested. Fears about the ability of Greece and other countries, such as Ireland, Portugal, and Spain (and even Italy and France), to be able to avoid default on their debt grew stronger. These fears were all the more so significant that EU members had entered a currency union with the Euro without entering a fiscal union, which would have required more policy (and political) coordination.

The challenge for the European Union lay, once again, in finding a common political narrative about the reasons to save what had become far more than just a common currency. Thanks to the creation of the European Stability Mechanism, a eurozone rescue fund, and proactive monetary policy of the European Central Bank, EU members were able to contain the crisis. The most vulnerable economies like Greece are now borrowing, once again, on financial markets. But these economic fixes have not provided the European Union with a broader common political narrative. In fact, the extent to which the European Union has been reactive rather than proactive throughout this crisis is rather striking: the real drivers of EU action were the realities relayed by financial markets that assess economic and financial risks, but that provide little feedback on the reality of the political divergence. The capacity of the European Union to reinvent its political *raison d'être* is fundamental—and a widely open question in this context.

What to Look for in the Forces of the Present

Ultimately, feedback is the process through which we determine the right indicators to anticipate and to adjust as the business environment moves. The bottom line is that your business environment is never static and requires constant strategic adjustments as a result. Feedback can help you confirm that your strategy will guarantee your ability to remain agile.

In the case of the European Union, the issue of economic convergence has played a critical role in providing insights on the overall health of the project. In particular, the spread between the rates at which members of the Euro area are borrowing has been extremely indicative of the extent to which financial markets have shared the view that this project is viable. More structural indicators, like investments in these economies' future, are also telling when it comes to measuring the commitment of EU governments to making the European project work and their ability to make the necessary efforts to fully leverage its benefits. This issue is both economic and political in nature: we have seen how the institution is able to find short-term political fixes to economic problems, but it has become increasingly clear that long-term fixes are likely to be political, with greater coordination of fiscal policies for example. Those open questions that current forces are putting forward are very likely to shape the future of the European Union as a result.

Horizon Scanning

Among the tools that we can use to understand what the future holds, horizon scanning is perhaps the most straightforward one.

Identifying Issues over the Horizon

It is about identifying the issues over the horizon that could profoundly shape the future landscape, though they may not be doing so currently. One governmental report in the United Kingdom defined horizon scanning as "a systematic examination of information to identify potential threats, risks, emerging issues and opportunities, … allowing for better preparedness and the incorporation of mitigation and exploitation into the policy making process."[14] Horizon scanners in the policymaking world are therefore interested in determining how emerging issues could lead decision-makers to think about what they could do so as to better adapt to future needs and challenges. Horizon scanning should also make current strategies less vulnerable to future uncertainty.

The same holds true for the private sector. As managers consider the emerging trends and developments that matter to them, they can adapt their long-term strategic approach. Indeed, they can identify the future sources of value and growth that will matter most to them in the future. And in both the private sector and the policymaking world, the take-away lesson should be the same: every future development need not be a strategic surprise. With thorough analysis, with a little bit of curiosity and imagination, we have ways of identifying and anticipating the threats and the opportunities to think about for the future of our activities.

Identifying the Convergence of Trends

In Chap. 5, we discussed how different trends in telecommunication, entertainment, and portable devices were shaping profoundly the cinema experience for a wide range of consumers. The discussion showed how trends that might have seemed quite distinct to our grandparents are now interacting with each other to create a whole new setting and a whole new experience. Horizon scanning can help us identify the potential for trend convergence. This objective can be reached through various (and non-mutually exclusive) methods.

The first is brainstorming. This method may sound trivial and trite; yet, with the support of very talented individuals who all put their minds to a collective objective, namely trying to identify how seemingly unrelated trends today may converge to lead to a perfect storm or a very enviable outcome, new insights and novel ways of thinking about a problem are bound to emerge. The real challenge lies in acting on what the session actually uncovers.

In addition, the extent to which data is getting increasingly accessible is striking. The so-called big data revolution can shed light on what drives the behavior of key stakeholders and can help us understand how a very significant number of incentives may interact and shape outcomes ultimately. Increasingly sophisticated data can also help uncover underlying trends that may not have been obvious before, or shed light on causal links that help us better understand the dynamics shaping the business environment. In particular, it can help us generate alternative hypotheses about how the world works—including some that we may have naturally overlooked without the assistance of big data.

Furthermore, experiences in the field and close links with active players can also contribute to our understanding of issues and opportunities over the horizon. At the turn of the twentieth century, as he made his case in favor of maintaining a free-trade approach and against the protectionist turn many politicians in his country were arguing for, British economist Alfred Marshall contended that:

> It is absolutely necessary, if England wants to maintain a high international rank, that she neglects no opportunity to increase the vigilance of her industrial population in general and that of her producers in particular. With this objective in mind, there is no other efficient way than maintaining her markets open to the new products of other nations, and more specifically to those which came from America's inventive genius or from the German systematic thought and scientific training.[15]

In other words, it is hard to imagine for anyone to maintain a good handle on the key topics that are likely to shape the future without being constantly confronted with the business environment's realities.

This philosophy is a tradition that governments across the world, in the United States, in the United Kingdom, in the European Union, and in Singapore, share. Strikingly, in each instance, the private sector is consulted and can rely on the work that is done in order to better anticipate future trends. In the United States and in the EU, influential reports about the world in 15 years have focused on issues over the horizon that could shape the future landscape. These reports are well-known and debated in policymaking and business circles.[16] In Singapore, the Risk Assessment and Horizon Scanning (RAHS) program has developed a similar whole-of-government approach that is meant to help governmental agencies, with the support of the private sector, share and collectively analyze information in order to better anticipate the future.[17] In all these instances, a wide range of actors, coming from a wide range of industries and activities, look to discuss future realities that could emerge tomorrow and that can be identified as early as today.

An Application: The Issues That Could Rock the European Boat Tomorrow

As we saw previously in the European case, the short-term economic fixes for the issues caused by the Euro have not quelled political tensions across the continent as frustration with the European Union grew stronger. While the institution has always been, historically, an easy target for governments looking to exonerate themselves, it has not been able to convince public opinions of what it brought to the table.

In the words of former UK Prime Minister David Cameron in a January 2013 speech announcing the coming referendum on Brexit,

> there is a growing frustration that the EU is seen as something that is done to people rather than acting on their behalf. And this is being intensified by the very solutions required to resolve the economic problems. People are increasingly frustrated that decisions taken further and further away from them mean their living standards are slashed through enforced austerity or their taxes are used to bail out governments on the other side of the continent.

In fact, the most emblematic result of this frustration is the UK referendum on Brexit, in which the British population expressed its will to leave the European Union.

But demonstrations across the continent and the surge of so-called populist parties suggest that this trend is not confined to the United Kingdom. It suggests instead that the common political narrative still appears as a major piece of the European puzzle that is still missing. This issue may very well be a question of weak European leadership: the times at which the so-called Paris-Berlin axis was a key driver in the political construction of Europe seem long gone. The ability of the EU to find a new political driver for its construction will be key.

What to Draw from Issues over the Horizon

Horizon scanning is an exercise ultimately designed to reduce the likelihood of surprises. Because it requires thorough analysis, imagination, open-mindedness, and curiosity, it pushes us to consider a far wider array of trends and outcomes than what we would be naturally inclined to look at. It contributes to our awareness of the broader business environment.

As the case on the European Union suggests, it may be difficult to maintain an economic reality (a single market and a common currency) without a common political narrative; yet, past attempts to offer an overarching political narrative for the European project have failed, in particular because these never created any consensus within Europe and often seemed like realities that were imposed on the people rather than democratically decided. This is one key issue over the horizon the institution will need to face.

Scenario Analysis

Relying on the three tools we have just discussed, as well as their application to the case of the European Union, we can generate a set of scenarios on the future of the institution and consider how we can act on the result of this analysis.

What the Future Holds for the European Union

This very brief discussion of the European Union suggests that there are two major dimensions shaping the future of the institution.

The first is economic in nature and concerns the ability of the European Union to further the integration of the continent's diverse economies and allow for these economies to converge. If convergence does occur fully, we can imagine a future in which EU economic integration is not a dream or an ideal but a reality that the institution can rely on in order to fully leverage its assets. If impediments to convergence continue to create economic tensions inside the continent, the notion that EU members share the same economic fate might crumble, thereby fueling additional risks of economic disintegration.

The second is political in nature and focuses on the ability of European Union members to develop a common political roadmap for the future—and rely on that roadmap to coordinate agendas and policies, so as to be stronger, in times of crisis in particular. Increased political integration can enhance the ability of EU members to coordinate their policies and their strategies, thereby increasing the overall impact of the institution inside the continent—and beyond. Political disintegration, at the other extreme, driven by the absence of a common political roadmap, and even increased political rivalries resulting from contradictory policy objectives, would dramatically increase the number of obstacles to decisive action on the part of the EU (Fig. 9.2).

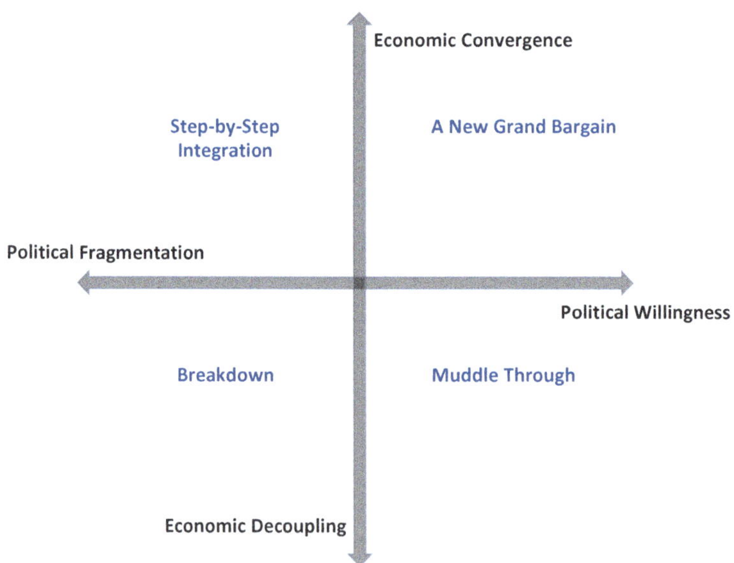

Fig. 9.2 Four scenarios for the future of the European Union

These two dimensions each point to two broad possibilities. Taken together, they generate four distinct scenarios.

The Breakdown

The first scenario is one in which the European Union disintegrates as a result of the lack of economic convergence among EU members and an absence of a common political roadmap. At the onset of the crisis, many observers believed that the difficulties of a weaker member, like Greece in particular, combined with the inability (or the unwillingness) of other EU members to act or to help, would trigger a domino-like process in which each piece of the institution would fall, one by one.

But as the crisis developed, growing frustration in public opinions of relatively stronger economies of Northern Europe and Germany led observers to question whether the breakdown would not come with the exit of one of the stronger EU partners. The vote in favor of the Brexit suggests this process is no less likely.

Muddle Through

The second scenario is one in which there is no real economic convergence between EU members, but in which a shared sense of history and political proximity keeps the institution together.

At each crisis, relying on this political proximity, EU members are able to find a compromise and a short-term fix to the problem. But the absence of economic convergence undermines the European Union's ability to have a long-term impact and to provide meaningful solutions to its members, muddling through crises, one after the other. In this scenario, the European Union does not disintegrate. Instead, it drifts into irrelevance.

Step-by-Step Integration

The third scenario is one in which the European Union lacks political cement because geopolitical rivalries overshadow, once again, the will of some EU members to build a common political roadmap; but in this scenario, private sector actors recognize the benefits of economic integration across the continent and look to further the process through initiatives of their own. They can leverage benefits of economic integration by looking for new partners and new opportunities to consolidate their activities. (EU regulation might create obstacles along the way, but in absence of political cement, it is open to debate whether the European Union would still have the means to enforce competition laws.)

Strikingly, this scenario resembles the historical process of the European construction: a step-by-step approach, based on common economic interests. But it differs from what has happened in the past in the sense that it is the private sector, not states, driving European integration.

A New Grand Bargain

The final scenario is one in which EU members are able to redefine the terms of their economic union as well as their political purpose.

This leads to a new grand bargain, akin to the one struck in the aftermath of the Second World War, but reinvented to meet the challenges and the opportunities of the current environment of the institution. This grand bargain would be based on a common recognition among European countries of a shared set of interests amid the spectacular rise of China and the rest of Asia, and the growing unwillingness on the part of the United States to play the global role the country has played since the end of the Second World War. This scenario would be the rebirth of the European Union.

Generating Scenarios in a Turbulent Business Environment

With these four scenarios, we have a meaningful view of what the future of the European Union may hold.

A Set of Outcomes We Can Easily Grasp

This brief example shows how analysis can generate set of four, mutually exclusive scenarios that cover a wide range of future possibilities, by uncovering two fundamental dimensions shaping the future of Europe: economic integration and political convergence. This analysis comes in three forms in the brief discussion of the European Union: historical analysis, study of current issues, and an exploration of issues over the horizon that the institution is facing. Each of these three forms of analysis can help in uncovering any dimensions shaping the future of any actor by providing political, economic, social and societal, as well as legal and technological indicators showing where the institution falls on both axes. The next section of this chapter explores each.

One is often tempted to argue that more than two dimensions can shape the future of an organization, and this would be a legitimate claim. But if we consider not two but three dimensions, we would generate not 4, not 8, but 12 scenarios. And in this author's experience, the human brain is not well-wired to manage more than five scenarios. In addition, more often than not, many of these 12 scenarios actually look alike and are not mutually exclusive. When there is a legitimate claim to considering not two but three dimensions, the solution lies in consolidating some scenarios in a meaningful way to obtain three to five scenarios that are telling about the future.

But in order to make this exercise as meaningful as possible, it is important not to focus on a single one of these scenarios believing that it is more "probable" than others—thereby exposing yourself to significant surprises if the future lands anywhere else. It is also critical to name each of these scenarios and appreciate their uniqueness and the key features: in doing so, the scenario will take a life of its own in any organization or team. Its members will all be able to contribute to each of these scenarios but relaying what they are seeing on the ground and what details would matter most to the organization or team in the given situation.

Addressing the Key Question: So What?

Ultimately, though, it is critical to remember that anticipation is not an end in itself. In fact, what is likely to give architects of change a meaningful edge in a turbulent business environment is their ability to draw implications from this exploration of the future. In doing so, they are able to ascertain how relevant they will be with the current strategies they have in place in a changing business environment and consider how they can reinvent accordingly.

As the leader of a large company in the big industry, for instance, this exploration suggests that no matter where the European Union ultimately ends up, a proactive approach to the European construction is likely to be helpful. It certainly is if the Union lacks political cement compared to the past and that there is no more sense of a shared fate. This outcome would result in states losing their traditional monopoly when it comes to boosting the European construction. In a world in which the Union finds new sources of cement, the ability of the private sector to shape the common political roadmap to bring to the table the new realities of the business environment that policymakers may not appreciate under the same light would be critical. In any case, these visions of the future provide pillars for your own reinvention that fits the transformation of a broader environment like the European Union.

As a banker, this exploration of the future suggests that there are plenty of risks to hedge against—but that there are plenty of opportunities to seize, at the same time. In particular, in spite of the recent crisis the European Union has gone through, it is remarkable that the degree of economic integration across European economies is higher than in any other region. In addition, the coordination mechanisms European governments can rely on to sync their policies are arguably stronger than anywhere else in the world. The real issue lies in understanding whether the European Union—and its members in particular—are ready to make the investments that would allow for this configuration to persist in the future. For the banker, addressing this question demands monitoring the right set of indicators so as to not overstate risks and underestimate opportunities, beyond the everyday noise and in times of crisis in particular.

Architects of Change: Acting on What You Anticipate

Anticipation is not about predicting the future, as we have argued, but about developing a better grasp of what the future might hold and to plan accordingly.

This is why architects of change are likely to find the exploration of the future to be a useful exercise. In particular, it can help them test the relevance of their current strategy or their approach given what the future could hold. In fact, everyone expects different sources of stress in the business environment; anticipation can help architect of changes stress test their strategies and adjust so as to remain as relevant as possible, regardless of what outcome actually materializes. Put differently, exploring the future can help architects of change become more flexible and increase their ability to adapt to the evolution of the business environment.

In addition, this exercise also helps architects of change identify the key dynamics shaping the future and shed light on the most meaningful levers of reinvention—the sort that is grounded in analytics rather than in wishful thinking. Instead of relying on the dogma of the day or the preoccupation that is on everyone's radar screen, but that could very well fall off of it as quickly as it came, exploring the future can help architects of change go beyond the noise and account for the forces that are really shaping the business environment—beyond what the headlines say. To this extent, anticipation is a very pragmatic exercise.

It does have limits, especially when events that one could not anticipate do occur and rock the boats of even the most flexible actors out there. In particular, it is worth noting that by design, scenario analysis brings your attention on what is known and what is tangible, not on the unknown and/or the unexplored. Flexibility may therefore be essential, but as the next chapter suggests, it may be not enough. Architects of change do need a second leg to stand on.

Greg Treverton is the former chairman of the US National Intelligence Council, which provides the country's intelligence community with long-term strategic analysis to address the questions of policymakers. The Council's Global Trends Reports, which is written up for an incoming president and his administration, is perhaps one of the most public and important pieces of work of the Council. In this exchange, he talks about the key features of the global business environment and what it takes to be successful.

Considering the work you did on Global Trends, what would be the changes in the global strategic landscape that you found most striking?

There are two things that I found most striking. One was the increasing importance of individuals in small groups. Of course, you think of terrorists. But when you see that Bill Gates, through the Gates Foundation spends more money on health in Africa than the World Health Organization, you see that things have changed. We still have this inter-governmental view of the world, but the world isn't like that anymore. Single individuals have effective vetoes that need to be taken into account. The full geometry of international relations has changed in a way we have not yet fully appreciated.

The second factor that emerged in Global Trends report during my tenure was the various forms of disconnect between the people and their governments. In the United Kingdom, there was Brexit. In France, the Yellow Vest movement. In the United States, there was Trump. All of these are different forms of the same phenomenon that is too easy to call "populism," but there is some of that. There is also to some extent a loss of faith in the liberal ideal.

What does that say, in your opinion, about those that will likely make a difference in the future?

Those making a difference will understand that these trends are afoot and find a way to turn them into a positive game-changer rather than just complain about them because they make life and governance harder.

It is easy to put these trends in the negative. For instance, increasing empowerment of individuals in small groups has a negative side to it: it is harder to build a coalition because more people have to be considered, more people have veto power. But the trend also has lots of power: those who figure out how to harness the immense energy that has been created for interesting public purposes will be able to bring game-changing transformations to the landscape. We don't see too much of that yet, but we see some philanthropists buying newspapers and playing a more public role.

So what skills will you need to be successful in that environment?

This business environment requires a degree of foresight that may not come naturally to most people. Executives say they spend 40% of the time thinking about the future but I'm always skeptical of that. This environment requires a lot more people doing foresight, comparing the advantages and disadvantages against a rapidly changing landscape. You want organizations to be more nimble. Who can be against that? But it's not just that: it's also thinking about capacity in relation to trends and goals.

As a public manager, I think about this like a triangle. One leg was what you wanted to do, your personal goals and aspirations in an organization. A second was what capacities an organization has, what is it good at. A third was what is the broader authorizing environment, and how much could you interact with it in order to change or broaden your mandate. This triangle describes a set of constraints that people will need to manage in order to be successful in this environment.

What does engineering the future require ultimately?

There are plenty of interesting examples of actors doing it. In one sense, a lot of the big innovations we've seen have been not so much driven by foresight than by asking "why not" questions. A recent example is Netflix: why pay by the film? You do not pay by the workout in a gym: you have a subscription and you can go as much as you want. With that "why not," Netflix was able to revolutionize the film industry. When you ask "why can't we do this," you start to make a difference.

Think of yesterday's giants, like Kodak, Nokia, and IBM. Or today's giants, like the tech companies. Or the giants of tomorrow, like, perhaps, Netflix. What is most likely to determine which one survives, and which one does not?

The question for me is whether the things that made the big ones fail before will be the same things that will make the big ones fail today—and that is failure to anticipate dramatic changes in business practice or technology. IBM and PCs, Kodak and digital cameras ... If you imagine the big ones now, they are extremely reliant on data for their business power. So in the future, you might wonder how their access to data might be restricted or whether data becomes less important. The immediate challenge would be a backlash against the tech business model that is not illegal but borderline immoral.

What would be your advice to the next generation when it comes to shaping the future landscape? The list of Dos and Don'ts?

It is easy to see the trends. Take the Arab Spring: we all knew that Arab countries were very fragile. But what we couldn't predict was what could trigger change. There would be something pretty inevitable. Hard to say what it would be or how it might happen. You need to be at least open to trigger events, perhaps by asking: what might be a trigger? No one would have guessed that a street vendor setting himself on fire would be a trigger for riots in Tunisia. But it is worth recognizing that trends are going to play out in unpredictable ways. Trends are pretty predictable but the triggers for dramatic change are not.

Ultimately, open-mindedness and nimbleness, as well as a breadth of vision, looking across aspects of culture, psychology, but also technology will matter most.

You shouldn't get too comfortable with the story you like. Everybody thought Saddam Hussein has weapons of mass destruction, including people like me who opposed the war. But we failed to ask: why might he pretend to have something he doesn't have? You need to be careful about the story.

In addition, when I teach about intelligence, I tell my students that when I made an assessment, I asked myself why was this assessment popular with me, and the reasons why I like it. Sometimes, it is because it is convenient for me. And you also need to ask yourself what it would take to change my mind.

What would be the most single important lesson you draw from this assessment of the world landscape in terms of education for parents out there?

It would be easy to say that more is better than less but I'm not sure that's right! Something we don't do very well (and helicopter parents do it even worse because they are all always trying to raise their kids to meet the existing conventional standards) is encourage creativity. We knock creativity out of kids too often. Our system takes kids that were often quite creative and makes them less so. This means not giving too much attention to traditional metrics and provide more opportunities to gain experiences and to things that don't involve looking at screens.

Notes

1. "Africa Rising," *The Economist*, December 3, 2011, https://www.economist.com/leaders/2011/12/03/africa-rising.
2. "Aspiring Africa," *The Economist*, March 2, 2013, https://www.economist.com/leaders/2013/03/02/aspiring-africa.
3. The quote is from former RAND Corporation long-term policy analyst, Jim Dewar, quoted in Gregory F. Treverton and Jeremy J. Ghez, *Making Strategic Analysis Matter*, RAND Corporation Conference Proceedings Series CF287-NIC (Santa Monica, CA: RAND, 2012).
4. "The Folly of Prediction," *Freakonomics* (blog), June 30, 2011, http://freakonomics.com/2011/06/30/the-folly-of-prediction-full-transcript/.
5. Daniel Kahneman, *Thinking, Fast and Slow*, 1 edition (Farrar, Straus and Giroux, 2011).
6. See in particular Jerker Denrell, "'Experts' Who Beat the Odds Are Probably Just Lucky," *Harvard Business Review*, April 1, 2013, https://hbr.org/2013/04/experts-who-beat-the-odds-are-probably-just-lucky.
7. Philip E. Tetlock and Dan Gardner, *Superforecasting: The Art and Science of Prediction*, Reprint edition (Broadway Books, 2016).
8. See for instance George Friedman and Meredith Lebard, *The Coming War with Japan*, 1st edition (New York: St Martins Press, 1991).
9. Only two days before Ben Ali's ouster, then-French Minister of Foreign Affairs Michèle Alliot-Marie suggested that France could assist Tunisia in containing the ongoing riots that would later be known as the beginning of the Arab Spring. Her offer is often seen as very telling of the lack of understanding of Western governments of what was actually happening in the region at the time.
10. Thomas Schelling, *The Strategy of Conflict*, Reprint edition (Cambridge: Harvard University Press, 1981).
11. Dehio, Ludwig, *The Precarious Balance: The Politics of Power in Europe, 1494–1945*, London, UK: Chatto & Windus, 1963, p. 19.
12. Tetlock and Gardner, *Superforecasting*.

13. See for instance Guido Jouret, "Inside Cisco's Search for the Next Big Idea," *Harvard Business Review* 87, no. 9 (September 2009): 43–45.
14. John Day, "Review of Cross-Government Horizon Scanning" (London, UK: Cabinet Office, January 21, 2013), https://www.gov.uk/government/publications/review-of-cross-government-horizon-scanning.
15. Quoted in Paul Bairoch, Jean-Charles Asselain, and Anne Saint-Girons, *Mythes et paradoxes de l'histoire économique* (Paris: La Découverte, 2005).
16. In the case of the United States, see the National Intelligence Council's Global Trends Reports: "Global Trends Home Page," Office of the Director of National Intelligence, accessed April 12, 2019, https://www.dni.gov/index.php/global-trends-home. For the European Union, see European Strategy and Policy Analysis System (ESPAS) and its Global Trends to 2030 reports: "European Strategy and Policy Analysis System (ESPAS)," accessed April 12, 2019, https://espas.secure.europarl.europa.eu/orbis/espas.
17. See: "The National Security Coordination Secretariat (NSCS)," accessed April 12, 2019, https://www.nscs.gov.sg/events.html.

10

Case Study: Getting Ready for the World in Five Years

Yu Yan was very proud: she had just been named chief political scientist in a big Chinese tech giant and she was the first female to ever reach that position. Now, she was a woman on a mission: for all the talk about how turbulent the global business environment had become, and about how there was no "small topic" because every single local crisis could ultimately have a huge effect on her company, she felt that no one, in her team or among the consultants her company had hired for a hefty price, was really feeding her with any thinking about what her world would look like in the near future.

And yet, her colleagues and fellow members of the board of directors needed to make strategic decisions based on what that world would look like five years down the line. As we all know, she thought, if you want something done right, you have to do it yourself; so it was time to act and get the analytical effort going within her team, the only set of individuals she could trust to be honest.

The challenge lay in determining how she and her team could achieve this goal. In particular, she wondered about the themes she and her team should have on their radar screen. She also thought about where should she put the emphasis in her analysis: on the global consensus, and thus what seemed like the most "likely" scenario? Or on the disagreements among global observers, in order to underscore the issues that were most likely to surprise down the line since there was no real unanimity about outcomes?

Another challenge was the way in which she and her team could not only provide meaningful and impactful analysis for the company right now but also how this effort could be continuous over time by feeding the company with updated analysis. Her objective was to ultimately make the work of her

J. Ghez, *Architects of Change*, https://doi.org/10.1007/978-3-030-20684-0_10

team about the future of the business environment part of the company's bloodstream, in a way that would almost be invisible because it would be so natural and omnipresent. The ultimate challenge, of course, was to get the company to account for this work in a systematic way so that it could get prepared for the future her team was anticipating and strategize upon her analysis.

In a nutshell, this effort of the analysis of the future had been delayed too often. It was now time to act.

Choosing Themes

The first challenge was about deciding what type of topics to monitor over time.

A Regional Approach

Yu Yan's company had vested interests across a very wide region, all along the new Silk Road that runs across the Asian continent and in the Indian Sea, through the Caucasus and the Middle East, into Europe and Eastern Africa. This new Silk Road, or the "One Belt, One Road" (OBOR) as it was named by Beijing officials, was one of President Xi Jinping's flagship projects. It was designed to economically integrate regions that were east of China with the objective to provide the country with new markets to Chinese excess production capacities.

Her firm was not strategizing in a political vacuum as a result. And yet, the region that the OBOR initiative affected covered a very wide range of political, economic, and social realities. She could count at least ten geographical entities of interest:

1. China	6. The Middle East
2. South East Asia	7. Turkey in particular
3. India	8. East Africa
4. Russia	9. Eastern Europe
5. The Caucasus	10. Western Europe

Her team would need expertise in each of these regions in order to ascertain the relevant trends in this extremely diverse set of countries and economies. But would that be enough? Though the United States was still off bounds for her company, Yu Yan knew that any decisions in Washington D.C. were bound to shape the regulatory dimension of the global business environment, at the very least. As the popular saying reminded her, a flap of a butterfly's wing in D.C. could set off a tornado in Asia. In particular, she expected that any economic slowdown in the United States would affect the rest of the planet.

A Thematic Approach

In addition, there were key, overarching issues that transcended any regional consideration. The most obvious one on her mind was automation and the effects the process would have on consumer behavior, on her firm's organization and, more generally, on mobility. A second transformation that was on her mind was 3D printing: would this transform global trade and retail, by triggering a shift away from goods to 3D blueprints?

Needless to say, Yu Yan knew there were plenty of other issues over the horizon, but that it would be impossible to make an exhaustive list at this point. It was certainly worth thinking about how she and her team could update that list over time. Another open question struck her: instead of thinking where to put the emphasis, on regions or on themes, could her team not focus on how the first would interact with the second?

In any case, it was clear to her that she and her team were unlikely to get everything right on the first try. What mattered most was to have enough intellectual flexibility to adjust over time and to revisit their positions so as to redefine their assumptions and the indicators they were monitoring. Preserving a margin of error was essential in the first few months at least.

What to Look for

The second challenge lay in deciding the format of the final output she and her team would deliver to the rest of the company.

Scenarios Are Unavoidable ... or so Everyone Seems to Think

One expectation seemed quite natural to her fellow members: her team would be in a position to provide the company with a set of scenarios that would help the company and all its business units plan ahead. With all the expertise she had been able to put together, she felt her team had the means to put these together. The challenge would probably lie in making them accessible and operational enough to provide all business units with meaningful food for thought on how to act on them. This would likely require different sets of presentations for different types of actors within the firm.

But would she have enough influence and clout to make sure that they were properly interpreted and used throughout the company? And would delivering a set of scenarios, along with some food for thought on their implications for the firm really be the impactful outcome she was looking for? She did not care much for the hackneyed expression of "thinking out of the box"; yet one had to recognize that scenarios did offer a "box" that may prove difficult to distance yourself from once they were put on paper—and looked as if they were engraved in stone. As a result, thought Yu Yan, this final output needed to be provocative and be an invitation to think, rather than a way to force feed the analysis of her team to the rest of the firm.

Identifying or Breaking the Consensus?

In particular, it seemed a natural reflex for people looking at a set of scenarios to seek what the global consensus was saying, what everybody agreed upon. This phenomenon was particularly striking in the realm of finance in which the market consensus was about looking at the average of estimates provided by analysts and considering it as the most likely truth. After all, was that not the best we could do in terms of anticipation? If surprises did happen, were they not by definition unpredictable?

Yu Yan could not help but think that this view was excessively simplistic for two reasons.

First, in some cases, there was no consensus. In those cases, the nature of the disagreements was as informative, if not more, about the state of the world and the open questions that remained unsolved—and that could therefore be the sources of surprise for some active players down the line. Representing those disagreements, or even the variance around a single consensus, could be critically useful to show the range of possibilities beyond a single expectation.

The Human Risk

In addition, was the future exclusively driven by mega-forces? And was the ability of some players (institutions or individuals) with hidden agendas to weigh in on final outcomes really impossible to anticipate?

As two fellow political scientists from America had put it quite eloquently once, "political risks are generated by individuals, people with particular and identifiable sets of motivations and limitations. This makes them predictable—and not black swans."[1] More generally, every individual had incentives; and, at times, some had the ability to punch above their weight for a limited amount of time, because of sheer coincidence or because of clever maneuvering on their part. Either way, it was important to identify these temporary power players and think about how the firm could make them allies. But how did you identify them?

She was particularly struck by the results of what was now called "red team analysis": When a set of members of her team, or within the company, played the role of devil's advocate, the overall conclusions of her team's analysis became increasingly robust. As one author put it,

> red teaming is a structured process that seeks to better understand the interests, intentions, and capabilities of an institution—or a potential competitor—through simulations, vulnerability probes, and alternative analyses. Though red teaming has subsequently been adopted in a wide range of fields and tailored to various needs, it remains woefully underexplored and severely underutilized by corporate boardrooms, military commands, cyber-security firms, and countless other institutions that find themselves facing threats, complex decisions, and strategic surprises. By employing a red team, institutions can get a fresh and alternative perspective on how they do things. It can help them reveal and test unstated assumptions, identify blind spots, and potentially improve their performance.[2]

In fact, it was not only about the mega-forces shaping the landscape. It was also about identifying the key incentives of individual people or organizations, among the firm's stakeholders or competitors, that could have a vested interest in shaping the world of the company. It was about having enough tact to understand how people see themselves and the business environment they find themselves in. For instance, would the Chinese government react well to the firm's stated ambitions for the next five years? If Yu Yan adopted the viewpoint of the government and looked at the world with its incentives and objectives, would the firm's ambitions collide with its intentions, or to the contrary, would they be complementary? If there was the risk of a collision, could Yu Yan's firm mitigate them in any way by acting proactively? It occurred to Yu Yan that she could undertake this effort with a wide range of public and private actors to stress-test her approach, beyond measuring the relevance of her company's strategy against the scenarios her team anticipated.

Ultimately, identifying those potential power players would play a key success in the ability of the firm to keep an eye on influencers and power players that could become the greatest allies or the biggest foes the firm would need to deal with. This approach seemed the most meaningful to be an actor of change, rather than just adopt a "wait-and-see" attitude and remain a passive player in a chaotic landscape.

Time to Get Geared Up, Architects of Change

Yu Yan's mentor had once observed that it was pretty easy to build a network, but far harder to maintain it over time. She felt that this effort set a similar dilemma: it was not very hard to put together an analysis of the future; the ultimate challenge lay in making the effort durable. In fact, Yu Yan thought, this effort needed to be institutionalized to the extent that it was engraved in the company's culture, making it a natural, not an extraordinary, exercise. Analyzing the future so as to consider what it meant for the strategy of the firm needed to become part of this company's bloodstream. How could she get the analysis of her team to be absorbed horizontally and vertically in the elaboration of the firm's strategy? As it has been pointed out before, and as Yu Yan asks herself this question, it occurs to her that being an architect of change is as much a mindset as being an action-driven character. One is not an architect of change on a one-shot basis but on a full-time basis.

Reaching the objective of getting her team's analysis to be absorbed horizontally and vertically in the elaboration of the firm's strategy would undoubtedly be the result of a very long-term effort within the business anyway. Yu Yan knew that she needed to network within the company, not only to make the benefits of her analysis known but also to better understand what the men and women on the ground actually needed in terms of information in order to do their jobs better. It was not enough for the analysis to be "good"; it needed to be actionable and easy to understand in a very short time span. Those were the challenges she needed to solve. Her ability, like that of all architects of change, to show empathy in this complex process, was key.

In the longer run, Yu Yan also wondered about the network of experts she could put together to better serve her colleagues. The need for regional and technical expertise was clear to her at the onset of the project. But what other profiles would help her achieve her goals? It seemed as if people with imagination and curiosity, like novelists and philosophers, could also enlighten her on the trends that were shaping the world under our very eyes, but that we may not be paying attention to, because we are so obsessed with the flames of the day. This effort was not only about changing the culture of the company; it was also about changing her mindset to broaden horizons. Because ultimately,

Yu Yan knew, an architect of change does not know it all but certainly knows a wide range of people that are collectively quite knowledgeable about a wide range of questions.

Justin Vaïsse is the former director of Policy Planning at the French Ministry of Foreign Affairs and a former senior fellow in Foreign Policy at the Brookings Institution. Understanding how the world and the global environment were evolving was his business. In this testimonial, he shares his experience.

You were the director of Policy Planning at the French Ministry of Foreign Affairs for six years. What does it take to anticipate global trends effectively?

First a good dose of humility. If you don't have it naturally, it comes with age once you've gotten a few trends wrong. But if you are a historian, you already know that life is made up of both necessity and contingency. For this reason, there is just no effective way to predict the future, and no method guarantees success. Some well-known tools or recipes are useful, however, including the scenario method, the Delphi method, historical analogy, predictive markets, or the use of big data. I also think that theory helps in many cases, especially in international relations, although with limits. At the end of the day, what works is intuition, keeping an open mind, and listening to many different parties.

What are the most salient trends that you observed during your tenure?

There are the ones we call "systemic," having to do with the international system itself. In the past 20 years, the repartition of power has started shifting away from the United States and the West and towards emerging countries, especially China. This evolution towards multipolarity has had profound implications for relations among great powers, multilateral institutions and global governance. In the Middle East for example, America's retreat has created a vacuum of power and the turbulent rise of new actors to fill the void. But global social change has also been an important factor, especially the reaction to globalization and rising inequalities, with nationalism and populism staging a comeback in various forms.

What were the biggest strategic surprises?

There were the ones created by single actors having maximum agency, like terrorists and strongmen. For example, we were often blindsided by Vladimir Putin, because, thanks to his dominant position in the Russian political system, he could decide single-handedly to grab a territory from a neighboring country, with no warning signs, only very weak signals. Terrorist attacks are also impossible to predict and can have high impact.

Notes

1. Ian Bremmer and Preston Keat, *The Fat Tail: The Power of Political Knowledge in an Uncertain World*, Reprint edition (Oxford ; New York: Oxford University Press, 2010).
2. Micah Zenko, *Red Team: How to Succeed By Thinking Like the Enemy* (Basic Books, 2015).

11

The Purpose of Imagination

Imagination may strike us as in complete contradiction with analysis and the need for pragmatism when doing business. And yet, it is an activity that occupies a significant chunk of our life—and it may be the ultimate solution to a chaotic landscape. This chapter explains why.

There is arguably a lot to learn from available information from the past, from what we know and from what we see. In fact, through analysis and careful consideration of the information we have at hand, there are truths to uncover and realities to shed light on—in particular because these truths and realities are triggered by well-identified causes, making the causal link clear. Not everything is chaotic and unpredictable in this business environment, in other words, and the search for the exact causal link should be what analysts seek to establish as precisely as possible in order to help their organizations adapt to the evolutions and the pressures of the business environment. Chief examples include demography, a science that is able to measure how fast a population is growing or ageing with precision, or meteorology, which is able to predict the weather (as opposed to the climate) in the short and medium run.

But the very existence of chaos and uncertainty in the landscape also mean that in many other areas causal links are not *absent* but are so complex that our human brains are ill-equipped to process them appropriately: there are so many different actors and stakeholders, as well as drivers of change, that the past, the known, and the observable will not be of great help in any effort to uncover complex causal links. Our experience may, at times, make it even harder for us to uncover those causal links because they lead us to generalize lessons that

J. Ghez, *Architects of Change*, https://doi.org/10.1007/978-3-030-20684-0_11

may not hold true in the future; they may point to patterns that may not reappear tomorrow; they may not shed light on other phenomena that are not manifesting themselves yet but that could matter more than we know; they may overshadow, ultimately, the pieces of information that will be truly decisive in tomorrow's landscape.[1]

In addition, our experience, our information, and our knowledge of the world around us may overshadow the visions of other stakeholders that have a vested interest in shaping outcomes. What is more, if we surround ourselves with people who think exactly like us, we may profoundly fail in our effort to grasp the complexity of the business environment and the diversity of individual or group incentives shaping it. In particular, it will be harder for us to understand how the world looks to others because we will not have the means to actually imagine that. From this comes one of the critical benefits of diversity and empathy. Imagination comes with that ability to admit that it will be hard for any one individual to fully grasp all of the facets of the business environment, and that prospects and conclusions about the world may vary greatly across actors.

As a result, imagination may become one of the most critical tools for those looking to make a difference by helping them to avoid relying excessively on easily accessible information and, thus, to consider what might not be on our collective radar screens. The popular expression "uncharted waters" takes a whole new meaning in this logic: imagination is the tool to explore places that no one has ever explored before; it the best ally to conceive a world that is not necessarily our world but one that could result from our collective intelligence (or stupidity), our collective movements (or inaction) and our collective aspirations, in a way we may not be able to anticipate if we do not drop our current assumptions about the world. Imagination helps us explore what we do not know, beyond our traditional zone of comfort. It helps us generate new ideas, or, said differently, different variations of current realities in order to enable us to select those that are likely to make us stronger down the line.

Imagination, in a nutshell, may be the ultimate tool to face global uncertainty. This chapter explores how, in practice. It opens up with a discussion of the meaning of uncertainty. It then explores what uncertainty demands from us, in particular by putting the emphasis on the differences between flexibility and resilience. It concludes with implications for would-be actors of change who, if they ever lack imagination, might experience difficulties adapting to a chaotic and turbulent world. That is what may distinguish them from true architects of change ultimately.

Defining Uncertainty

The definition of uncertainty is not as straightforward as intuition would suggest. In fact, the word increasingly seems hackneyed because the viewpoint that the world is uncertain may be widely shared, but such statement is neither informative about the actual state of the business environment, nor is it very telling of the implications this has for actors looking to bring about transformative change. Unpacking the concept may help.

A (Very Brief) Historical Perspective

Humanity's struggle with uncertainty is not new. In the realm of business and broader human interactions in particular, there are traces of insurance mechanisms that date back to Ancient times, when the development of economic activity and trade required people to hedge against the hazards of everyday life.

What We Do Not Control

This struggle took on a whole new dimension though when economic activity and trade expanded significantly with the beginning of the industrial revolution in Western Europe, as early as the seventeenth century.

What is striking is that it is at that time that French mathematician and philosopher Blaise Pascal develops his argument, known as Pascal's wager, about the existence of God: it is rational to bet on the existence of God because if you do not and lose that bet, your losses are likely to be infinite; but if you do make that bet and lose, your losses, defined by the less than recommendable activities you engage in on earth, are finite. Hedging against uncertainty was not just about protecting your tangible assets; it was also about protecting yourself against far greater losses that went beyond earthly matters.

This explains why our relationship to uncertainty is a true struggle: it is about our inability as individuals to fully control every factor that will ultimately shape our future prospects.

The Modern Distinction

American economist Frank Knight's seminal work on uncertainty has produced a well-accepted modern definition of the concept. In a 1921 book, the economist offered a distinction between risk and uncertainty.[2]

In Knightian terms, risk is quantifiable: we may regard one particular situation as "uncertain" when there is a known risk; but the outcome of that single situation is actually predictable "in accordance with the laws of chance," because we know, or we can estimate the likelihood of any possible outcome. We may make mistakes in those predictions, but the prediction error becomes negligible, or even nonexistent, when we do not consider one single situation but many—that is, when the number of cases increases significantly. This process is at the heart of diversification in the insurance industry which is able to hedge against any particular individual risk by combining a wide range of cases whose outcomes it can predict on average, especially relying on existing data.

By opposition, uncertainty is not measurable because there is no objective probability distribution to rely on: whereas risk is what you face playing the roulette or rolling the dice, games in which you know before the fact the likelihood that you may win upon placing a bet, uncertainty is what you face when you play poker, a game in which likelihoods are far more complex and in which there is far more room for gambling and bluff. More generally, the possibility of extreme scenarios, beyond what was a priori probable, means that we may not always be able to fully understand the nature of the best we are making before the fact: in the case of uncertainty, we do not know what the likelihood distribution looks like because there is no existing data. This is perhaps because the industry we are studying is profoundly changing and we lack perspective, or perhaps because the interactions we are considering are so complex that it may be difficult for us to fully understand the nature of causal links and therefore correctly anticipate outcomes.

A Complex Reality

The distinction between risk and uncertainty is crucial, in particular because the two concepts do not have the same operational implications for actors looking to trigger change in their business environment: while risk will require agility to deal with prediction errors, uncertainty will demand resilience and imagination to deal with the unknown. Current debates about strategies and policymaking in a turbulent environment shed light on these implications.

Former US Defense Secretary Donald Rumsfeld famously observed that:

> There are known knowns; there are things we know we know. We also know there are known unknowns; that is to say we know there are some things we do not know. But there are also unknown unknowns—the ones we don't know we

> don't know. And if one looks throughout the history of our country and other free countries, it is the latter category that tend to be the difficult ones.

What is striking about this observation of a controversial US political figure is that it captures in just a few words all the complexity of the concept of uncertainty, what it means and what it does not mean, and, even more significantly, what it may require from all actors looking to bring change to their environment.

The Past, the Known, and the Seen

In fact, consider Rumsfeld's classification. First come the known knowns or the "things we know we know," that is, the facts of the business environment that we can draw from analysis and research. We certainly know who the president of the United States is; we know the agenda of the next European Summit; and we may not know by heart the current price of a barrel of oil, but we certainly have the tools to learn that piece of information in a quasi-instantaneous way. Statements about the need to maintain a good grasp on these facts may sound as straightforward as they may seem trivial; yet, as discussed in Chap. 7, in the age of ideological polarization and dogma, one should not underestimate the power of analysis.

Next come the known unknowns, that is, the variables or the open questions. As complex as the business environment might look at a first glance, there are still a wide range of questions that we can *formulate*. In particular, we may wonder who the next president of the United States might be; we may ask what political priorities the European Union may have tomorrow if its frontiers ever change; and we may develop sophisticated econometric models (or rely on those others developed) to consider the possible price of a barrel of oil tomorrow. These "known unknowns" represent all of the moving pieces that are on our radar screen and that we need to monitor over time.

In both of the cases, "known knowns" and "known unknowns," we are dealing with risk, to use Frank Knight's terminology, to the extent that we can quantify what we know and do not know. Put differently, there is no real difficulty to define a question in the case of "known knowns" and "known unknowns" because we have the historical perspective and the data to formulate expectations about what is or what may be tomorrow. Furthermore, the implications of risk should be clear: the existence of risk means that the business environment will evolve over time as facts and variables change, and, with this evolution will come new opportunities or new sources of pressure that will lead us to change and to adapt. These processes are what you can expect in a very linear world, requiring you to remain as *flexible* as possible in order to adapt.

The Real Uncertainty

There are, finally, the unknown unknowns, in Rumsfeld's classification—the things "we don't know we don't know"—and this additional comment, which many pundits seem to forget about when quoting the former US Defense Secretary: historically speaking, these events are usually the hardest ones to deal with. This is particularly true because they are hard to define in specific terms by essence—because if we could, they would not be unknown to us. Some analysts have called these events "black swans," considering that they are random events whose a priori likelihood is quite low, but once they materialize, are highly influential and transformational. Their significance is therefore appreciated only *after* the fact. They are hard to deal with because economies and societies usually react to them rather than proactively develop a cure to mitigate them or avoid them all together.

They are therefore particularly common in a business environment in which actors ignore all together the existence of uncertainty—the way it was defined by Knight. In this case, in fact, we cannot rely on existing data, because there is none and, perhaps more importantly, because we would not know where to look for it: unlike the case of risk, in that of uncertainty, we cannot even formulate a question given our lack of understanding of the phenomenon at stake. The implications of uncertainty should also be very clear: uncertainty means that there will necessarily be unforeseen disruptions in the business environment that will force actors to transform the way they approach issues or do business. Some of these transformations may be successful while others will fail. But all these transformations are needed to generate new ideas and insights on possible variations of existing realities, so as to help organizations, activities, and people evolve over time in a very chaotic world. That world requires a lot of *resilience* as a result.

Flexibility and Resilience

The life of architects of change is unlikely to be an easy one, in particular because transforming the business environment means bringing themselves and their activity in a setting that is, by essence, unknown. Adjusting will be critical to deal with the traditional hazards of life, but it may not be enough to face the events that go *beyond* those traditional hazards.

Flexibility Is Never Infinite

The effects of risk and uncertainty on an individual or an organization in a turbulent business environment are akin to what happens to a rubber band when you pull on it. You can pull on it repeatedly and the rubber band is likely to get back to its original shape because it is elastic.

Similarly, the stress of a turbulent business environment on individuals or organizations is likely to have limited effects on more agile actors that are able to adjust. Therefore, risk requires you to be conscious of the multiple trajectories that can occur in the future. This is why it demands flexibility, both physically and intellectually speaking: because it is crucial to maintain an ability to adjust by both being able to reallocate your resources on the ground accordingly and to keep an open mind about what the future may hold, by avoiding to focus on a specific trajectory that fits your plans more than others.

Failing to avoid that temptation will make the effects of those stresses that a turbulent business environment induces all the more so greater—in particular because the differences between expectations and realities will be so great. This reasoning is at the heart of hedging strategies, designed to dodge the expectable risks that you may encounter along the way.

When the Rubber Band Breaks

Yet, if you pull this elastic a very significant number of times, or worse, if you pull too hard, the rubber band may break—and it will hurt your fingers. Likewise, if the stress induced by a turbulent business environment becomes too significant, the tensions a firm or an individual will need to face may require more than mere adjustments: if they transform the business environment in a way that is unforeseen and/or unprecedented, past strategies and approaches are likely to be moot. This is particularly true when trajectories land you in a place that you did not anticipate, leading to a set of existential questions for you and your organization. Firms and individuals may face existential crises if they prove unable to reinvent accordingly, that is, if they lack imagination and fail to explore the so-called uncharted waters.

Donald Rumsfeld's classification is important because it unpacks the concept of uncertainty and reminds us of the effort we need to undertake to face the different realities of the concept: in particular, while the first two challenges of known knowns and known unknowns require analysis and flexibility, the possibility that unknown unknowns will rock our boat reminds us that being agile may never be enough when the amount of stress our activity faces in a turbulent business environment is too big. In fact, this possibility requires resilience and enough imagination to completely rethink who we are and what we stand for, as well as transform the way we do business so as to better adapt to this new environment—a critical set of abilities of those players who will want to survive an existential battle to fight another day.

The Meaning of Bouncing Back

Resilience was initially a concept in physics, "the capability of a strained body to recover its size and shape after deformation caused especially by compressive stress," according to the Merriam-Webster dictionary. Psychology relies on the concept to describe the ability of a person to bounce back after a significant misfortune or a devastating loss, like an unhappy childhood or a tragic past event for instance.

In more recent years, social sciences have relied on resilience to describe the ability of an economy or a political system to withstand shock, that is, the time it takes for it to resume proper functioning after a crisis. In particular, an organization that has the ability to rebound and fight another day once a catastrophic or game-changing event has occurred can reinvent itself by redefining what it stands for in the new landscape. In this sense, resilience is accepting that the previous cause and effect paradigm that an activity or a strategy was based on has failed and that a new one needs to be rebuilt. It is arguably the most radical form of creative destruction discussed in Chap. 5, as a form of continuous redefinition of your activity and of your purpose in a turbulent business environment. In fact, Schumpeter's vision of entrepreneurs is those individuals who creatively destroy and who do not wait for groundbreaking events to happen; instead, they look to generate them themselves. This makes them far less vulnerable to fundamental changes in the landscape—and far more resilient as a result.

This social science definition of resilience is not as straightforward as it seems though. In particular, it sets the question of the potential difference between "resilient" and "elastic." A 2010 controversy regarding what Barack Obama actually meant to say about the state of US-Turkish relations illustrates how significant this difference can be: seeking to reassure Turkish public opinion and authorities about America's commitment to its relationship with

Turkey, the then US president said that the partnership between the two countries was "resilient." The Turkish daily newspaper *Hürriyet* that interviewed Barack Obama translated resilient as "elastic" into Turkish. But as another now-defunct Turkish daily, *Today's Zaman*, observed, elastic means being able to go back to one's original shape after being stretched, deformed, or expanded—whereas Barack Obama was referring to the strength of the relationship, who "could be expanding the horizons of the partnership each day rather than returning to its previous shape after each crisis,"[3] argued the newspaper. Bouncing back, in other terms, does not necessarily mean elastic, that is, returning to your previous shape after each crisis and carrying on, business as usual. Instead, it means the ability to reimagine what you stand for in order to be able to carry on while not fearing similar crises anymore.

This discussion over the actual meaning of resilience is therefore not trivial because it affects the way we think about what an individual, an activity, or even a system needs in terms of features and ability in order to carry on, in spite of game-changing events. Lebanese-American scholar Nassim Nicholas Taleb argues that in fact, resilience and robustness may not be enough in the long run in the world of random events, given that

> in the long run everything with the most minute vulnerability breaks, given the ruthlessness of time—yet our planet has been around for perhaps four billion years and, convincingly, robustness can't just be it: you need perfect robustness for a crack not to end up crashing the system. Given the unattainability of perfect robustness, we need a mechanism by which the system regenerates itself continuously by using, rather than suffering from, random events, unpredictable shocks, stressors, and volatility.[4]

Resilience, in other words, means unaffected by a crisis, whereas what is required to bring transformative change is the ability to feed oneself off of global chaos. This property is what Taleb calls "antifragility," or the ability to see shocks as a source of information that was previously unknown and as an opportunity to reinvent oneself or a system in consequence. Adjustment is not just incremental or meant to let the system function *as it did* but to draw the lessons of the crisis in a way that modifies the way it actually operates.

Taleb's argument in favor of a concept that goes beyond resilience or robustness because we cannot just be resistant to shocks, we also need to feed off of them to improve, is an additional reminder that flexibility (or elasticity) is never infinite. But independent of the word we choose to characterize this property, it is ultimately the human ability to imagine that helps us bounce back: when the current system is broken and past recipes fail to work, there is no real alternative than to rethink and reinvent the system as a whole without yesterday's assumptions that have been proven wrong.

Living Like an Architect of Change

This discussion on resilience gives the notion of "reinvention" a whole new flavor as a result, in particular by enlightening us on the purpose of imagination: it is this ability to envision a new model, a new paradigm that makes us more fit to survive in a transformed landscape, so as to be able to fight another day, stronger. In practice, lack of resilience may result from the fact that collectively, we lack imagination about our business environment and about the future. If we showed more imagination, the propensity of the business environment to surprise us and catch us off guard may be far smaller—and our ability to seek a beneficial radical option, that is, one that helps us maintain a definite edge, would be stronger.

Resilience is no substitute for flexibility; instead, it is a close cousin. The challenge lies in understanding what in your landscape relates to known unknowns and to risk on the one hand, and what relates to unknown unknowns and to uncertainty on the other hand. In fact, not everything in the business environment is complex and unpredictable: when causal links are identifiable (like in the examples of demography and meteorology discussed above), we can formulate some reasonable expectations about outcomes. In those cases, flexibility is enough to withstand small variances compared to what you expected: the environment changes at the margin, and you adapt accordingly by responding to those pressures and those incentives coming from the outside. But, because this is a business environment full of surprises and disruptive moments, bluff, gambles, and extreme scenarios are likely to rock the boats of those who are ill-prepared to think beyond the traditional hazards of life and who exclusively rely on extrapolation and anticipation. Turbulence in the business environment means that we cannot always identify a clear causal link, making any anticipation exercise quite difficult—if not useless. Mere adaption is insufficient in those cases that require more profound evolutions as we enter truly uncharted waters.

As Taleb and American professor Mark Blyth once eloquently observed,

> Humans simultaneously inhabit two systems: the linear and the complex. The linear domain is characterized by its predictability and the low degree of interaction among its components, which allows the use of mathematical methods that make forecasts reliable. In complex systems, there is an absence of visible causal links between the elements, masking a high degree of interdependence and extremely low predictability.[5]

Architects of change (like everyone else) live in two worlds at once. What makes them different is their ability to understand what is linear and what is complex, and leverage and surf on the first, while keeping in mind the second as an incentive to constantly conceive (rather than merely anticipate naïvely) what comes next. Ultimately, the purpose of imagination is to develop the ability to live in a world in which uncertainty exists. It may not be a coincidence if imagination occupies such a big chunk of our daily routine: it may be the best solution nature has found to help us survive.

Joel Barbier is the Director of Thought Leadership at Cisco. In this capacity, he has worked extensively on the changing business and technological environment of firms and the transformations that this will entail down the line. These transformations may feel like a "tornado" to those actors that are unprepared—or, in other words, like the chaotic world that the previous chapter described. This is an important testimonial that provides hints to the disruptions one could expect in the future and the coming showdown between incumbents and disruptors. It serves as a powerful illustration of uncertainty in a digitalized world and the usefulness of imagination in this context.

What is the Digital Vortex?

The Digital Vortex is the market context of disruption, characterized by an irresistible force that pulls all organizations toward a point where "everything that can be digitized is digitized."[6]

As we researched digital disruption, its potential to reshape competition and markets faster than ever before became evident. Our team looked for a simple metaphor that could summarize many months of research. The image of a vortex, the physical phenomenon involved in a tornado, was helpful to describe what was happening across industries. Digital disruption, like a vortex, is the inevitable movement of industries toward a "digital center" in which offerings, business models, and value chains become digitized, and where physical components that inhibit competitive advantage (such as legacy investments, physical infrastructures, and manual processes) are shed...

The threat is spreading fast. New rivals are attacking incumbents' value chains, gaining market share, eroding margins, and changing the competitive landscape in every industry. Even those that seemed unlikely to be affected by technologies, such as taxis and hotels, were disrupted quickly by the likes of Uber and Airbnb .... Disruptive companies like Tencent and Amazon are using digital capabilities to quickly cross industry boundaries, blurring traditional delineations between value chains.

Industries expecting to experience the most disruption over the next five years have one thing in common: their offers, products or services, can be digitized. Media and entertainment, technology products and services, and retail, in particular, are the three most disrupted industries. They are already experiencing dramatic market share shifts, a high intensity of venture capital investment, and waves of incumbent consolidation and bankruptcies. Other industries less immediately affected are at the periphery. However, all are at risk, as the digital vortex keeps churning, and organizations must perpetually reimagine their business and operating models.

Based on the research we conducted for Digital Vortex, we recommended that incumbents emulate key capabilities in their disruptive competitors—in particular, their ability to create customer value and their level of operational agility.

How will it shape tomorrow's business environment?

For insights into how the competitive environment is evolving, an understanding of how digital disruptors are impacting companies, both inside and outside their own industries, is the first step. With the help of digital technologies, disruptors are changing the way they create, deliver, and capture value. Research from the Global Center for Digital Business Transformation (DBT) revealed that nearly four in ten incumbents will be displaced by disruptive competitors in the next five years. To address this threat, companies must rethink how they provide value to customers. They can do this by emulating specific capabilities of today's most effective disruptors. Those disruptors are harnessing 15 business model innovations, to create three main forms of customer value: cost value, experience value, and platform value (Table 11.1).

Table 11.1 Fifteen digital business models create three forms of value

Cost value	Experience value	Platform value
Free/ultra-low cost	Customer empowerment	Ecosystem
Buyer aggregation	Customization	Crowdsourcing
Price transparency	Instant gratification	Communities
Reverse auctions	Reduced friction	Digital marketplaces
Consumption-based pricing	Automation	Data orchestrator

Source: Global Center for Digital Business Transformation, 2015–2017

Disruptors create cost and experience value for customers by offering products and services at very low cost, or by placing a premium on customer experience: unbundling incumbents' offerings and empowering customers to select and pay only for what they need; tailoring experiences to their unique preferences; delivering goods and services in real time; and automating processes using analytics and low-cost labor. Disruptors also create value by providing a conducive environment in which users can create value for themselves and others. Platforms are the new value-creation model of the digital economy. Platform-based business models have fundamentally changed how companies can do business. Disruptors create ecosystems that enable platforms to scale in ways that traditional businesses cannot. Providing scalability to bring millions of users onboard quickly through positive network effects results in significant value for users. Platforms are also disrupting the traditional competitive landscape by removing inefficiencies and unlocking new sources of value. By creating digital marketplaces, platforms facilitate the exchange of goods and services or fulfill social needs by removing intermediates, gatekeepers, or any other kind of barrier.

The most successful disruptors *combine all three* kinds of business models to create value for their customers—an approach that is, by its very nature, disruptive, and which we have dubbed "combinatorial disruption." Disruptors also depart sharply from incumbents, not just in their business models but in the organizational elements that enable business models—that is, a company's "operating model." Disruptors are not encumbered by the limitations of traditional value chains. As a result, disruptors are "unbundling" entire industries, carving off incumbents' most profitable business segments in the process. This is happening in banking, for example, where hundreds of startups (called "Fintechs") are reinventing loans, mortgages, payments, wealth management, and more. They provide their services without physical branches and financial advisors, which lowers their distribution costs and eliminates middlemen and high-touch service models.

A subset of digital disruptors, "value vampires," blends compelling forms of cost value with experience value and platform value to undercut incumbents and quickly win significant market share. Simply put, a value vampire is a company whose competitive advantage shrinks a market's overall revenue or profit pool (or both).

For incumbents, however, digital disruption is not all bad news. In fact, as industries move toward the center of the Digital Vortex, meaning where digitization and disruption are most intense, another scenario may arise: the possibility of capitalizing on "value vacancies." A value vacancy is a market opportunity that can be profitably exploited via digital disruption. Companies can enjoy a period of fast growth, high margins, and a privileged market position, but these are increasingly short-lived. Established competitors from other industries, start-ups, and value vampires soon intrude. To maintain growth, companies must find and exploit a succession of value vacancies. Apple provides a prime example of how to capitalize on value vacancies. The company successfully moved into a value vacancy in digital music distribution because it satisfied a market need that music labels and retailers had an interest in not meeting.

What type of people and organizations are most likely to succeed in that business environment?

At its most basic, digital disruption occurs because disruptors adapt quickly to changing conditions and develop innovations in a better and faster way, creating or enhancing customer value. What are the strengths of disruptors? Which organizational capabilities do they have that most incumbents do not? The DBT Center's research reveals that to defend their businesses from disruption and exploit new opportunities to create customer value, incumbents must develop an organizational competency we refer to as "digital business agility."

Digital business agility can be summarized in three attributes: hyperawareness, informed decision-making, and fast execution.

- **Hyperawareness** is a company's ability to use technology to sense key changes taking place in its environment. It includes collecting and integrating information from customers, partners, and employees (behavioral awareness), along with sensing changes in the operating environment and keeping abreast of technological and competitive changes (situational awareness).
- **Informed decision-making** is the ability to transform information collected during the hyperawareness sensing phase into actionable insights using advanced analytics (augmented decision-making) and employees' expertise, irrespective of their role and location (inclusive decision-making).
- **Fast execution** is the ability to implement the decisions taken during the previous phase effectively, and in a timely manner. This involves rapid acquisition, management, and deployment of human, financial, and technological resources to meet emerging business needs (dynamic resources), along with creation of new organizational capabilities and adjustment of day-to-day operations in real time to capture value (dynamic processes).

While implementing these capabilities is good business practice for any organization, disruptors are deploying them at a scale and maturity level that sets them apart.

Redefining Competitive Advantage

As companies determine how to transform, they must consider how to create (1) new value for customers (cost, experience, and platform value), and (2) how to develop the capabilities to compete (hyperawareness, informed decision-making, and fast execution). Our research tells us that the ability to combine multiple business models with organizational agility creates the largest value for customers. It is the key to competing in the Digital Vortex.

We define competitiveness as the advantages companies acquire to create more recognizable customer value and preference than their rivals, to grow faster, and to deliver products and services more rapidly and efficiently—ultimately generating more profits and sustaining that profitability over time. Until the digital era, leading management thinkers held that there were two principal ways to achieve sustained competitive advantage:[7] through greater efficiency and scale, offering lower-cost options for buyers, generally with higher sales volumes; or by providing premium features that command a higher price—that is, through differentiation. For instance, in the automotive industry, the most profitable companies are Toyota (again, low cost with high volume) and Porsche (premium vehicles, high-quality experience).[8]

Our analysis of disruptive startups, however, contradicts this broadly accepted principle. Disruptors using platform value to gain competitive advantage, for example, are also capable of offering lower prices than their competition and of providing a differentiated experience. This is the essence and power of combinatorial disruption. Whether it is Netflix or Amazon, Uber or Apple, these companies compete through better prices, a broader choice of products or services, greater convenience and flexibility, and technology that allows them to match supply and demand and to expand globally at unprecedented speed and scale.

From understanding disruption to leading transformation

While *Digital Vortex: How Today's Market Leaders Can Beat Disruptive Competitors at Their Own Game*, explored the "why" and "what" of digital business transformation in depth, it did not focus on "how" organizations should conduct a transformation. The research focused mainly on the changes technology and business model innovation is bringing to the nature of competition among firms. Today, digital business transformation has become a pressing imperative for large and mid-size firms. This is the raison d'etre for a second book, *Orchestrating Transformation: How to Deliver Winning Performance with a Connected Approach to Change*.

Over the past few years, through thousands of conversations with business leaders, new questions arose: *How to transform? Where should we begin? What are best practices and approaches we can follow? What is success and how do you measure it?* This new book offers a practitioner's perspective for leaders driving digital business transformation—ambitious strategic changes beyond the scope of individual functions or incremental organizational improvements. Research shows that the vast majority of transformation initiatives fail to deliver their expected benefits, and that executives misunderstand what digital transformation is about. This is causing billions in unnecessary costs and hindering organizations' readiness to compete.

Many organizations consider transformation as an episodic, one-time effort, very much like the change initiatives required by ERP deployments or Y2K bug fixes, as if they could metamorphose like butterflies. This conception of change is in fact an obstacle to grasp the nature of innovation and change, and what makes these programs successful ... *Transformation is not an event; it's an essential and perpetual task of leadership.*[9] The survey conducted by the DBT Center in 2018 shows that business model innovation—new ways to create, deliver, and monetize value for an organization's customers—is accelerating, from a phenomenon taking place every few generations to every one to five years.

Few leaders also recognize the *connected nature of change*. Too often, they underestimate the complexity and *entanglement* of their operations—the interdependence, dynamic nature, and scale of the organization's elements. Piecemeal strategies and pilot projects are hopelessly inadequate to address the intricacies of most companies.

Transformation practitioners need a different mindset, a new approach, and a set of execution competencies and tools to succeed. With a more holistic, connected approach, leaders can recognize the challenge of connectedness, and harness it to their advantage. *Orchestration—"mobilizing and enabling so as to achieve a desired effect"*—provides this new view of organizational resources and how they work together to drive change synergistically.

Notes

1. This is an argument omnipresent in Nassim Nicholas Taleb, *The Black Swan: The Impact of the Highly Improbable*, 1 edition (New York: Random House, 2007).
2. Frank Knight, *Risk, Uncertainty and Profit* (Chicago, IL: University of Chicago Press, 1921).
3. "Despite Challenges, US Ties Prove to Be Resilient in 2010," *Today's Zaman*, December 25, 2010.
4. Nassim Nicholas Taleb, *Antifragile: Things That Gain from Disorder* (Random House, 2012), https://www.amazon.com/Antifragile-Things-That-Disorder-Incerto/dp/1400067820/ref=sr_1_1?crid=16W3XT1K91FBD&keywords=antifragile+by+nassim+taleb&qid=1555080290&s=gateway&sprefix=antifragile%2Caps%2C191&sr=8-1.
5. Nassim Nicholas Taleb and Mark Blyth, "The Black Swan of Cairo," *Foreign Affairs*, May 2011, https://www.foreignaffairs.com/articles/egypt/2011-04-15/black-swan-cairo.
6. Source: *Orchestrating Transformation: How to Deliver Winning Performance with a Connected Approach to Change*. Wade, Macaulay, Noronha, Barbier, 2019.
7. Michael Porter's *Competitive Advantage: Techniques for Analyzing Industries and Competitors* became a bible of business thinkers in the late 1980s. Echoing the ideas of comparative advantage expounded by David Ricardo, a nineteenth-century economist, this book provided managers with a framework for strategic thinking about how to beat their rivals. Porter argued that competitive advantage is a function of either providing comparable buyer value more effi-

ciently than competitors (low cost), or of performing activities at comparable cost but in unique ways that create more buyer value than competitors and, hence, command a premium price (differentiation). You win either by being cheaper or by being different (which means being perceived by the customer as better or more relevant). There are no other ways. Source: *The Economist,* 2008.

8. While the average automotive industry operating margin (EBIT) was 5.9% over the last three years (2014–2016), Toyota had an average operating margin (EBIT) of 9.7%; Porsche AG operating margin (EBIT) was 16.3%, Source: Capital IQ, Cisco analysis.
9. Source: *Orchestrating Transformation: How to Deliver Winning Performance with a Connected Approach to Change.* Wade, Macaulay, Noronha, Barbier, 2019.

12

Case Study: Conducting a Pre-Mortem

A consultant who runs business war games worldwide and who teaches and writes about strategic thinking once observed that "Nobody has data about the future." Anita, a Moscow-based consultant begged to differ: you don't, *unless* you can actually generate that data.

Anita was looking for new ways to identify obsolete business models, industries ripe for disruption, or companies that enjoyed an aura of excitement but that would not be as long-lasting as conventional wisdom and market consensus seemed to believe. In particular, she thought, take any Fortune-500 company (see Table 12.1), especially one that seems particularly robust and successful today because it is profitable, innovative and/or has shown a strong ability to adjust over a long period of time. That company is likely to make the headlines because of the headway it made on a particular market, because of the game-changing technology, product, or service it developed, or just because it is the new hype in the Silicon Valley or elsewhere. In short, pick the company that you believe is the least likely to go bankrupt, anytime soon.

Then, smiled Anita, consider the impossible: imagine it does go bankrupt. And ponder the question: what in the world happened?

The Pre-Mortem Exercise

There are two major steps to achieve this.

J. Ghez, *Architects of Change*, https://doi.org/10.1007/978-3-030-20684-0_12

Welcome to the Future

First, invite some of the brightest minds you know, whether they are from your team or outside. Welcome them to the future: use the current date and tell them that we are actually ten years into the future. Lock the doors. And announce the unthinkable: this seemingly robust, innovative, and game-changing company is about to disclose an explosive piece of information in a few moments: it is going bankrupt. Ask each person to think individually or in small teams to address a simply stated but immensely difficult question: what happened? Relax, and watch what happens, decided Anita.

In an hour or less, each individual or each team is likely to come up with a story about how this seemingly strong company went down. It is important to get them to focus on but also differentiate between the company's potential internal vulnerabilities *and* the exogenous forces that led to this fateful outcome. The debrief of this first part of the exercise is critical: it can help all participants share notes and cross-check their assumptions, and help the group identify where there may be consensus, but perhaps more importantly, where there may be disagreements about the firm's prospects. This debrief should help all participants think about how relevant, founded, and robust their assumptions about the company and its business environment actually are.

Back to Present

Next, welcome the group back to the present.

What a nightmare this was for the company. Well, think back to the last time you had a nightmare. If you are anything like me, Anita tells the group, you wake up with two distinct feelings: first, you feel relieved that this bankruptcy is not a situation that you will need to deal with; second, you tend to wonder how in the world did you imagine such an outlandish story. This is an opportunity to start from scratch and to bounce back, she states, by going back to the whiteboard: imagine that the CEO of that company is on the line and asking how can it reinvent itself, what idea or ideas could help it strengthen its resilience—or become antifragile—so as to avoid the imagined scenario—or any other extreme future. In other words, she asks, what types of *variations* of this firm are most likely to help the company survive in a turbulent landscape.

Again, thought Anita, relax and watch what happens.

The Final Debrief

At the end of the session, you should have three sets of meaningful results.

First, you may think that you know which industries are ripe for disruption and which business models are undeniably obsolete in the current business environment—and you may very well be correct in your assessment. But it is equally likely that this list of industries and business models is incomplete, not necessarily because you lack imagination but because daily urgencies prevent you from using the full force of that imagination. This exercise can help participants broaden horizons, in particular by getting them to consider extreme scenarios and reducing the likelihood of surprises in the longer run. It is an invitation to think about the future and about scenarios that may seem outlandish today, but that are not impossible, by any stretch of the imagination: it may feel like a bizarre setting, a never-ever land at this moment that may just be "uncharted waters" in a future that is closer than what you might believe.

Second, this exercise can generate a set of ideas that can help business analysts and decision-makers, as well as those advising them, understand where a company or an industry is going. Overall, the company may not be interested in one but in a set or in all of the ideas generated all together. To a large extent, creative destruction requires a large number of ideas given the uncertainty there is about the ultimate success of some or all of them, about the possibility that any will be *selected*. The more groundbreaking ideas you generated, the more geared-up you are in a non-linear world in which you expect plenty of disruptive moments without necessarily understanding what they will look like and what they will entail in practical terms. In addition, generating ideas can help people not be taken hostage by the flavor of the day and measure how innovative their project is when compared to a set of aspirations of very ambitious people.

Last, Anita came back to the original point, namely that "nobody has data about the future." This is not entirely correct, given that the pre-mortem exercise is unlikely to generate a full string of numbers, but if it is carried out correctly, it can generate a set of key points about the coming transformation of industries, about the untold vulnerabilities of some companies, and about how the interactions between both can create the perfect storm in the near future—a perfect storm that those lacking imagination will definitely miss. This exercise is the form of mental gymnastics that can only encourage imagination and help shed light on data points that we can anticipate more easily than we might have thought initially.

The Constant Pre-Mortem of the Architect of Change

The pre-mortem is by no means a pessimistic exercise.

Into the State of Mind of Architects of Change

Instead, it is about the necessary and constant rebirth of an idea, which, no matter how good it was in the beginning, will need to not merely adjust but to live and feed off the business environment over time—and even feed off its chaos. This is why anticipation may be helpful but insufficient in a world bound to surprise us in ways we did not foresee. This is also why those looking to bring about meaningful change in their business environment should not consider this exercise as a one-off effort, but one they should consider undertaking on a quasi-constant basis.

In fact, it is arguably a hallmark of the state of mind of architects of change to constantly reinvent their model: a combination of significant awareness of the business environment, a strong will to act, to change and to fix, *and* solid knowledge about the levers to pull is what transforms a candidate for change-making into a true architect of change. And ultimately, this is what the pre-mortem helps them uncover, by reducing uncertainty, that is, what is not possible to anticipate, to its most incompressible level.

Other Forms of Pre-Mortem

Pre-mortem has been used elsewhere in different ways.

American psychologist Gary Klein's way is arguably the most notable one. Klein usually works with a set of key decision-makers inside a company, who are all on board when it comes to a specific project that triggers the enthusiasm of everyone in the firm. Klein tells these decision-makers to imagine that a year from now, the project was actually a miserable failure, and asks them to take a few minutes to think about why. Though this project is a source of enthusiasm and these decision-makers are all on board, it turns out that many of them actually have quite a few non-negligible qualms about it. This effort helps generate plausible reasons on why the project could fail.

Gary Klein observed that the rate at which projects fail is spectacular, in particular because "too many people are reluctant to speak up about their reservations during the all-important planning phase. By making it safe for dissenters who are knowledgeable about the undertaking and worried about its weaknesses to speak up, you can improve a project's chances of success."[1] It is easy, psychologically speaking, for an overinvested manager to press on with a project regardless of its weaknesses, whether these are known, ignored, or even unknown. To this extent, pre-mortems help teams shed light on these weaknesses.

Nobel Prize recipient Daniel Kahneman describes himself as Klein's "adversarial collaborator" given their disagreements on the influence of human biases and the viability of algorithms as substitutes. But Kahneman has shown some enthusiasm for pre-mortems, that he sees as "partial remedy" to overconfidence because "it unleashes the imagination of knowledgeable individuals in"[2] by pushing them to look for threats—and opportunities one could add—in places where people may not have looked before. It reduces surprises and the damages they could cause. And ultimately, they help legitimize doubt which is perhaps the only tangible piece of evidence we may have about the existence of uncertainty.

Do Not Lack Imagination!

Anita's approach in this example has similar aims. Ultimately, like Klein and Kahneman, Anita is looking to break the consensus that can characterize thinking and hinder our ability to remember that we do live in a world of chaos—not just in a linear world. It is also similar in the sense that by design, this version of the pre-mortem sheds light on the factors that do not come to mind when we strategize, because we are lazy, because we lack imagination or because these factors result from such complex mechanisms, in terms of causality in particular, that they are very hard to grasp. Like other versions, this form of pre-mortem can help uncover the channels of transmissions of shocks and shed light on how weaknesses can interact with the broader environment and compound the effects of a disruptive moment in an unexpected or unforeseen way.

In fact, in this author's experience, when conducting pre-mortems with executives, it is very rare that there is a single factor in anyone's mind that leads to the company's demise. The image of the "perfect storm" is far more illustrative of what happens in their minds, as they come up with a wide range of factors, which, taken one by one, are very straightforward; complexity comes with the multiple interactions between these factors that they imagine.

Sheer analysis can seldom uncover those possibilities of interactions, making imagination a key element of this exercise.

This format of the pre-mortem is less focused on groupthink—though it partly aims at breaking the consensus—and puts greater emphasis on uncovering the nature of what we do not know we do not know. By design, we can *never* formulate what that actually is—and I have never met participants who feel that the scenario they imagined in the first part of the exercise claim will materialize exactly in the way they describe it, so this is *not* a game of prediction. But we can get closer to uncertainty by thinking about the factors that are driving it and the complex interactions that are shaping it. In this way, we can limit the actual amount of uncertainty by broadening horizons and widening effectively the elements of risk (and opportunity) we monitor on a radar screen.

Reinvention in the Making

Recall what Donald Rumsfeld had to say about certainty and uncertainty. In his categorization, there were the known knowns, that require analysis and fact-checking, and the known unknowns, the variables that require hedging and mitigating strategies. Knowledgeable and flexible actors will know how to navigate a linear world that changes, that produces new opportunities or pressures to adapt and that leads to incremental change as a result. This was the key message of the giraffe parabola, in which the animal adapts to incremental changes in the environment so as to survive.

But let us remember what Joseph Schumpeter argued about creative destruction: this is the driver of the capitalist system because it does not trigger marginal changes in a firm's cost structure; instead, it transforms the product, the service, or the organization itself in a way that provides the firm with a definitive edge. Pre-mortems trigger a wide range of ideas—enough for the best to ultimately survive in a world that also experiences chaos and Darwinian processes—that are arguably the most radical options a team could potentially imagine. If a company regularly carries out this pre-mortem effort, it may be able to increase the likelihood that it will ultimately bounce back.

Ultimately, the pre-mortem exercise is how architects of change transform raw information into meaningful implications for a turbulent environment (Table 12.1).

Table 12.1 List of Fortune 500 companies

1	Walmart	101	DuPont	201	Molina Healthcare	301	Lennar	401	Charles Schwab
2	Exxon Mobil	102	Avnet	202	WellCare Health Plans	302	GameStop	402	Calpine
3	Apple	103	Macy's	203	CBS	303	Reliance Steel & Aluminum	403	CMS Energy
4	Berkshire Hathaway	104	Enterprise Products Partners	204	Visa	304	Hormel Foods	404	Alliance Data Systems
5	McKesson	105	Travelers Cos.	205	Lincoln National	305	Celgene	405	JetBlue Airways
6	UnitedHealth Group	106	Philip Morris International	206	Ecolab	306	Genworth Financial	406	Discovery Communications
7	CVS Health	107	Rite Aid	207	Kellogg	307	PayPal Holdings	407	Trinity Industries
8	General Motors	108	Tech Data	208	C.H. Robinson Worldwide	308	Priceline Group	408	Sanmina
9	Ford Motor	109	McDonald's	209	Textron	309	MGM Resorts International	409	NCR
10	AT&T	110	Qualcomm	210	Loews	310	Autoliv	410	FMC Technologies
11	General Electric	111	Sears Holdings	211	Illinois Tool Works	311	Fidelity National Financial	411	Erie Insurance Group
12	AmerisourceBergen	112	Capital One Financial	212	Synnex	312	Republic Services	412	Rockwell Automation
13	Verizon	113	EMC	213	Viacom	313	Corning	413	Dr Pepper Snapple Group
14	Chevron	114	USAA	214	HollyFrontier	314	Peter Kiewit Sons'	414	iHeartMedia
15	Costco	115	Duke Energy	215	Land O'Lakes	315	Univar	415	Tractor Supply
16	Fannie Mae	116	Time Warner Cable	216	Devon Energy	316	Mosaic	416	J.B. Hunt Transport Services
17	Kroger	117	Halliburton	217	PBF Energy	317	Core-Mark Holding	417	Commercial Metals
18	Amazon.com	118	Northrop Grumman	218	Yum Brands	318	Thrivent Financial for Lutherans	418	Owens-Illinois

(continued)

Table 12.1 (continued)

19	Walgreens Boots Alliance	119	Arrow Electronics	219	Texas Instruments	319	Cameron International	419	Harman International Industries
20	HP	120	Raytheon	220	CDW	320	HD Supply Holdings	420	Baxalta
21	Cardinal Health	121	Plains GP Holdings	221	Waste Management	321	Crown Holdings	421	American Financial Group
22	Express Scripts Holding	122	US Foods Holding	222	Marsh & McLennan	322	EOG Resources	422	NetApp
23	J.P. Morgan Chase	123	AbbVie	223	Chesapeake Energy	323	Veritiv	423	Graybar Electric
24	Boeing	124	Centene	224	Parker-Hannifin	324	Anadarko Petroleum	424	Oshkosh
25	Microsoft	125	Community Health Systems	225	Occidental Petroleum	325	Laboratory Corp. of America	425	Ameren
26	Bank of America Corp.	126	Alcoa	226	Guardian Life Ins. Co. of America	326	Pacific Life	426	A-Mark Precious Metals
27	Wells Fargo	127	International Paper	227	Farmers Insurance Exchange	327	News Corp.	427	Barnes & Noble
28	Home Depot	128	Emerson Electric	228	J.C. Penney	328	Jarden	428	Dana Holding
29	Citigroup	129	Union Pacific	229	Consolidated Edison	329	SunTrust Banks	429	Constellation Brands
30	Phillips 66	130	Amgen	230	Cognizant Technology Solutions	330	Avis Budget Group	430	LifePoint Health
31	IBM	131	U.S. Bancorp	231	VF	331	Broadcom	431	Zimmer Biomet Holdings
32	Valero Energy	132	Staples	232	Ameriprise Financial	332	American Family Insurance Group	432	Harley-Davidson
33	Anthem	133	Danaher	233	Computer Sciences	333	Level 3 Communications	433	PulteGroup
34	Procter & Gamble	134	Whirlpool	234	L Brands	334	Tenneco	434	Newell Brands

(continued)

Table 12.1 (continued)

35	State Farm Insurance Cos.	135	Aflac	235	Jacobs Engineering Group	335	United Natural Foods	435	Avery Dennison
36	Alphabet	136	AutoNation	236	Principal Financial	336	Dean Foods	436	Jones Lang LaSalle
37	Comcast	137	Progressive	237	Ross Stores	337	Campbell Soup	437	WEC Energy Group
38	Target	138	Abbott Laboratories	238	Bed Bath & Beyond	338	Mohawk Industries	438	Marathon Oil
39	Johnson & Johnson	139	Dollar General	239	CSX	339	BorgWarner	439	TravelCenters of America
40	MetLife	140	Tenet Healthcare	240	Toys "R" Us	340	PVH	440	United Rentals
41	Archer Daniels Midland	141	Eli Lilly	241	Las Vegas Sands	341	Ball	441	HRG Group
42	Marathon Petroleum	142	Southwest Airlines	242	Leucadia National	342	O'Reilly Automotive	442	Old Republic International
43	Freddie Mac	143	Penske Automotive Group	243	Dominion Resources	343	Eversource Energy	443	Windstream Holdings
44	PepsiCo	144	ManpowerGroup	244	United States Steel	344	Franklin Resources	444	Starwood Hotels & Resorts
45	United Technologies	145	Kohl's	245	L-3 Communications	345	Masco	445	Delek US Holdings
46	Aetna	146	Starbucks	246	Edison International	346	Lithia Motors	446	Packaging Corp. of America
47	Lowe's	147	Paccar	247	Entergy	347	KKR	447	Quintiles Transnational Holdings
48	UPS	148	Cummins	248	ADP	348	Oneok	448	Hanesbrands
49	AIG	149	Altria Group	249	First Data	349	Newmont Mining	449	Realogy Holdings
50	Prudential Financial	150	Xerox	250	BlackRock	350	PPL	450	Mattel
51	Intel	151	Kimberly-Clark	251	WestRock	351	SpartanNash	451	Motorola Solutions
52	Humana	152	Hartford Financial Services Group	252	Voya Financial	352	Quanta Services	452	J.M. Smucker

(continued)

Table 12.1 (continued)

53	Disney	153	Kraft Heinz	253	Sherwin-Williams	353	XPO Logistics	453	Regions Financial
54	Cisco Systems	154	Lear	254	Hilton Worldwide Holdings	354	Ralph Lauren	453	Celanese
55	Pfizer	155	Fluor	255	R.R. Donnelley & Sons	355	Interpublic Group	455	Clorox
56	Dow Chemical	156	AECOM	256	Stanley Black & Decker	356	Steel Dynamics	456	Ingredion
57	Sysco	157	Facebook	257	Xcel Energy	357	WESCO International	457	Genesis Healthcare
58	FedEx	158	Jabil Circuit	258	Murphy USA	358	Quest Diagnostics	458	Peabody Energy
59	Caterpillar	159	CenturyLink	259	CBRE Group	359	Boston Scientific	459	Alaska Air Group
60	Lockheed Martin	160	Supervalu	260	D.R. Horton	360	AGCO	460	Seaboard
61	New York Life Insurance	161	General Mills	261	Estee Lauder	361	Foot Locker	461	Frontier Communications
62	Coca-Cola	162	Southern	262	Praxair	362	Hershey	462	Amphenol
63	HCA Holdings	163	NextEra Energy	263	Biogen	363	CenterPoint Energy	463	Lansing Trade Group
64	Ingram Micro	164	Thermo Fisher Scientific	264	State Street Corp.	364	Williams	464	SanDisk
65	Energy Transfer Equity	165	American Electric Power	265	Unum Group	365	Dick's Sporting Goods	465	St. Jude Medical
66	Tyson Foods	166	PG&E Corp.	266	Reynolds American	366	Live Nation Entertainment	466	Wyndham Worldwide
67	American Airlines Group	167	NGL Energy Partners	267	Group 1 Automotive	367	Mutual of Omaha Insurance	467	Kelly Services
68	Delta Air Lines	168	Bristol-Myers Squibb	268	Henry Schein	368	W.R. Berkley	468	Western Union
69	Nationwide	169	Goodyear Tire & Rubber	269	Hertz Global Holdings	369	LKQ	469	Envision Healthcare Holdings
70	Johnson Controls	170	Nucor	270	Norfolk Southern	370	Avon Products	470	Visteon

(continued)

Table 12.1 (continued)

71	Best Buy	171	PNC Financial Services Group	271	Reinsurance Group of America	371	Darden Restaurants	471	Arthur J. Gallagher
72	Merck	172	Health Net	272	Public Service Enterprise Group	372	Kindred Healthcare	472	Host Hotels & Resorts
73	Liberty Mutual Insurance Group	173	Micron Technology	273	BB&T Corp.	373	Weyerhaeuser	472	Ashland
74	Goldman Sachs Group	174	Colgate-Palmolive	274	DTE Energy	374	Casey's General Stores	474	Insight Enterprises
75	Honeywell International	175	Freeport-McMoRan	275	Assurant	375	Sealed Air	475	Energy Future Holdings
76	Massachusetts Mutual Life Insurance	176	ConAgra Foods	276	Global Partners	376	Fifth Third Bancorp	476	Markel
77	Oracle	177	Gap	277	Huntsman	377	Dover	477	Essendant
78	Morgan Stanley	178	Baker Hughes	278	Becton Dickinson	378	Huntington Ingalls Industries	478	CH2M Hill
79	Cigna	179	Bank of New York Mellon Corp.	279	Sempra Energy	379	Netflix	479	Western & Southern Financial Group
80	United Continental Holdings	180	Dollar Tree	280	AutoZone	380	Dillard's	480	Owens Corning
81	Allstate	181	Whole Foods Market	281	Navistar International	381	EMCOR Group	481	S&P Global
82	TIAA	182	PPG Industries	282	Precision Castparts	382	Jones Financial	482	Raymond James Financial
83	INTL FCStone	183	Genuine Parts	283	Discover Financial Services	383	AK Steel Holding	483	NiSource
84	CHS	184	Icahn Enterprises	284	Liberty Interactive	384	UGI	484	Airgas
85	American Express	185	Performance Food Group	285	W.W. Grainger	385	Expedia	485	ABM Industries

(*continued*)

Table 12.1 (continued)

86	Gilead Sciences	186	Omnicom Group	286	Baxter International	386	salesforce.com	486	Citizens Financial Group
87	Publix Super Markets	187	DISH Network	287	Stryker	387	Targa Resources	487	Booz Allen Hamilton Holding
88	General Dynamics	188	FirstEnergy	288	Air Products & Chemicals	388	Apache	488	Simon Property Group
89	TJX	189	Monsanto	289	Western Refining	389	Spirit AeroSystems Holdings	489	Domtar
90	ConocoPhillips	190	AES	290	Universal Health Services	390	Expeditors International of Washington	490	Rockwell Collins
91	Nike	191	CarMax	291	Owens & Minor	391	Anixter International	491	Lam Research
92	World Fuel Services	192	National Oilwell Varco	292	Charter Communications	392	Fidelity National Information Services	492	Fiserv
93	3M	193	NRG Energy	293	Advance Auto Parts	393	Asbury Automotive Group	493	Spectra Energy
94	Mondelez International	194	Western Digital	294	MasterCard	394	Hess	494	Navient
95	Exelon	195	Marriott International	295	Applied Materials	395	Ryder System	495	Big Lots
96	Twenty-First Century Fox	196	Office Depot	296	Eastman Chemical	396	Terex	496	Telephone & Data Systems
97	Deere	197	Nordstrom	297	Sonic Automotive	397	Coca-Cola European Partners	497	First American Financial
98	Tesoro	198	Kinder Morgan	298	Ally Financial	398	Auto-Owners Insurance	498	NVR
99	Time Warner	199	Aramark	299	CST Brands	399	Cablevision Systems	499	Cincinnati Financial
100	Northwestern Mutual	200	DaVita HealthCare Partners	300	eBay	400	Symantec	500	Burlington Stores

Notes

1. Gary Klein, "Performing a Project Premortem," *Harvard Business Review*, September 1, 2007, https://hbr.org/2007/09/performing-a-project-premortem.
2. Daniel Kahneman, *Thinking, Fast and Slow*, 1 edition (Farrar, Straus and Giroux, 2011).

13

The Meaning of Creativity

Managers and executives seem to constantly hear, nowadays, injunctions to be creative and to look for novel and innovative solutions. Yet, these calls for creativity are so commonplace that they seem to be lost in the sea of unsolicited tips and advice that these managers and executives receive every day—to the extent that it remains unclear whether we, as humanity, still know or agree on what creative actually means. What is worse is that as a result of these empty injunctions, the idea of creativity often seems to feel trite: in a turbulent business environment, in which resources are limited and decision-makers need to account for budget constraints, the urgencies of the moment can easily overshadow any long-term benefits you can draw from being "creative" today.

And yet, this chapter argues, creativity does not have to be such an empty word—especially not in this business environment that can surprise and arouse our curiosity. In fact, our ability to continue to formulate questions, or, put differently, to refrain from taking anything for granted, is crucial to drive change, as previous chapters have hinted. Similarly, the ability to defy consensus and conventional wisdom, to challenge yesterday's rules, interpretations, and standards, to disrupt past patterns, approaches, and practices is at the heart of the discovery journey that any actor looking to drive change will need in order to be successful. The real challenge lies in determining how we can achieve this in a turbulent business environment, driven by the urgencies of the day.

There is good and encouraging news, which may seem straightforward and trivial, and yet too easily forgotten by actors who, because of their sophistication, tend to forget the obvious: as children, being creative was not a challenge

J. Ghez, *Architects of Change*, https://doi.org/10.1007/978-3-030-20684-0_13

for us but an existential need to survive in a world that we did not feel we knew as well as we do today. In other words, there was a time in all of our lives at which we knew how to ask questions because we did not take conventional wisdom, rules, explanations, and practices for granted; that is, there was a time in our lives when creativity was part of our bloodstream. As we become sophisticated, it disappears, progressively. The challenge, therefore, lies not in *being* more creative, but in finding once again the energy and the curiosity to question our business environment in a way we once did.

After discussing the definition of creativity and its implications for architects of change, this chapter explores how creativity can shape the way we network and influence our business environment. Ultimately, being "creative" may be hard because we confuse creativity with sophistication and because the latter may kill the former over time. Children show us how we may be able to take an alternative path which may be particularly critical in this dogmatic, polarized, and ideological landscape.

Defining Creativity

In definitions of creativity, there is an emphasis on an individual's intent, will, or aspiration: creativity is about imagining, inventing, bringing into existence, or producing through action or behavior something original and unusual.

Original and in Opposition to What Exists

It is the opposite of imitation since creativity is about producing and creating—rather than reproducing and recreating. This point is significant to the extent that it suggests that, by design, creativity entails a transition into an environment that is, partly at least, unknown, or even a transformation of the environment so as to avoid an obsolete status quo. As another definition puts it, creativity is "the ability to transcend traditional ideas, rules, patterns, relationships, or the like, and to create meaningful new ideas, forms, methods (or) interpretations,"[1] making the concept a synonym of originality and progressiveness. This definition connects creativity to the popular saying "thinking outside the box" that allows change in approaches or result.

As a result, creativity is also about willfully circumventing existing and accepted limits or norms. Creative solutions may look to transcend current regulations that may not allow actors to fully do what they wish to do. It can be seen through a positive light, when it brings improvement, or through a more pejorative prism, when the objective is to get around legal or regulatory standards. It is therefore the result of *both* innovation *and* analysis of the existing.

Taming Constraints

As a result, an alternative and purposeful way to think about creativity lies in placing the concept at the intersection of certainty, risk, and uncertainty: creativity is the outcome that results from a meaningful synthesis of facts, of open questions, and of the unknown that seeks to provide actors with a way forward.

There cannot be creativity without a solid understanding of constraints (facts), a good grasp of what can be negotiated or bent (open questions), and enough imagination about what can be invented as a result (uncertainty). Creativity is therefore about taming constraints so as to aim for an outcome that strikes a fundamental difference with today's reality. As two academics once argued, contrary to what conventional wisdom may suggest, it is not scarcity but constraint that is the mother of innovation: it is because we understand what the business environment will and will not allow us to do that we are able to bring about a new reality that fits that landscape in the most meaningful way.[2]

Implications for the Knowledge Economy

The definition of creativity has implications for the way we think about what organizations and businesses need to survive and thrive in this business environment.

Mind, Brain, and Ideas

In particular, there seems to be a consensus around the idea that we have now moved into a "knowledge economy," one in which mind, brain, and ideas matter more than matter, brawn, and things in the words of American academic Erik Brynjolfsson.[3]

The acceleration of globalization in the aftermath of the end of the Cold War, combined with the revolution of information technologies and the advent of the Internet, could suggest that the rise of the "knowledge economy" is a relatively new phenomenon; and yet, American management consultant Peter Drucker resurrected the concept as early as 1969, noting the increasing central role of knowledge in the economy and the workforce.[4] The demand for knowledge became significant, he concluded, because knowledge had become productive: "The systematic and purposeful acquisition of information and its systematic application, rather than 'science' or 'technology,' are emerging as the new foundation for work, productivity, and effort throughout the world," he argued.

The Quality of the Business Environment

What may be relatively more recent is our ability to measure the impact of knowledge in economic growth. In particular, there is part of residual growth that neither the increase of capital nor that of labor, can explain. Instead, the way an economy combines capital and labor (and other inputs), the ecosystem it creates for its economic activity, or, put differently, the quality of its business environment, is what matters for long-term growth.

For instance, the World Bank has found that in order for a country to be an active actor in the knowledge economy, it needs to rely on four fundamental pillars. First, education and training play a key role because an "educated and skilled population is needed to create, share and use knowledge." Second, solid information infrastructure is crucial so as to guarantee that information is accessible and easy to disseminate and process. Third, economic incentives and the rule of law provide economic actors with the incentive to invest and to adopt an entrepreneurial mindset which plays a key role in the knowledge economy. Last, a "network of research centers, universities, think tanks, private enterprises and community groups" plays a critical role by not only contributing but also harnessing the increasing amount of knowledge worldwide by assimilating it and adapting it to specific cases.[5]

The adaptation of this notion of efficient combination of factors of production is as telling at the firm level: it suggests that two firms with an equal amount of capital and labor at a given point in time may not know the same fate ultimately because one may get an edge over the other through a better combination of factors of production. This suggestion confirms the very intuitive notion that a firm's *business model* matters—and that the ideas that structures its approach to the market, as well as its management style can be decisive assets facing competition.

Knowing or Getting to Know?

Ultimately, what ties an economy's business environment and a company's business model is the question of how conducive is the ecosystem both can offer to generate new ideas for value creation and development. There may therefore be an ambiguity around the very concept of the "knowledge economy": it is less about the absolute amount of knowledge that one may master and more about the easiness with which you can access, adapt, and harness information to reach your goals. As a result, this may be less of a "knowledge economy" and more of a "creativity economy."

This "creativity economy" has implications for the way we think about networking and professional relationships: the challenge may lie far less in knowing it all than in building the right network and the right teams to not only *access* but also *process* information in due time. In the experience of this author in particular, it is striking that when young decision-makers (like MBAs) and more experienced ones (like Executive MBAs) think about their network, the most salient features that stand out is the immediately actionable contacts that they can rely on to hire, get hired, or obtain precise information pertaining to their industry. Having a sociologist, a historian, or an artist is not what may seem most practical—and rightfully so, in most cases: neither one of these profiles will ever be in a position to provide them with the business solution they desperately need. Yet, a sociologist like a historian could point to the social, historical and, more profoundly, the human dynamics that are driving a particular crisis. An artist who masters the science of symbols and analogies well could be well placed to offer interpretations that the urgency of the moment otherwise overshadows. They could all offer alternative perspectives that ultimately broaden the range of available options—in particular because they think about situations with a different kind of creativity than "operational" actors do.

This discussion can also inform the way we think about our own skills. The World Economic Forum anticipates a striking evolution in this regard, as it affects critical skills: the organization expects complex problem solving to remain the top skill to thrive in the Fourth Industrial Revolution, but also foresees critical thinking and creativity overtaking coordinating with others and people management as the second and third top skills respectively.[6] In other words, this economy provides us with the tools to be faster on a wide range of tasks; but the new sets of products, services, technologies, and management paradigms will only help unleash creativity to the extent that they reduce the amount of time we spend on those tasks. The challenge lies in putting that free time to the best use possible—and that process may involve at times very painful efforts at the individual level to reinvent, in particular for those whose specialty was to carry out those tasks. It is a process of self-creative destruction that will definitely place a substantial chunk of the workforce into uncharted waters, but which could also create enormous opportunities for impact. To this extent, creativity is not just imagination about abstract concepts; it is the ability to open up more doors in particular in a business environment in which actors often feel stuck in insurmountable stalemates.

Breaking the Rules

This "creativity economy" also has implications for the way we think about rules, standards, and practices, that is, the way we think about conventional wisdom and what it says about acceptable and less acceptable behavior. As underscored before, "creative" may have a pejorative connotation in some instances, when it involves, like in the case of creative accounting, efforts to undermine rules and regulations designed to protect the stability of the system. But "creative thinking" refers more often to breakthrough innovation solving a mind-boggling problem and/or breaking a consensus. In that sense, breaking "the rules" is another way to broaden the set of available options and consider some that we suppressed, perhaps unconsciously, but that might deserve more consideration.

Irrational or Strategic?

In particular, it has become very fashionable to wonder and worry about people's rationality. This debate has profoundly shaped the economics and psychology literature that has pointed out that our behavior is influenced by a wide range of cognitive biases—leading us, humans, to make mistakes. But this observation, namely that we make mistakes, often leads us to the conclusion that we must therefore be irrational—when making a mistake can actually be very rational, the cost of collecting all of the relevant pieces of information outweighs the benefits of *not* making a mistake. In addition, making mistakes can help us understand our own limits, as well as those of our organization. It can provide meaningful information on what we can and cannot achieve at any moment in time.

What is more is that it is very tempting to label someone whose behavior we do not understand as irrational. When someone acts in ways we do not understand or expect, it is far easier to blame it on the other's "irrationality," "craziness," or plain stupidity instead of wondering why you were not better able to see the world through an alternative set of eyes. That person may very well be irrational, crazy, or stupid—unless it is plain determined, in which case that person may already be one strategic step ahead of us. In the words of Economic Nobel Prize recipient Thomas Schelling,

> Even among the emotionally unbalanced, among the certified 'irrationals,' there is often observed an intuitive appreciation of the principles of strategy, or at least of particular applications of them. I am told that inmates of mental hospitals often seem to cultivate, deliberately or instinctively, value systems that make them less susceptible to disciplinary threats and more capable of exercising coercion themselves. … It may not be an exaggeration to say that our sophistication sometimes suppresses sound intuitions, and one of the effects of an explicit theory may be to restore some intuitive notions that were only superficially 'irrational.' … It may be perfectly rational to wish oneself not altogether rational, or—if that language is philosophically objectionable—to wish for the power to suspend certain rational capabilities in particular situations.[7]

Suspending "certain rational capabilities" is a way, in other words, to guarantee that our minds do not limit what we are actually able to achieve.

Many societies value predictability on the part of an individual, and frown upon unpredictable and erratic behavior. In fact, we are trained to be predictable. We are appreciated by colleagues because we are to some extent predictable. And we are loved by close ones because we are predictable. But it may be strategically harmful to be predictable all the time. In particular, one should be careful before labeling a rival or a mere counterpart as "irrational" or crazy. That irrational counterpart may have far more leverage than one actually thinks. It may have a far better grasp on the basic principles of strategic thinking and may very well be, therefore, a few steps ahead, nurturing a strategic edge one did not even realize.

The "irrational," in other words, may be the ones breaking the rules by breaking to pieces obsolete conventional wisdom and opening up broad avenues of action. In a turbulent business environment, breaking the rules may very well be something that is done to you, especially if you are not doing this to others.

Changing the Dynamics

Breaking the rules is, in particular, the theme American author Malcolm Gladwell uses to revisit the old, biblical tale of David and Goliath. The story of how David, the young shepherd kills the Philistine giant Goliath is a well-known illustration of a key theme of the Bible: those who have faith will ultimately prevail thanks to divine miracles.

Yet, says Malcom Gladwell, there may be a second interpretation to the story that we may be ignoring, namely that David was not the underdog that we thought he was: the sling he has turns out to be very effective weapon that he is able to turn into a strategic advantage. As Gladwell observes, "Once he decided to break the rules, he's the guy in charge." In addition, Goliath is not the impressive giant that we tend to think he is: he needs an attendant, he is slow, and he does not appear to fully understand the nature of the duel that is about to oppose him to David. According to Gladwell's interviews with endocrinologists, Goliath may suffer from acromegaly which triggers overproduction of human growth hormone, "a tumor on your pituitary gland that causes overproduction of human growth hormone, which is why he's so big, but also often has a side effect of constricting your optic nerves." This is a "lumbering giant who cannot see", concludes Gladwell, far from the underdog versus favorite narrative that the Bible may want to us to believe. Ultimately, notes Gladwell, once David decided to break the rules, he is able to reconfigure the combat to his advantage and to break the likely consensus about the outcome of a fight between what probably looked like an impressive giant and a small shepherd.[8]

The biblical story of David and Goliath is a cautionary tale to all actors who believe that a strategic advantage they may enjoy at some point in time will be permanent or even long-lasting. Companies like Kodak and Nokia, which had technology that was superior, if anything because what they offer is more user-friendly and attractive to customers, were never supposed to see their boat rocked by market forces. But their inability to reconfigure and reinvent that advantage over time played a critical role in their loss of influence or their bankruptcy—which were less an issue of financial means than the absence of an incentive to innovate and change with the business environment.

Architects of Change Engineer the Future

The story of reinvention begins and ends ultimately with creative destruction. In this particular case, breaking the rules is not merely about avoiding falling to market forces and ultimately to bankruptcy; it is about considering what we have too often taken for granted and what type of consensus will not survive to the changing business environment. This task is another hard one at which architects of change excel nevertheless.

In fact, ultimately, this effort is not one that only relies on analysis, nor on solid anticipation; nor is it only about lack of imagination; it is about engineering the future, that is, not seeing your business environment as a trap but as a setting you can influence and fundamentally change; it is about showing the empathy and the will to understand other stakeholders so as to co-create that future business environment and thus avoid being blindsided by the aspiration of other actors that you copiously ignored; and it is about accepting that you may not know everything, even if (or in particular when) you believe that the drivers of the business environment are straightforward. Architects of change are able to overcome all of this through the permanent exercise of mental gymnastics that they undertake not only to *prepare* for the coming world but also to *shape* it in a way that will make it easier for them to achieve their goals. Architects of change are rule-breakers as a result.

This effort to question the environment and its governing laws may look like a very ambitious and grueling one—and yet it is one that architects of change must constantly undertake. What is more, it is one that, as children, we constantly undertook as well. The challenge may lie in learning how to carry it out, once again. The conclusion of this book will explore this point in detail.

Jean-Noël Kapferer is an internationally renowned expert of brands and luxury. He is known in particular for his work on brand identity and on luxury management. In this stunning testimonial, he talks about the world's largest market for luxury, China—a country in which the word "luxury" does not exist. How does one convey the notion of luxury? It turns out that you better be able to understand your local constraints, anticipate the market's reactions, and imagine new avenues for development in a market that was left unexplored until quite recently. In other words, you'll need to be mightily creative to get your message across as a result, especially when the Chinese market represents such a substantial chunk of your sales.

Is luxury in China just a question of words?

Today, and even more so tomorrow, the most important customer for luxury will be Chinese. Chinese clients already account for 33% of sales of "personal luxury" that well-known brands of fashion and accessories, like Hermes, Gucci, Vuitton, Chanel, YSL, Dior, Balenciaga, Prada, Bulgari, Rolex, Van Cleef, all represent. The Chinese clients' share is bigger than that of the Japanese (10%), North Americans (22%), or Europeans (18%).

But here is a paradox: when a luxury brand looks to penetrate the Chinese market, one of the major difficulties lies in translating the word "luxury." In all western countries, the word luxury is the same or is derived from the same Latin word, *luxatio*, which is the same word as dislocation. It suggests that luxury, like a dislocation, is like a major split with regard to high-end or premium products, an excess that is impossible to justify rationally. Luxury is not simply being more expensive. It is being elsewhere.

Reality is different in China because the word "luxury" does not exist in Chinese—or, more to the point, there are many ways to talk about "luxury" products and brands, depending on which facet of luxury you want to put the emphasis on when you are talking about such products and brands. For instance, the word *Jing Pin* refers to a refined object from crafts, an exceptional product. It suggests that the object is a premium product, but the word does not contain any reference to dream or to social stratification that is central to luxury.

Ming Gouei means a well-known name that is expensive and precious. It applies to a jewel that is rare and valuable—but also to a wide range of other products, including products that are not necessarily luxury ones, like rare natural tea.

A more common term for luxury is *She Chi*, which means everything that only people in high society can afford. It is made up of two Chinese characters. The first reminds us of a tall or great man, while the second reminds us of a crowd. For the Chinese, luxury is therefore what distinguishes great people from the masses, as the first (great people) and their possessions are observed by the second (masses). Luxury is therefore clearly what belongs to others. This view is at odds with typical European demands for discreet luxury products that may not even bear any logo—in particular because the newly wealthy, the self-employed entrepreneurs and dynamic young people in China are driving the growth of demand for luxury. These populations are proud of their success and want to openly enjoy it as others look on.

But the term *She Chi* has recently suffered with President Xi Jinping's anti-corruption policies. Luxury brands once surfed on this corruption that required precious gifts, like watches and expensive alcohols, to strive. This explains why many luxury brands now chose a more neutral and less charged term of *She Hua* that doesn't incorporate the notion of long run which is nevertheless critical in luxury.

The internationalization of brands is now a pillar of modern management, as frontiers are increasingly deemed to be irrelevant. The instance of China reminds us of another reality: brands are global, but their clients are local. Undoubtedly, for reasons of economies of scale, it is rather hard to adapt products or marketing to niches, to small markets or countries. But the question is rather different when a country like China represents a third of your sales and a potential market of 220 million affluent clients!

Notes

1. "The Definition of Creativity," Dictionary.com, accessed April 12, 2019, https://www.dictionary.com/browse/creativity.
2. Teresa Amabile and Kramer, "Necessity, Not Scarcity, Is the Mother of Invention," *Harvard Business Review*, March 25, 2011, https://hbr.org/2011/03/necessity-not-scarcity-is-the.
3. Erik Brynjolfsson, *The Key to Growth? Race with the Machines*, TED Talks, 2013, https://www.ted.com/talks/erik_brynjolfsson_the_key_to_growth_race_em_with_em_the_machines.

4. As he pointed out then,

> Ninety per cent of all scientists and technologists who ever lived are alive and at work today. In the first five hundred years since Gutenberg, from 1450 to 1950, some thirty million printed books were published in the world. In the last twenty-five years alone, an equal number has appeared. Thirty years ago, on the eve of World War II, semiskilled machine operators, the men on the assembly line, were the center of the American work force. Today the center is the knowledge worker, the man or woman who applies to productive work ideas, concepts, and information rather than manual skill or brawn. Our largest single occupation is teaching, that is, the systematic supply of knowledge and systematic training in applying it.

5. "The Four Pillars of The Knowledge Economy," The World Bank, accessed April 12, 2019, http://web.worldbank.org/archive/website01503/WEB/0__CO-10.HTM.
6. "The Future of Jobs" (Geneva, Switzerland: World Economic Forum, January 2016), https://www.weforum.org/reports/the-future-of-jobs/.
7. Thomas Schelling, *The Strategy of Conflict*, Reprint edition (Cambridge: Harvard University Press, 1981).
8. Fareed Zakaria, "Gladwell: Why We've Got David and Goliath Wrong," *The Global Public Square* (blog), October 27, 2013, http://globalpublicsquare.blogs.cnn.com/2013/10/27/gladwell-why-weve-got-david-and-goliath-wrong/.

14

Case Study: Looking for Talent in a Chaotic World

Daniel Trainme, the managing partner in a major HR consulting firm, sat in his first-class seat, expecting his plane to take off at any moment. Over the years, he came to enjoy these long, quiet flights more than he ever thought he could: they gave him the opportunity to take a deep dive and reflect on very long-term trends that he would not have the luxury to think about otherwise, in more usual circumstances.

This time around, his most recent conversation with a client who was at the head of a major tech firm of the Silicon Valley was on his mind. This client was wondering about the type of talent and profiles she would need to attract in the future to thrive in such an unstable and uncertain global environment. This was a crucial question that could have significant ramifications, not only for this particular client but for its competitors as well. And, depending on the strategy that tech giants would choose, their decisions could not only shape these companies' ability to influence the future of technology but also influence global economic and political interactions, given how widely used their products and services were.

In fact, Daniel thought, it is clear that tech giants, and what he liked to call the GAFAs (an acronym that stands for Google, Apple, Facebook, and Amazon) in particular, had felt the laws of geopolitical gravity apply to them more than ever over the recent months. Would that not translate, at some point in the near future, into a fundamental need for a geopolitical strategy that would let them mitigate risk but also leverage new opportunities that the global landscape offered? What profile, and what competences would be required to develop such strategy? In particular, what would be the scope of the job? What would be the objective of this individual or group of individuals?

J. Ghez, *Architects of Change*, https://doi.org/10.1007/978-3-030-20684-0_14

How GAFAs Redefine the Rules of the (Geo)political Game

In the aftermath of the 2008 crisis, Daniel thought, we lived in a world in which the state did not necessarily have the financial means, the political mandate, and the basic will to fulfill the missions it carried out in the past. As one famous French entrepreneur, Xavier Niel, put it in an interview with the French magazine *Society* in June 2016, "the state may not have anymore money, but I do." In fact, the crisis had created a huge vacuum in which new power players, GAFAs in particular, looked to shape global outcomes. These tech firms seemed particularly effective at redefining a broad set of concepts like the meaning of power, the relationship to space and the broader notion of governance. By reinventing the rules of the game, they were also decisively shaping the business environment in an inexorable way—and this, Daniel thought, they needed to understand.

Redefining the Meaning of Power

The sheer size of these companies, Daniel noted, was humbling, first and foremost. All four of the GAFAs were among the world's biggest corporations, measured in terms of annual revenue: Apple ranked fourth, Amazon seventh, Alphabet (the parent company of Google) ninth, and Facebook twenty-first. Their annual revenue exceeded the GDP (gross domestic product) of poor and even middle-income countries, suggesting that they had more firepower than some states.[1] Furthermore, their increasing omnipresence and the fact that so many people across the planet relied on their services increased their influence worldwide. Facebook CEO Mark Zuckerberg once argued that his company was in fact the biggest country on the globe with more than two billion users, since the number of people on the social media exceeded the populations of the United States, China, and Brazil.

Moreover, the perception that these tech giants were challenging the state in its traditional missions was quite common. In particular, because technology is by nature "diffuse and decentralized," tech giants had the ability to "challenge two core functions of sovereign states," namely the ability to protect and the ability to tax, noted one analyst.[2]

On the security side, two features of the GAFA were particularly striking: (1) the ability to encrypt user data and keep it secure, including from the interference of public authorities and (2) the supply of cyber tools that can allow individuals or groups of people to launch cyber-attacks on key infrastructure. Both features illustrate the challenge of tech firms to the state's traditional mission of maintaining security on its territory. The existence of the GAFAs and their services undermines the state's monopoly in terms of surveillance and the political power's key assets—infrastructure in particular.[3] This was like a game of cat and mouse in which every time the government found a way to add additional constraints, the tech giants would find a way to overcome these until authorities imposed new measures. This could go on for quite some time. But, Daniel thought, the GAFAs would do well not to underestimate the potential for a political and public backlash against their overwhelming influence. It was not entirely clear, ultimately, who would, in this game, be the cat and who would be the mouse.

On the tax collection side, the challenge was perhaps even more straightforward, considering the ability of the GAFAs to develop complex schemes to limit their tax liability in any given country. But the same way, tax avoidance led these tech giants to become part of the political debate in ways that were not necessarily favorable to their image, and even less so their interests. Increased scrutiny did not only mean criticism and fines. It also meant changing policies on the part of governments that undermined their traditional ways of doing business. These policies, in turn, led tech giants to further engage in the political debate to protect their interests. They have done so repeatedly, including in the United States where they have voiced concerns over policies of the Trump administration, especially in the realms of free trade and immigration policy. Their strategy had political consequences, including on themselves.

Ultimately, this discussion over size and service users made the comparison with states all the more so powerful. In fact, the rise of these corporate superpowers (effectively stateless companies) was bound to redefine what power meant in the twenty-first century, especially in terms of who had the ability to act and to shape ultimate outcomes. But at the same time, these shifts would undeniably exacerbate the rivalry between big tech giants and traditional governments. It was about who could outsmart who. How long could any barrier or regulation stand in such a fast-moving environment in which the state had lost its monopoly on regulating economic and political interactions? One observer may have gotten it right when stating that "The world is entering an era in which the most powerful law is not that of sovereignty but that of supply and demand."[4] But again, Daniel thought: the power of these corporate giants did not mean that no backlash was possible—quite the contrary.

Redefining the Relationship to Space and to Others

The redefinition did not stop at power. It also seemed that these firms, through their actions, were redefining one's relationship to others, to space and perhaps to time.

This was particularly striking in the case of Facebook, which had given to basic terms such as "friend," "group," and "like," a whole new dimension. As a result, it was the whole concept of community that could ultimately be seen through a different light: those would not solely be the historical organizations with long-standing traditions as they could increasingly become virtual spaces where people could find alternative ways of communicating and sharing.

Amazon focused more on the time and the space issue. The company had now become famous for its relentless efforts to reduce time of delivery, in particular by increasingly relying on non-traditional means of delivery, including drones and taxis. The ultimate (and ironic) twist may have come when the firm—an Internet company *par excellence*—decided to open up a brick and mortar store in the middle of New York city, perhaps implicitly admitting that one also needed to be physical to some degree in order to fully leverage geography. Reorganizing space and geography to serve broader strategic objectives seemed to become the firm's specialty.

The case of Apple was perhaps slightly more subtle but nonetheless as striking. The company had revolutionized the way people listened to music, with the iPod and the development of iTunes. It reinvented the way we think about and what we expect from a phone, with the iPhone. It redefined what portability meant, through the development of the iPad. It was also hoping to get people to reconsider what to expect from a watch. By targeting basic products that individuals used almost on a daily basis, the company had the potential to redefine the way people shared information, and, perhaps more importantly, mobilized their resources and coordinated their efforts. The significance of social media in the unraveling of the Arab Spring had been widely discussed in the past. Whether Apple could bring this to a whole new level seemed like a rather legitimate question. Was the digital world really the place where citizens wanted to live in the long run?

The whole buzz around the Netflix series *Black Mirror* was interesting to Daniel: it looked like an all-too-real horror show that people watched to better exorcize their fears. The world that tech giants offered did not really seem to create genuine momentum when the logic of the societal organization they offered was pushed to its limits. The awe that some of us feel in the wake of the impressive technological feats that these companies were able to achieve may ultimately not be sufficient, concluded Daniel, to durably convince public opinions that there was nothing to fear.

Redefining Governance and Standards Across the Internet

The GAFAs did not only have the potential to rethink how people coexisted and interacted on line; they were also trying to redefine the way societies were organized, both in business and in societal and political terms. Some attempted and succeeded. Others tried—but failed.

This was particularly striking in the case of Amazon. As one observer of the industry noted, "Mr. Bezos has created a transaction engine that is reinventing the way entrepreneurs can do business," and speculated that the Amazon CEO's "ambition is to colonize the entire infrastructure of consumption," since the company's technological skills were basically limitless.[5] This was less about the creation of a mere marketplace or exchange platform and more about the emergence of a whole new paradigm of value creation that could challenge the relevance of domestic and global public goods.

But this effort did not stop at the supply chain or at the business level. Facebook also tried to become an alternative political forum and broadcast platform, that was increasingly becoming a rival to traditional media like radio and television[6]—which left little room for individuals to weigh in. No more corner newsstand from which you could read the headlines of the day:[7] Facebook attempted to go an extra mile by not only offering live information to each voter, but by also providing a megaphone that could give any individual far more influence than she would have had without social media.

But there were several issues that could transform into existential crises for Facebook. First, even the algorithm of news feeds was becoming political.[8] That was a fundamental limit of technology, Daniel thought: it seemed as if it, too, was not able to break down ideological barriers between people. Facebook may be more like an echo chamber than a megaphone.[9] In addition, suspicions that the network had been manipulated by ill-intentioned actors seeking to influence the outcome of elections undermined Facebook's ability to reach these goals—as well as its reputation. Worse of all, perhaps, was the Cambridge Analytica scandal that damaged the reputation of the firm further in this realm: Cambridge Analytica used the data it collected on 87 million Facebook users to influence their votes—without the users knowing.

Offering governance solutions was not as straightforward as it sounded, especially in a business environment in which consumers valued their privacy far more than what these tech giants may have initially imagined. This placed the Silicon Valley at the heart of one of the most defining technological *and* societal debates of the century that it willingly took part in. In fact, with these successes and failures, it was becoming increasingly apparent that these tech giants may not be traditional businesses: they were undeniably looking to maximize profits, but as they did, an increasing number of them seemed to look to affirm a set of political values along the way. Indeed, these companies had become forceful proponents of libertarian values, placing the protection of private data and privacy on top of their public agenda, even against the will of usually powerful governments.

This is what Apple did by refusing to help the FBI access data on the phone of a suspected terrorist involved in a deadly shooting in December 2015 for instance.[10] In a letter to customers, Apple CEO Tim Cook argued that "while we believe the FBI's intentions are good, it would be wrong for the government to force us to build a backdoor into our products. And ultimately, we fear that this demand would undermine the very freedoms and liberty our government is meant to protect."[11] If there was ever the possibility of a backdoor on any device or in any system or platform, as former National Security Agency (NSA) contractor Edward Snowden had revealed, consumers would not trust these companies and their expansion would be impeded. This explains why Apple, in its struggle against the FBI, was able to garner so much support, even from its traditional Silicon Valley rivals—somewhat of an unusual phenomenon.[12]

Tim Cook later doubled down on that idea at the World Economic Forum in Davos in 2019, calling "on the U.S. Congress to pass comprehensive federal privacy legislation—a landmark package of reforms that protect and empower the consumer," based on four principles: "the right to have personal data minimized," "the right to … know what data is being collected and why," "the right to access" in order to correct and delete personal data, and "the right to data security."[13]

This is also the change that Mark Zuckerberg has tried to set in motion in the wake of the different scandals that his social media was involved in. In March 2019, the very person who, years back, had declared that privacy was dead, now offered a "privacy-focused vision for social networking."[14] Instead of being a public square, Facebook was to become more of a living room, where users could enjoy privacy and less scrutiny from third parties, thanks to technologies like encryption and standards like postings that would disappear over time. This change of heart on the part of the Facebook CEO stumped many observers who remembered the social network for wanting to make everything public.

But the debate was pointing to new standards that could influence the industry as a whole. In particular, both Zuckerberg and Cook's contributions to the privacy debate suggested that encryption was becoming the new orthodoxy.[15] This seemed like the tech giant's way of addressing the key issues that had been raised in recent years.

Nevertheless, it was all but clear to Daniel that tech giants would successfully convince other stakeholders they had a satisfactory response. It may be time for these tech giants to start understanding why, in particular by getting a better grasp of their customers' *technological* needs, but also their expectations as *citizens* and *humans*. Daniel was reminded of the work of two Economics Nobel Prize winners, Richard Thaler and Jean Tirole. Thaler built his research around the idea that consumers and investors are not the rational actors economic theory says they are. Understanding what motivates them requires far more savviness than understanding their utility function.[16] Similarly, Tirole argued that human beings follow a far more complex decision-making process than what economists of the past century have argued. In addition to psychology, those economists neglected lessons from sociology, from anthropology, from history, from law, from political science and from biology when they studied the rational decision-maker.[17] These were the actors tech giants were interacting with in this new business environment after all. Understanding them was not a luxury anymore.

The Birth of a New Society

In practice, were these big tech giants looking to sign a new social contract, guaranteeing individual freedoms in a way traditional governments were not doing anymore, with their consumers? It certainly seemed as if that was the ambition of these companies which, like none of its predecessors, were keen on participating in philosophical debates on the role of the state, especially when it came to questions related to privacy. But were they succeeding?

On the one hand, some argued, even if this was a marketing statement on the part of some of these tech giants (something that Apple flatly denied),[18] seeing in encryption a way to differentiate themselves by providing to their consumers real guarantees in terms of data protection, were they not succeeding in addressing a clear societal need that governments did not offer? Whether governments liked it or not, these new tech giants were now filling the void, in particular by influencing the debate on the balance between security and privacy—and far more so than any other private sector agent had done in the past. And ultimately, the competition that these big tech giants were engaging in would lead them to find new ways of innovating, especially in the realms of connectivity and artificial intelligence. This competition was likely to shape the societies we lived in, far more so than traditional powers.

Who Supervises the Empire?

On the other hand, given the repeated scandals and controversies they were repeatedly involved in, it seemed as if these tech giants lacked the human resources to think about these issues beyond the only dimension of business. Their rise to power may seem unstoppable given the means they have and the ability to challenge traditional regulators. But it did not mean that the regulators would remain passive.

In fact, who would be the counter-powers to these nascent empires?[19] Counter-powers are, after all, the hallmark of democratic, free-market economies in which the tech giants prospered in the first place. In addition, it would be foolish, thought Daniel, to believe that this story would end with tech giants dominating the day for the rest of time. So again, he repeated to himself: beware of the backlash.

The Necessary Regulator

In fact, Daniel thought, tech giants were at times able to leverage the fact that they moved far faster than regulators did. As a result, the rules of the game were unclear, leaving room for political and business instability—or for creative thinking, depending on how you thought about it. But, at the same time, these very same states that tech giants could seemingly challenge could also take very painful measures in terms of fine and regulations that could undermine these companies' dominance: it was clear that the interest of tech giants and governments did not necessarily coincide, and could lead to politically motivated and protectionist policies that were easy to justify to the public in the short run, even if they had harmful long-term implications for consumers.

Tech giants have to tread carefully in handling their power moving forward as a result, thought Daniel.

As one analyst put it,

> technology companies often enter (and in some cases create) markets and industries in which regulatory regimes are barely formed—the 'rules of the game' are unclear not only to the company, but also to the regulators themselves. While this kind of blank slate certainly brings opportunity, it also

brings unpredictability—especially when the broader political, cultural, and economic dynamics in a market are unknown.[20]

Breaking into any market and sustaining a long-term position required political savviness, cultural awareness, and a solid understanding of the local context. Instead of a "new global order" that these big tech firms may have imagined, reality suggested that fragmentation, not integration, was the rule, even in this industry. As one journalist put it,

> [The] backdrop of social anxiety explains why Europe is on the march against American tech giants. European governments have been at the forefront of an effort to limit the reach of tech companies, most often through privacy regulations and antitrust investigations. … Over the next few years, we are bound to see increasing friction between the tiny group of tech companies that rule much of the industry and the governments that rule the lands those companies are trying to invade. What is happening in Europe is playing out in China, India and Brazil and across much of the rest of the globe, as well.[21]

(In practice, since 2010, the European Commission launched three separate investigations against Google for instance, fining the tech giant for a total sum that now exceeds €6 billion euros).

The GAFA looked like all-mighty businesses ready to take over the global economy in countries in which social anxiety was significant. But the reality was that these firms were actually far more vulnerable to political changes, driven by real economic needs or by evolving political sentiments, that, either way, they needed to monitor.

The Not-so-Weak Consumer

Daniel also knew that, since he had become so dependent and so enthusiastic about them. But that same enthusiasm, Daniel thought, can also be ephemeral: the same consumers (including him) who relied so much on these tech firms' services could be the very same who decided that the social contract they offered was not satisfactory or had been breached.

As one pundit put it, "Apple is innovative. Its products look nice. But civilisation would survive the absence of iPads and iPhone."[22] And while the debate on the tension between privacy and security is relevant, there does not seem to be any real justification for Apple, rather than society as a whole, to solve it by itself: Neither Apple nor its competitors can claim the status of "custodians of the digital future … that should grant them immunity from the meddling of courts or the judgments of elected politicians."[23] And as another report added, there was no guarantee that the consumer would necessarily trust these big giants more than the government when it came to data protection and safety. A backlash could be possible if the data crunching that these big tech giants engaged in did not provide satisfaction to the consumer or was considered inadequately safeguarded.[24]

In fact, it occurred to Daniel that history teaches us that empires are never eternal. In practice, these tech giants' influence could be undermined if their own constituents refused, at some later point, to play ball: in other words, if the consumer ever decided to pull the plug, the empire could fall. The answer to the question of these firms' counterweight could be far simpler than most people thought.

The Changing Global Landscape May Require More than Geeks to Strive

It was therefore crucial for GAFAs to consider the ultimate effects of their strategy on their relationship with governments and on the broader, global business environment. Without careful consideration, the potential for backlash was huge.

Forces, Unite?

Could tech giants and business work together?

Proceed with caution, Daniel thought once again. The alliance between tech giants and states made sense on key political hot topics, like when it came to the fight against religious extremism and efforts to counter the narratives of terrorist groups for instance. This could be a problem though when the government in the partnership had a questionable approach to human behavior, as Egypt did. The country's government requested Microsoft's assistance in countering extremist narrative of the Islamic State in Iraq. While the task was laudable, Egypt's dubious track record when it came to human rights made it no less tricky.[25]

Other cases suggested that, in practice, the partnership could and did work, on the religious extremism issue,[26] as well as on others like when it came to protecting a country or a region's infrastructure, especially in the cyber domain. This type of cooperation on key strategic issues seemed in everyone's interest.[27] Countries needed these businesses in order to foster growth-friendly environments. Conversely, in case of a breach and/or an attack led by a foreign entity, as this has happened in the past, any of these firms would require government assistance.[28]

In the end, it was a matter of getting these significantly different profiles to talk to each other. As two analysts put it,

> Policymakers need to shape intelligent integration of promising technology solutions, and commercial technology companies will want to reap the most benefit from these vast and burgeoning markets. For this to occur, tech geeks and policy wonks need to shed the hackneyed 'disruptors versus regulators' paradigm and focus on the ways they can work together.

They concluded, ultimately: "When geeks and (policy) wonks reach across the divide, both policies and products will benefit."[29]

Beyond the Geeks

But as Daniel's analysis of the situation had pointed out, though they could be temporary partners, states and governments were bound to be competitors.

Competition did not necessarily mean the collision course that some stark opposition suggested. In fact, they could be healthy competitors. As it became increasingly hard to force big tech companies to abide by current standards and regulations, traditional governments would have the incentive to adapt and to spend more resources to beat these firms at their own game. As a result, some, including former NSA director Michael Hayden, even thought that this competition would turn out to be healthy: technological progress, that guaranteed privacy for instance, made everyone safer. If governments wanted to circumvent the technological safeguards for legal and monitoring purposes, they would need to invest the money in research and development to achieve their goal. By uncovering vulnerabilities in operating systems or adapting regulations, those governments would provide in turn private stakeholders with the incentive to continue to improve their products and strategy. Overall, the rivalry makes regulations more relevant in a changing context.

In any case, whether competition was healthy or harsh, Daniel reached the same conclusion, over and over: being politically savvy, culturally aware, and having a solid understanding of the local context were the key. So what types of profiles were best suited to monitor these uncharted waters, understand the evolving nature of policies and political calculations, and ultimately help define the business–government relationship? This landscape was undoubtedly filled with risks, but it could also be full of opportunities for the most agile, imaginative, and clever actors.

Next Steps: Finding the Talent to Address These Challenges

Building the right team with the relevant talent, training (or re-training) the workforce to help it adapt to the changing landscape, and identifying and seeking the new types of talents needed to tackle the new challenges of the business environment is the ultimate task of architects of change.

The example of tech giants is quite meaningful from this perspective: they set in motion a transformation of our business environment which, in turn, may very well be forcing their own transformation. This case study raises the issue of the kind of staff that these companies—and arguably others from the tech sector and beyond—need in order to manage the new business environment they contributed to bring about. In particular what type of skills and competences will they now need, beyond the technical and engineering skills they will most likely require to further develop their products? The case sheds light on this debate by pointing to three fundamental sets of human resource issues that these firms will need to address.

First comes the question of the overall sets of skills you need from your workforce. As the previous chapter showed, the World Economic Forum expects critical thinking and creativity to play a relatively more important role alongside of complex problem solving, compared to people management and coordinating with others. What is noteworthy is that both critical thinking and creativity are skills that affect a wide range of positions inside a firm: any decision, product or service improvement, or broader shift in strategy has the potential to have broader ramifications. Those who understand those ramifications and who can design strategies so as to better control their consequences are likely to maintain an edge over competitors. This is what critical thinking is designed to help a manager achieve: by "using logic and reasoning to identify the strengths and weaknesses of alternative solutions, conclusions or approaches to problems,"[30] tech giant executives, and, more broadly, architects of change, should be able to challenge more effectively some of the prevailing consensus in the industry that could shape its future. The fact that the process through which a social network like Facebook had to go through on the issue of private data was particularly painful shows that challenging these consensuses is no easy task. Creativity, or the "ability to come up with unusual or clever ideas about a given topic or situation, or to develop creative ways to solve a problem,"[31] is all the more crucial to challenge those preconceptions. And strikingly, in yesterday's world, neither creativity nor critical thinking was necessarily the first quality of tech experts. This is a first source of change.

Second comes the very related question of the new breed of talents that may be needed to tackle the challenges of *today's* business environment. The example of data scientists is telling from this standpoint. As two American academics have argued, "Data scientists are the people who understand how to fish out answers to important business questions from today's tsunami of unstructured information." While their most basic skill is coding, they are also very curious profiles and show "a desire to go beneath the surface of a problem, find the questions at its heart, and distill them into a very clear set of hypotheses that can be tested." They are not, in fact, merely statisticians, but data experts with an eye turned towards the social reality they are trying to uncover, that is, data experts with a consciousness of the human complexity of the business environment they are looking to help their business tame. Reconciliating very technical fields like data analysis with the understanding of changing realities is another human resource challenge for architects of change as a result.

Third, and not unrelated challenge either, is the question of talents when you know full well that you are entering uncharted waters. By definition, defining the talents and skills you will need in order to survive and strive in this world is difficult, not to say impossible. It is at this point that it becomes critical for resilience and creativity to be part of an institution's bloodstream: there may be deep uncertainty about the environment that you will end up in tomorrow, but there is far less uncertainty about the need to use logic to identify alternative solutions and to identify creative, clever, and unusual ways to solve problems. Encouraging that mindset in an institution to the extent that it becomes standard practice is easier to state as a goal than to actually implement. And yet, this is the mindset that characterizes architects of change who, in the end, recognize that the process of creative destruction ultimately applies to them—and requires them to invest in their teams and in themselves to continue bringing change.

Notes

1. David Francis, "The Top 25 Corporate Nations," *Foreign Policy*, April 2016.
2. Mark Y. Rosenberg, "Tech Giants Who Keep Ignoring Geopolitics Do so at Their Peril," *Quartz* (blog), March 4, 2016, http://qz.com/631560/tech-giants-who-keep-ignoring-geopolitics-do-so-at-their-peril/.
3. Rosenberg.
4. Parag Khanna, "These 25 Companies Are More Powerful Than Many Countries," *Foreign Affairs*, April 2016, http://foreignpolicy.com/2016/03/15/these-25-companies-are-more-powerful-than-many-countries-multinational-corporate-wealth-power/.

5. Barney Jopson, "From Warehouse to Powerhouse," *Financial Times*, July 8, 2012, https://next.ft.com/content/cc3a0eee-c1de-11e1-8e7c-00144feabdc0.
6. Derek Thompson, "Facebook and Fear," *The Atlantic*, May 10, 2016, http://www.theatlantic.com/technology/archive/2016/05/the-facebook-future/482145/.
7. Geoffrey A. Fowler, "What If Facebook Gave Us an Opposing-Viewpoints Button?," *Wall Street Journal*, May 18, 2016, sec. Tech, http://www.wsj.com/articles/what-if-facebook-gave-us-an-opposing-viewpoints-button-1463573101.
8. Farhad Manjoo, "Facebook's Bias Is Built-In, and Bears Watching," *The New York Times*, May 11, 2016, http://www.nytimes.com/2016/05/12/technology/facebooks-bias-is-built-in-and-bears-watching.html.
9. Fowler, "What If Facebook Gave Us an Opposing-Viewpoints Button?"
10. Eric Lichtblau and Katie Benner, "Apple Fights Order to Unlock San Bernardino Gunman's IPhone," *The New York Times*, February 17, 2016, http://www.nytimes.com/2016/02/18/technology/apple-timothy-cook-fbi-san-bernardino.html.
11. Tim Cook, "A Message to Our Customers," Apple, February 16, 2016, http://www.apple.com/customer-letter/.
12. Tim Bradshaw, "Apple Gains Support from Tech Rivals in FBI Case," *Financial Times*, accessed June 7, 2016, http://www.ft.com/cms/s/0/5be5dc14-e1aa-11e5-8d9b-e88a2a889797.html.
13. Tim Cook, "It's Time for Action on Privacy, Says Apple's CEO Tim Cook," *Time*, January 16, 2019, http://time.com/collection-post/5502591/tim-cook-data-privacy/.
14. Mark Zuckerberg, "A Privacy-Focused Vision for Social Networking," *Facebook* (blog), March 6, 2019, https://www.facebook.com/notes/mark-zuckerberg/a-privacy-focused-vision-for-social-networking/10156700570096634/.
15. Cade Metz, "Forget Apple vs. the FBI: WhatsApp Just Switched on Encryption for a Billion People," April 4, 2016, http://www.wired.com/2016/04/forget-apple-vs-fbi-whatsapp-just-switched-encryption-billion-people/.
16. Carol Tavris, "How Homo Economicus Went Extinct," *Wall Street Journal*, May 15, 2015, sec. Arts, https://www.wsj.com/articles/how-homo-economicus-went-extinct-1431721255.
17. Jean Tirole, "L'homo economicus a vécu," *Le Monde*, October 5, 2018, https://www.lemonde.fr/idees/article/2018/10/05/jean-tirole-l-homo-economicus-a-vecu_5365278_3232.html.
18. Holman W. Jr Jenkins, "Encryption Answer Is Spy vs. Spy," *Wall Street Journal*, March 29, 2016, sec. Opinion, http://www.wsj.com/articles/encryption-answer-is-spy-vs-spy-1459291538; "Answers to Your Questions about Apple and Security," Apple, accessed June 8, 2016, http://www.apple.com/customer-letter/answers/; Philip Stephens, "Silicon Valley Should Step out of

the Cloud," *Financial Times*, March 3, 2016, http://www.ft.com/cms/s/0/075be1b2-deed-11e5-b67f-a61732c1d025.html.

19. The comparison between these giant tech companies and empires is recurrent. Referring to Facebook's "like" button, *The Economist* observed: "Not since the era of imperial Rome has the "thumbsup" sign been such a potent and public symbol of power." It added: "A mere 12 years after it was founded, Facebook is a great empire with a vast population, immense wealth, a charismatic leader, and mindboggling reach and influence. The world's largest social network has 1.6 billion users, a billion of whom use it every day for an average of over 20 minutes each. In the Western world, Facebook accounts for the largest share of the most popular activity (social networking) on the most widely used computing devices (smartphones); its various apps account for 30% of mobile internet use by Americans." See "Imperial Ambitions," *The Economist*, April 9, 2016, http://www.economist.com/news/leaders/21696521-mark-zuckerberg-prepares-fight-dominance-next-era-computing-imperial-ambitions.
20. Rosenberg, "Tech Giants Who Keep Ignoring Geopolitics Do so at Their Peril."
21. Farhad Manjoo, "Why the World Is Drawing Battle Lines Against American Tech Giants," *The New York Times*, June 1, 2016, http://www.nytimes.com/2016/06/02/technology/why-the-world-is-drawing-battle-lines-against-american-tech-giants.html.
22. Stephens, "Silicon Valley Should Step out of the Cloud."
23. Stephens.
24. "Imperial Ambitions."
25. Colum Lynch, "How to Defeat Extremism Without Becoming Egypt's Microserf," *Foreign Policy* (blog), May 10, 2016, https://foreignpolicy.com/2016/05/10/how-to-defeat-extremism-without-becoming-egypts-microserf/.
26. Julia Harte and Dustin Volz, "U.S. Looks to Facebook, Private Groups to Battle Online Extremism," *Reuters*, February 25, 2016, http://www.reuters.com/article/us-internet-militants-countermessaging-idUSKCN0VY01O.
27. Elias Groll, "SecDef to Silicon Valley: Can't We Just Be Friends?," *Foreign Policy* (blog), March 2, 2016, https://foreignpolicy.com/2016/03/02/secdef-to-silicon-valley-cant-we-just-be-friends/.
28. Michael Schrage, "How Amazon or Apple Could Cause a War with China," *Harvard Business Review* (blog), May 6, 2011, https://hbr.org/2011/05/how-amazon-or-apple-could-caus.
29. Lillian Ablon and Andrea Golay, "How the 'Wonks' of Public Policy and the 'Geeks' of Tech Can Get Together," *TechCrunch* (blog), March 17, 2016, http://social.techcrunch.com/2016/03/17/how-the-wonks-of-public-policy-and-the-geeks-of-tech-can-get-together/.
30. "The Future of Jobs" (Geneva, Switzerland: World Economic Forum, January 2016), https://www.weforum.org/reports/the-future-of-jobs/.
31. "The Future of Jobs."

15

A Tribute to My Kids (the Ultimate Architects of Change)

Meet Daniel, 7, and Emilie, 4, partners in crime. At the end of a long day, it is not unusual for their father to sit on the couch, thankful that he can finally rest for a few minutes—that is, until he hears a big noise coming from the room of our two little friends. The father, like any father, is likely to rush to their room, praying (like any father again) that tonight will not be the night when he will need to rush to the emergency room (again). Yet, more often than not (and thankfully), when he gets to the room, he is not the witness of some grave accident. Instead, in that room, there may be chaos, there may be racket, there is often a huge mess—but there are as well (and invariably) two little children laughing and surprised to see their dad come so fast. And that very laugh has often left this author wondering: why a laugh, and no other form of reaction?

This question may feel extremely philosophical or trivial depending on your own experience. But its ramifications for the way we think about the business environment and the way we bring about change are actually phenomenal. As children, we did not lack curiosity, imagination, or creativity. We constantly questioned and challenged the world that surrounds us. Yet, as we grow older, we stop doing that; and as we do, our ability to become architects of change weakens. This brief conclusion explains why this might be.

What Science Says About a Child's Brain

Over the course of the past half-century, our beliefs about children, their behavior and their thinking, have profoundly evolved: scientific research has suggested that they probably have far more empathy, are far more rational and

J. Ghez, *Architects of Change*, https://doi.org/10.1007/978-3-030-20684-0_15

are far more interested in and able to figure out causal links than what we used to think. In fact, anyone who has interacted with children knows the feeling of being struck by their outright ability to deal with complex machines, understand how to get them to work and to use them. This ability suggests that their thinking may be far more subtle and complex than what we can imagine: though they may not do it consciously, they not only act as if they are constantly looking to refine their understanding of how the world works but also look to incorporate what they learn along the way in their reasoning so as to avoid making mistakes again.

The Power of Open-Mindedness

Take, for instance, what cognitive scientist, psychologist, philosopher Alison Gopnik has shown about children being far more open-minded than what we used to think. In particular, because they have a basic understanding of the laws of physics and biology, they are not only able to recognize statistical anomalies; they also have the ability to ponder those anomalies and think about what they mean, instead of looking to confirm what they initially thought as adults would do.[1] Evidence that contradicts what they know is like an opportunity to refine their understanding, rather than some insurmountable event that could lead an adult's world to crumble. In a nutshell, children display a far greater ability to update their understanding than we do.[2]

Gopnik argues that these remarkable abilities children have to learn is a result of evolution. Humans remain children for a much longer period of time than most species, and the division of labor between childhood and adulthood is quite remarkable: as Gopnik puts it, "Babies get a protected time to learn about their environment, without having to actually do anything. When they grow up, they can use what they have learned to be better at surviving and reproducing—and taking care of the next generation."[3] Children learn under the protection of adults who guarantee their existence, through reproduction, and their survival, by caring for them.

Evolution at Play

But in order for this division of labor to function properly, babies and young children must have remarkable learning abilities; otherwise, they would not be able to care for the next generation once they become adults. On this matter, the evolution of the brain, from childhood to adulthood, is quite insightful, Gopnik tells us. In fact, the region of the brain that helps adults concentrate, plan, and be productive is the prefrontal cortex that takes an especially long time to mature—up to 25 years. Whereas the ability to concentrate, to plan, and to be productive may be fundamental for adults, would children have it too, they would experience far greater difficulties in learning: as Gopnik puts it,

> being uninhibited may help babies and young children to explore freely. There is a trade-off between the ability to explore creatively and learn flexibly, like a child, and the ability to plan and act effectively, like an adult. The very qualities needed to act efficiently—such as swift automatic processing and a highly pruned brain network—may be intrinsically antithetical to the qualities that are useful for learning, such as flexibility.[4]

In other words, unless children are curious, imaginative, and creative, unless they always try to experiment and test, they cannot possibly learn about the world that surrounds them and ultimately cannot survive. This division of labor between children and adults works because children have a remarkable ability to learn and to remember lessons for adulthood.

So, back to the initial question: why are Daniel and Emilie laughing? Perhaps because they are learning or refining their understanding of what gets their dad running to their room—in this particular case, a huge noise. That laugh is an expression of their satisfaction of having learned something new, something that will let them refine their comprehension of the world. Science suggests that adults tend to lose that ability as they grow older and become more fit for tasks such as planning and acting effectively, because they become more "inhibited" to use Gopnik's term. A short exploration of fiction can help us better understand why this is.

What Fiction Has to Say About a Child's Intelligence

The story that award-winning American novelist Jonathan Safran Foer tells in one of his books, *Extremely Loud & Incredibly Close*, can particularly enlighten us on why adults may be far more "inhibited."

Smart Versus Knowledgeable

Oskar, a nine-year-old boy, is the main character of the book. His father (and closest friend), among the victims of the 9-11 attacks, left an envelope containing a key in his closet. The book tells the story of Oskar's investigation to determine what that key is for and who it belongs to. Just like an investigator, the boy looks to collect evidence, and recalls, on the day of his father's funeral, a specific conversation he had with him about the family retail jewelry business. As he recalls it, "Dad constantly used to tell me I was too smart for retail. That never made sense to me, because he was smarter than me, so if I was too smart for retail, then he really must have been too smart for retail." But his father begs to differ, telling his son: "I'm not smarter than you, I'm more knowledgeable than you, and that's only because I'm older than you. Parents are always more knowledgeable than their children, and children are always smarter than their parents."[5]

Oskar's father provides us with a meaningful insight about human psychology: we may be confusing intelligence and knowledge, or worse, intelligence and sophistication. In fact, as we grow older and as we become more knowledgeable, we legitimately feel more sophisticated: we arguably have more analytical tools at our disposal and a greater ability to grasp the complexity that surrounds us.

The Surprising Effects of Our Sophistication

This makes us feel more sophisticated because we possibly rely less on speculation, on fantasy, or on irrational explanations to give sense to the world that surrounds us. But this sophistication comes at an unlikely and unexpected price: it undermines our ability to *question* the world that surrounds us. It means that we are less likely to challenge ideas that seem far more straightforward than they should and that are far less consensual than they really are. It also means that we are more likely to underestimate the power of observation: As American financier Bernard Baruch once observed, "I'm not smart. I try to observe. Millions saw the apple fall but Newton was the one who asked why." As a result, this sophistication shrinks the array of options we consider in order to solve a problem. In sum, this sophistication makes us less intelligent and less creative—not more. (This sets an interesting question for the western education system: as children grow older, they ask increasingly less questions at school, even though the fields they study become increasingly complex. This is a real challenge that this book does not tackle, but that is certainly worth pondering.)[6]

Again, back to the initial question: why are Daniel and Emilie laughing? It is not only because they have refined their comprehension of how the world works and that they are able to improve their understanding of the probability distribution that governs their surroundings. It is also because they have further evidence of the fact that their ability to learn is intact, and that they are doing their job as children, namely learning to understand what is happening around them through exploration. Coming to that conclusion can only be the cause of satisfaction.

Think Like a Child? The Ultimate Challenge for Architects of Change

The encouragement to think like a child should not be confused with an invitation to act in a childish manner—quite to the contrary. This encouragement is about abandoning dogma and preconceptions about how the world works and about generating a wide range of ideas, even outlandish ones, in order to look a little more like children when we approach and try to tackle issues.

Striking Resemblances

That we live in a complex world is a (quite trivial) fact that everyone seems to agree on; but in doing so, we may take for granted the notion that this very complexity that we both love, given the technological achievements it allows for, and fear, given the instability it can generate, requires complex solutions. This may very well be true, most of the time—but not necessarily, because complex solutions require sophistication, the very kind of sophistication that kills curiosity, imagination, and creativity.

In fact, if you consider the major characteristics and tasks of architects of change—those very people who are best equipped, both in terms of skills and in terms of mindsets, to bring solutions to the world's most pressing and mind-boggling problems—you may notice how much they resemble that of children.

In particular, as this book argued, architects of change develop an ability to think more like Q and not just like James Bond, looking to develop alternative views of the world (Chap. 2). They question the world they live in and try to make sense out of it, in order to decide how to act appropriately (Chap. 3). They look to reinvent by developing alternative uses for existing assets whose purpose they thereby redefine (Chap. 5). They are analytical, not ideological, in their quest to determine what the facts are (Chap. 7). They try to anticipate what is coming, in particular by shedding light on drivers and on causal links, including complex ones (Chap. 9). They do not fear to put their imagination to good use and to explore the unknown—or what *they* do not know, their unknown (Chap. 11). And in the end, they see in creativity the only possible response to a turbulent business environment, as they look to break rules and consensus that lost their relevance over time (Chap. 13).

It is striking that there is no single characteristic or task in this list that children could not decide to undertake naturally, on their own, because survival dictates that they do in order to accomplish their goal, namely learn about the world they live in—in order to better tame in the future. Children may very well be, as a result, the ultimate architects of change.

The Solution May Be Closer Than You Think

Daniel, Emilie, and all the others often turn to us to learn because it is their job to do so and because they know that they do not know. Our job, in turn, lies not only in educating them but also in emulating them. In fact, if we do not emulate them, stagnation and status quo may be the least of our problems: as babies and as young children, we explore freely and learn in order to be more fit to survive and to reproduce, so as to better care for the generation that comes next; if we are really failing to continue exploring freely and learn, our ability to survive may be compromised.

In fact, this learning process does not stop the world from changing, at times in dramatic ways, as we grow older and become adults—making what we have learned as children potentially obsolete. The notion that we could stop learning, or, worse, that we could believe our sophistication exempts us from needing to learn and to be curious, could be fatal as a result, in the end. Worse, believing in simple solutions that are sold to us by demagogues, that are the undebatable dogma of the tribe, or that are dictated by the ideology of a generation which overlooks the risks of nonchalance and complacency may provide short-term relief—but will also be the reason of our long-term hardship that we will deserve if we do not make an effort to go beyond those simple solutions and if we find comfort in indifference about the world that surrounds us. In the words attributed to the late writer Elie Wiesel, "The opposite of love is not hate, it's indifference. The opposite of art is not ugliness, it's indifference. The opposite of faith is not heresy, it's indifference. And the opposite of life is not death, it's indifference." The only way to continue having an impact on this landscape is to avoid indifference. Curiosity and learning are the only policy insurances we can believe in.

In fact, when we stop taking the world for granted and when we stop relying on assumptions we do not question anymore, that is, when we do emulate any child that we know, we remove the ultimate barriers to becoming true architects of change.

Notes

1. Alison Gopnik, "Little Scientists: Babies Have Scientific Minds," *Scientific American*, July 2010, https://doi.org/10.1038/scientificamerican0710-76.
2. As Gopnik argues,

> Adults suffer from 'confirmation bias'—we pay attention to the events that fit what we already know and ignore things that might shake up our

preconceptions. Charles Darwin famously kept a special list of all the facts that were at odds with his theory, because he knew he'd otherwise be tempted to ignore or forget them. Babies, on the other hand, seem to have a positive hunger for the unexpected. Like the ideal scientists proposed by the philosopher of science Karl Popper, babies are always on the lookout for a fact that falsifies their theories. If you want to learn the mysteries of the universe, that great, distinctively human project, keep your eye on those weird eggs.

See: Alison Gopnik, "How 1-Year-Olds Figure Out the World," *Wall Street Journal*, April 15, 2015, sec. Life, https://www.wsj.com/articles/how-1-year-olds-figure-out-the-world-1429111159.

3. Gopnik, "Little Scientists."
4. Gopnik.
5. Jonathan Safran Foer, *Extremely Loud and Incredibly Close* (Penguin Books, 2005), https://www.amazon.com/Extremely-Loud-Incredibly-Close-Novel-ebook/dp/B003K16PXC/ref=sr_1_2?keywords=Extremely+Loud+and+Incredibly+Close&qid=1555166947&s=gateway&sr=8-2.
6. Hodgson, Philip, and Randall White. Relax, It's Only Uncertainty: Lead the Way When the Way Is Changing. 1 edition. Harlow: Pearson Ft Press, 2001.

Index[1]

NUMBERS AND SYMBOLS
9-11 (date), 219
1929 crisis, 34
1998 Russian Debt Default, 52
2008 Great Recession, 72, 113, 118

A
Africa, 127, 128, 147
Alibaba, 18, 50, 121, 122
Alice in Wonderland, 67, 68
Allison, Graham, 118
Alphabet, 202
Amazon, 111–123, 169, 172, 202, 204, 205
Anticipation, 13, 127–149, 154, 168, 178, 196
Antifragility, 167
Architect of change, 9, 11–13, 16, 18, 19, 24, 38, 63, 65–66, 75, 93, 106–108, 123, 146, 156, 157, 168–173, 178–180
Artificial intelligence (AI), 3, 45–50, 55, 83, 85, 92, 208
Asimov, Isaac, 69
Automation, 3, 48, 49, 92, 112, 153

B
Barbier, Joël, 169
BBC, 108
Ben Ali, Zine el-Abidine, 131, 149n9
Big data, 55, 64, 139, 157
Black Mirror, 204
Black swan, 155, 164
Blair, Tony, 52
Brand, 18, 91, 197, 198
Brexit, vii, 32, 66, 108, 140, 141, 143, 147
Broken system, 2, 11, 12, 65
Business environment, vii, viii, 1, 2, 3, 7–13, 15–20, 23–26, 31, 33–38, 41, 43, 45, 48–51, 62–65, 67, 70, 73–75, 79, 82–85, 95–100, 112, 114, 116, 117, 122, 123, 127, 128, 130, 131, 137–141, 144–147, 151–153, 155,

[1] Note: Page numbers followed by 'n' refer to notes.

J. Ghez, *Architects of Change*, https://doi.org/10.1007/978-3-030-20684-0

159–166, 168, 170–171, 176–178, 189–197, 202, 205, 207, 210, 212, 213, 217, 221
Business models, 1, 11, 44, 84, 93, 122, 148, 169, 170, 172, 173, 175, 177, 192, 193

C

Cambridge Analytica, 205
Cameron, David, 140
Carroll, Lewis, 67–69
Central bank, 56
Chicago Board Options Exchange Volatility Index, 119
China, 3, 27–29, 33, 42, 47, 50, 55, 56n3, 72, 112, 113, 116–118, 121, 131, 144, 152, 157, 197–198, 202, 209
Climate change, 3, 38, 39, 41–47, 56, 121, 123
Cold War, 3, 4, 31, 117, 122, 191
Competition, 54, 63, 68, 70, 72, 75–87, 144, 169, 172, 192, 207, 208, 211
Cooperation, 24, 34–38, 45, 51, 81, 85, 114, 210
Corporate superpowers, 203
Creative destruction, 70, 74, 75, 83, 86, 166, 177, 180, 196, 213
Creative economy, 191–194
Creativity, 13, 63, 66, 74, 99, 149, 189–198, 212, 213, 217, 221
Curiosity, 8, 9, 13, 15, 19, 20, 139, 141, 156, 189, 190, 217, 221, 222

D

Darwin, Charles, 83, 84, 86, 87, 223n2
Data scientist, 213
David and Goliath, 195–196
Dehio, Ludwig, 133
Diaz, Carlos, 104, 120
Differentiation, 77, 78, 81, 83, 172, 174n7
Digital Vortex, 169, 171, 172
Disconnect, 1, 2, 147
Disruptive moments, vii, 25, 33, 66, 95, 106, 115, 123, 131, 132, 168, 177, 179
Diversification, 162
Dogma, 10, 15, 19, 40, 95, 101, 129, 146, 163, 221, 222
Dysfunctional, 1, 9, 12, 38–41, 45–47

E

Economic growth, 3, 8, 42, 44, 120, 192
The Economist, 17, 111, 113, 118, 121, 127
Efficiency, 4, 39, 45, 73, 75, 98, 105, 172
Egypt, 131, 210
Elasticity, 167
Empathy, 61, 66, 74, 156, 160, 197, 217
Empowerment, 7, 39, 147
Encryption, 206, 207
Eurasia Group, 53, 54, 58n29
Euro crisis, 117, 133, 134
European Union (EU), vii, 29, 32, 33, 35, 36, 77, 111, 116–118, 128, 131–135, 137, 138, 140–146, 163
Evolution, 20, 28, 36, 43, 68, 69, 83, 86, 87, 96, 100, 102, 103, 113, 146, 157, 159, 163, 168, 193, 218–219
Extrapolation, 87, 131, 168

F

Facebook, 41, 64, 114, 202, 204–206, 212, 215n19
FBI, 206

Feedback, 128, 131, 135–138
Fintechs, 170
Fireman, 8, 9
First-mover advantage, 85
First-past-the-post, 108
Flexibility, 147, 153, 160, 164–168, 172, 219
Focal points, 131–133
Foer, Jonathan Safran, 219
4G, 64
Fourth Industrial Revolution, 45, 193
France, 5, 31, 111, 115, 132, 137, 147, 149n9
Friedman, Thomas, 63, 66n5, 124n8

G
G7, 52, 56n3, 117
G8, 52
G20, 117
GAFA (Google, Apple, Facebook, and Amazon), 50, 201–210
Game-changer, 11, 103, 132, 147
General Agreement on Tariffs and Trade (GATT), 117
Geopolitical rivalries, 24–34, 43, 46, 47, 50, 51, 56n3, 117, 118, 133, 134, 143
German reunification, 133
Germany, 5, 132–134, 143
Gladwell, Malcolm, 195, 196
Globalization, 3, 56n3, 72, 73, 83, 111–123, 157, 191
Global warming, vii, viii, 24, 41, 42, 51
Google, 41, 114, 202, 209
Gopnik, Alison, 218, 219, 222n2
Greece, 133, 134, 137, 143
Gross domestic product (GDP), 4–6, 25, 27, 113, 115, 116, 202
G-Zero, 34

H
Hayden, Michael, 211
Hegemon, 25–27, 33, 37
Historical analysis, 128, 131–133, 135, 144
Horizon scanning, 128, 131, 138–141
Human Development Index (HDI), 5, 6

I
IBM, 17, 148
Identity politics, 24, 51
Ideology, 40, 47, 101, 222
Imagination, 9, 13, 19, 20, 31, 66, 95, 132, 139, 141, 156, 159–173, 177, 179–180, 191, 194, 196, 217, 221
Inequalities, 24, 39–41, 51, 121, 157
International Labor Organization, 74, 75
Irrationality, 194

J
James Bond, 12, 15–20, 221
Japan, 127, 131
Jobs, Steve, 84, 102

K
Kahneman, Daniel, 86, 129, 179
Kapferer, Jean-Noël, 197
Klein, Gary, 178, 179
Knight, Frank, 161, 163, 164
Knowhere News, 47
Knowledge economy, 13, 191–194

L
Lamarck, Jean-Baptiste de, 83, 84
Lee, Harper, 62

Lehman Brothers, 52
Linearity, 95, 100
LinkedIn, 64
Luddite, 48
Luxury, 9, 23, 122, 197–198, 201, 207

M

Ma, Jack, 121
Maastricht Treaty, 132
Maddison, Angus, 5
Made in China, 18
McAfee, Andrew, 49
Media, 19, 41, 47, 54, 55, 101–103, 108, 169, 202, 204–206
Megatrends, 23, 62
Mental gymnastics, 20, 62, 63, 123, 177, 197
Metaphors, 69–70, 104, 105, 135, 169
Microsoft, 210
Millennium Development Goals (MDG), 39
Mitterrand, François, 133
Monopoly, 78, 86, 111, 145, 203
Morgan, Gareth, 104, 105
Mubarak, Hosni, 131

N

National Security Agency (NSA), 206, 211
Netflix, 148, 172, 204
Network, 17, 19, 50, 54, 84, 102, 130, 133, 136, 156, 170, 190, 192, 193, 205, 206, 212, 215n19, 219
Newton, Alastair, 51–55, 58n28, 58n29–59n33, 60n36, 220
Nomura, 52
Non-state (non-governmental) actors, 25, 29, 32
North Atlantic Treaty Organization (NATO), 31, 37
Nye, Joseph, 32

O

Obsolete, 1, 9, 12, 23, 76, 93, 98, 99, 175, 177, 190, 195, 222
One Belt, One Road (OBOR), 152
Organization for Economic Co-operation and Development (OECD), 6, 52, 56n3, 113
Organization of the Petroleum Exporting Countries (OPEC), 81

P

Pascal's wager, 161
PESTLE (Political, Economic, Social, Technological, Legal, and Environmental), 96–100
Picq, Pascal, 83
Polarization, 3, 39–41, 102, 107, 108, 118, 163
Political analyst, 51–55, 59n31, 59n33
Populist, vii, 8, 112, 115, 116, 118, 141
Porter, Michael, 72, 73, 173n7
PowerPoint, 55, 59n34
Power struggles, 24, 33, 34, 105
Prefrontal cortex, 219
Pre-mortem, 13, 175–180
Prisoners' dilemma, 80
Privacy, 38, 205–207, 209, 211
Procurement, 10, 73
Productivity, 3, 45, 71, 72, 192
Profit maximization, 11, 70, 206
Profits, 10, 11, 17, 70, 73, 77, 81, 82, 84, 171, 172

Q

Q, 12, 15–20, 221

R

Red Queen, 67–70, 78, 83, 84
Red team analysis, 155
Regulator, 18, 29, 77, 79, 99, 208–209, 211
Reinvention, vii, 7, 13, 15, 67–87, 145, 146, 168, 180, 196
Renaissance, 7, 8
Republicans, 108
Resilience, 8, 13, 46, 112, 160, 162, 164–168, 176, 213
Rue des Rosiers, 76, 78
Rule breaker, 197
Rumsfeld, Donald, 162–165, 180

S

Scenario, 38, 85, 114, 128, 130, 131, 141–145, 151, 153–155, 157, 162, 168, 171, 176, 177, 180
Scenario analysis, 129, 131, 141–146
Schelling, Thomas, 42, 131, 132, 195
Schumpeter, Joseph, 70, 75, 78, 86, 87, 92, 166, 180
Selection, 84, 87, 105, 134
Shared value, 11, 37, 72, 73
Silicon Valley, 84, 120, 175, 201, 206
Singapore, 140
Skills mismatch, 74
Skype, 64
Slowbalisation, 111, 112, 121, 122
Smart power, 32
Snowden, Edward, 206
Social demotion, 4, 8, 39, 40
Social entrepreneur, 65
Soft power, 32
Spain, 133, 137
Status quo, 10–12, 26–29, 33, 34, 39, 104, 190, 222
Sustainable Development Goals (SDG), 39, 44, 46–47

T

Taleb, Nicholas, 167, 168
Technology, 17, 18, 24, 38, 45–51, 70–72, 74, 87, 91, 98–99, 101, 103, 104, 120, 128, 148, 169, 170–172, 175, 191–193, 196, 201, 202, 205, 206, 208, 211
Tetlock, Philipp, 129, 130, 136
Thomson, James A., 107
3D printing, 123, 153
Thucydides Trap, The, 124n18
Time horizon, 76, 81, 127
Today's Zaman, 167
To Kill a Mockingbird, 62
Toyota, 172, 174n8
Trend convergence, 102–103, 139
Treverton, Greg, 21n1, 147
Tribalism, 40
Trump, Donald, vii, 66, 104, 111, 117, 120, 147, 203
Truth decay, 101–102
Turkey, 167
Twitter, 55, 64, 84

U

Uber, 17–18, 169, 172
Uncertainty, 8, 30, 35, 37, 102, 138, 159–165, 168, 169, 177–180, 191, 213
Uncharted waters, 8, 9, 160, 165, 168, 177, 194, 211, 213
United Nations Children's Fund (UNICEF), 7
United Nations Development Programme (UNDP), 6, 39
United States (US), 2, 5, 26–33, 37, 40, 50, 52, 55, 58n29, 71, 74, 77, 101, 102, 107, 108, 111, 116–118, 121, 131, 140, 144,

147, 152, 153, 157, 163, 202, 203
Unknown, 1, 11, 132, 147, 162–164, 166–168, 179, 180, 190, 191, 209, 221

V

Vaïsse, Justin, 157
Value, 10–12, 19, 29, 31–33, 35, 37, 54, 62, 63, 65, 69, 72, 73, 87, 93, 104, 107, 116, 129, 135, 139, 169–173, 173–174n7, 193, 195, 205, 206
Vandehei, Jim, 18–19
Variation, 84, 87, 160, 164, 176

W

Wall Street Journal, 61, 63, 116
World Bank, 7, 192
World Economic Forum, 63, 117, 193, 206, 212
World Trade Organization (WTO), 36, 72, 116, 121

X

Xi Jinping, 117, 152, 198

The manufacturer's authorised representative in the EU is Springer Nature Customer Service Centre GmbH, Europaplatz 3, 69115 Heidelberg, Germany. If you have any concerns regarding our products, please contact ProductSafety@springernature.com

Printed and bound by CPI Group (UK) Ltd, Croydon, CR0 4YY
24/04/2026
02096336-0006